The Magic Number

The Magic Number

Inside Obama's Chase for the
Presidential Nomination

Jeff Berman

ORDWAY
HOUSE

THE MAGIC NUMBER

Library of Congress data will be made available upon request.

ISBN 978-0-9849340-0-3 (hard back)
ISBN 978-0-9849340-1-0 (paperback)
ISBN 978-0-9849340-2-7 (ebook)

For Trish, Joe, Cassie, Annie, Molly
Mom, Dad and Alan

Table of Contents

Preface

"NINE TIMES OUT OF TEN, Hillary Clinton beats Barack Obama for the presidential nomination. Our challenge is to find that one path to victory."

David Plouffe, Campaign Manager
Obama for America, early 2007

At the start of 2007, Barack Obama's fledgling presidential campaign was working to develop its plan for winning the Democratic presidential nomination. Campaign manager David Plouffe was concerned that Obama's competition with Hillary Clinton could turn into a complex war of attrition if no candidate delivered a knockout blow in the opening primaries and caucuses. The nomination goes to the presidential candidate who controls a majority of delegates at the Democratic National Convention, regardless of who wins the Iowa caucuses, the New Hampshire primary—or even the biggest primaries in the country.

Assembling this delegate majority was to become my job. I had toiled in five previous presidential elections as a presidential delegate hunter, every one of them a failure. In each case, my candidate was knocked out of the race early or never even made it out of the campaign starting gate.

I never took this lack of success personally because presidential campaigns are large operations, with hundreds of staffers, and of course, a unique candidate who must sell him or herself to voters throughout the country. Each one of my presidential campaign losses was like an investment, allowing me to gain valuable experience and the opportunity to test new approaches in strategy and day-to-day tactics. By the time the 2008 presidential cycle arrived, I was ready for what nobody expected—the longest and most intense nominating struggle in modern presidential history.

This is the story of the high stakes struggle of the Obama presidential campaign to take on the Clinton fighting machine in the battle for the 2008 Democratic presidential nomination. Hillary Clinton, we all knew, was the candidate to beat. The nomination was hers for the taking, or so the television talking heads told us. They said a novice candidate, two years in the Senate, an African-American with a foreign sounding name, would get run over by the tough, seasoned Clinton political apparatus.

But the presidential nominating process is long and unpredictable, and Barack Obama had his own set of unique strengths that counterbalanced those of Hillary Clinton. His magnetic personality and message of hope and reform drew a level of grassroots support that exceeded anything Hillary Clinton or his other rivals could muster. Obama supporters organized via the Internet, flooded his campaign with money and turned out to participate in every imaginable campaign venue.

This book is written from my vantage point, that of the national delegate director. Rarely has the work of the chief delegate hunter mattered more in determining the outcome of the presidential nominating contest. The historic 2008 Democratic presidential race was a seemingly unending confrontation fought in every community and state to control a sprawling national delegate battlefield.

We moved decisively months before the first round of primaries and caucuses to prepare for a long, national battle for the nomination. Given Hillary Clinton's early political strength, the Obama team needed to establish a foothold in the race as soon as possible—in Iowa—the first state to vote. Next, we had to secure Obama's position in the other key early contests to establish his presidential bona fides. If we could make it out of the early states, we'd have the opportunity to convert the incredible enthusiasm of Obama's grassroots supporters into winning delegate results.

Our efforts and those of the Clinton campaign engaged voters like never before, producing an explosion of public interest in the historic candidacies of both Hillary Clinton and Barack Obama. Huge numbers of people registered to vote and jammed local voting halls and caucus sites. Voters donated unprecedented sums of money and consumed every morsel of information they could find on broadcast and cable television, in newspapers and magazines, and over the Internet.

This torrent of public participation sometimes disrupted the election system, as did unexpected challenges to the rules for the nominating process. We improvised one solution after another, always working to keep our path to the nomination clear from obstruction.

In the end, our success was founded on our candidate, our grassroots supporters and our campaign management all working together toward one common goal. That goal was to reach the Magic Number—the number of National Convention delegates needed to nominate Barack Obama to be the 44th President of the United States.

Prologue

IT'S FRIDAY, MAY 2, 2008, and the nation is mesmerized by the titanic struggle between Barack Obama and Hillary Clinton for the Democratic presidential nomination. Hillary, as she is universally known in Democratic circles, has just won the Pennsylvania Primary by an easy ten percentage points. Obama, who won a slew of earlier primaries to build a slim but persistent delegate lead over Hillary, is fighting to regain the political initiative.

On Tuesday, four days from now, the candidates will clash in the upcoming primaries in North Carolina and Indiana. The national press corps is holding a constant electoral vigil in these two states, as Democrats nationwide wait to see how they vote.

My interest in the vote on Tuesday is as strong as anybody's, but I have other business on my mind. I'm on an airliner to Columbia, South Carolina. Tomorrow, Democrats in the state will convene at their State Convention to elect their delegates to the Democratic National Convention. Nearly all of South Carolina's delegates will be awarded to Obama, Clinton and even John Edwards based on the vote in the state's January 26th primary that captured so much national attention months earlier.

One delegate position, however, will be filled tomorrow without regard to the primary election results. This delegate, known in the jargon of the Democratic Party as an "unpledged add-on" delegate, will be elected by a vote of all the delegates at the State Convention. Since the new delegate will not formally be pledged to any presidential candidate, the State Convention can pick any Democrat it wants for the position. I don't care who the delegate is—as long as he or she will vote to nominate Barack Obama for president at our National Convention.

I've been waiting for months for this delegate to be selected. Unknown to the rest of the country, South Carolina Democrats have been running a full state caucus and convention system beginning in the weeks after the state's January 26th primary. Rank-and-file Democrats convened in precinct meetings in February and elected delegates to county conventions. March county conventions, in turn, elected delegates to attend tomorrow's May 3rd State Convention.

While Democrats nationally turned their attention away from South Carolina after its January primary, I continued to keep one eye on this state and its complex caucus and convention system. In regular calls with our state Obama leaders, I've stayed abreast of the levels of support among participants in this system for the two presidential candidates.

Now, on the eve of the State Convention, I'm confident that, when the delegates gather tomorrow, a majority of them will favor Barack Obama for president.

There is a problem, though, in using this majority support to obtain the unpledged add-on delegate for Obama. It turns out that the highest-ranking Democrat in South Carolina wants to fill this position—and he is uncommitted in the Democratic presidential race. His name is Jim Rex and he is the South Carolina Superintendent of Education.

Worse yet, Rex has the complete support of Carol Fowler, the chair of the South Carolina Democratic Party to be the unpledged add-on delegate. Carol is supporting my candidate for president. But Rex is Carol's top-ranked Democrat in the state and she is going to get him elected to be a delegate if that's what he wants—whether or not he intends to remain uncommitted.

Carol is married to Don Fowler, the legendary South Carolina Democrat who served as chairman of the Democratic National Committee for none other than President Bill Clinton. Don is understandably 100 percent for Hillary Clinton in her campaign for the presidential nomination. While Carol is not encumbered by Don's loyalty to the Clintons, she also won't drop her support for Rex in order to deliver the delegate position to Obama.

The next morning, I head straight to the convention hall for a walk-thru of the facility and to meet with my top state Obama advisors. We gather around a tiny cocktail table in the bar area outside the convention room to talk. We need a plan to win the unpledged add-on position for Obama, and there are no better people to come up with one than this group.

Going around the table are former Governor Jim Hodges, who is now an Obama Campaign National Co-Chair, Dick Harpootlian, the wisecracking former South Carolina Democratic Party chair, Joe Erwin, another highly regarded former state Democratic Party chair, and former State Superintendent of Education and U.S. Senate candidate, Inez Tenenbaum, along with her husband Sam, a retired business leader and philanthropist.

After a lengthy session of energetic banter and occasionally ribald humor, we get down to business. I begin by laying out the situation.

"Ok, guys, we need to elect an Obama supporter to be the unpledged add-on delegate. The only question is how we're going to do it. I have no problem with Jim Rex getting this position. I've never met the man and have nothing against him. I don't even care that he hasn't been supporting Obama despite our big win in the state's primary. But he has to agree to get behind Obama if he wants our help getting elected to the delegate position. He's your top Democrat. If Rex will back Obama, we should back Rex. Does anyone disagree?"

One by one, each of the strategists around the table provides his or her comments and nods in agreement to this approach. We'll offer the delegate slot to Rex, but he has to commit to Obama for the presidential nomination in order to gain our backing.

Governor Hodges warns me, "Rex is proud, maybe too proud sometimes. He knows Barack swept this state's primary, but I won't be surprised if Rex refuses our offer. He'll want the delegate position his way, without a commitment to Barack or Hillary."

Dick Harpootlian chimes in: "We'll need a backup plan for when he turns us down. And it better be good, because there is going to be a lot of unhappiness if a fight breaks out over this delegate position."

"No doubt about that, Dick," I respond. "But I think we've got a real good Plan B with us right here at this table."

Everyone starts looking around the table. My eyes land on Inez.

"Oh, no, don't even think about it, Jeff Berman," Inez says.

"Come on, Inez." I protest. "I'm not a South Carolinian, but I know enough to know you're one of the most beloved Democrats in this state. We may need you to carry the Obama banner and win this thing for us."

Inez turns to her husband. "Sam, you're not going to let them do this to me are you?" she asks with a grimace. "How can I be the one to block Jim Rex, my immediate successor as the Superintendent of Education, from going to the National Convention? Please! This would be way too awkward."

Sam cuts right to the point: "Inez, I hate to say it, but Jeff has a good point. You're probably the best person to try to win this position. If Jim Rex makes the right decision, you won't have to run. But if he doesn't, you should do it for Barack. You've been working for Barack for months. In for a penny, in for a pound."

With that, everyone at the table playfully congratulates Inez on her good fortune in being the state's next delegate to the National Convention. Of course, she is hoping against hope that Rex will relent and serve as an Obama delegate.

I can't blame her one bit. It's very aggressive on our part to try to possibly displace South Carolina's only statewide elected Democrat. But we have no choice. We're in a dogfight for the presidential nomination and we have to push the envelope in every corner of the country to preserve our narrow national delegate lead. If Jim Rex refuses our proposal, she'll have to run against him to save this delegate position for Obama.

With our plan set, it's time to send an emissary to Rex. Will he pledge for Obama? To assure Inez that we made an honest attempt to convince Rex to join us, we need an emissary she'll know went to the mat to get the deal done. Who better than her husband Sam, who blessed the decision to draft her in the first place?

So, off Sam goes, with the mission to convince Rex to be for Obama and avoid a face-off against Inez.

It doesn't take Sam long to return to our hallway hangout, and his news is not good: "Rex was blunt. He's not committing to Barack. Rex says the position is for an uncommitted delegate— and that's the way he wants it. And he's not happy that Inez is going to be the one to run against him."

Dick Harpootlian, on the other hand, is not particularly displeased: "Damn! We're going to have a floor fight."

As happy as Dick might be, Carol Fowler is no doubt unhappy. This is the delegate position she wants to direct to Rex, and now she's facing an all-out fight against the Obama juggernaut for it. True to her character, Carol doesn't get emotional about it. If Rex doesn't want to support Obama just yet, then she's not going to make a federal case out of it. She'll make sure Rex gets his chance to win the delegate position, and she'll do what she can to help him.

Well, I'm not going to get upset about this either. Instead, I'm going to focus on winning the delegate fight.

Governor Jim Hodges volunteers to accompany Inez to each of the six congressional district caucuses that will be held just before the start of the State Convention. At each caucus, Jim makes his way to the center of the mingling crowd and jumps up on a folding chair and calls everyone together. Jim is universally recognized and respected among South Carolina Democrats. It's fun to watch him pull the delegates together, letting them know what a fine person Inez is and, for all the Obama delegates, what a strong supporter she's been for Barack Obama.

"Inez was the first major Democrat in South Carolina to endorse Obama and her selection is backed by his national campaign," he says. Then Jim gestures in my direction and I nod and confirm that Inez is indeed the choice of the national Campaign. We repeat this routine for Inez six times, once at each congressional district caucus.

Finally, we get to the start of the State Convention. A number of uninteresting votes are taken before we get to the showdown vote on the unpledged add-on delegate. First, several candidates for the unpledged add-on position speak on their own behalf, with more people competing for the slot than I anticipated.

The convention hall is filled with so many delegates that the officials decide to use a standing vote count, where delegates stand to vote when their candidate's name is read and tellers circulate around the hall to count heads. Carol Fowler is running the vote and calls off the names of some of the minor candidates before getting to the major two candidates, Inez and Rex.

After the first couple of minor candidates have their votes counted, I realize that some Obama delegates, out of hometown loyalty, are standing up for the delegate candidate from their county even if the candidate has no chance to be elected.

"Damn it!" I shout to Hodges and Harpootlian. "We need these wasted Obama votes to be cast for Inez. Wave our delegates to sit back down before they get counted."

Carol then announces Rex's name for a vote and quite a large number of delegates rise all over the hall. I'm concerned.

After the vote for Rex, Carol returns to voting for a run of minor candidates, each one again carving off odds and ends of Obama delegates loyal to their home county candidate. Finally, after what seems like endless bleeding of our numbers, Carol moves to put Inez up for a vote.

Inez's name is announced, and the room immediately explodes with cheers. Throngs of Obama delegates rise up in unison throughout the sprawling convention hall. The Obama delegates see their numbers are far greater than those won by Jim Rex, and know they've delivered South Carolina one more time for Obama.

Rex had erred in his gamble. His stature as the state's senior elected Democrat was no match for the pull of Obama's historic presidential candidacy among the State Convention delegates.

Inez is relieved to have won and proud to have carried the banner for Barack Obama at the State Convention. She takes no pleasure, however, at the embarrassment that Rex has suffered. Inez is mindful that Rex was her successor as Superintendent of Education and that they share a common legacy in South Carolina public service. She's still perplexed that Rex would refuse to back Obama—even after his sweeping victory in the South Carolina Primary—and pained that she had to run against Rex to save the delegate position for Obama.

For my part, I'm no happier than Inez at having to defeat Rex to win the last available South Carolina delegate. He's the highest-ranking Democrat in the state and I'd have preferred him to simply back Obama and take the delegate position without a fight. But Rex declined, and we did what we told him we would do—deny him the delegate position.

★   ★   ★

Given the incredibly tight contest in 2008 between Obama and Clinton, the presidential nomination was on the line every time a delegate position such as the South Carolina add-on was up for grabs. Famed former Senator Everett Dirksen once said, when evaluating the growing cost of federal programs, "add a billion dollars here and a billions dollars there, and before you know it, you're talking real money." In 2008, during our nearly tied Democratic delegate contest, I was saying, "gain a delegate here and a delegate there, and before you know it, we're talking a real delegate lead."

Throughout the country, winning delegates was possible only because of our grassroots strength. In South Carolina, we needed the votes of the delegates on the State Convention floor to have any chance of winning the state's add-on delegate. The majority of these delegates backed Obama for the nomination, but probably were unaware they could select their own choice to be the add-on delegate, instead of a top officeholder unwilling to support Obama's candidacy. The national Obama campaign was able to provide the guidance these delegates needed to work their will on the State Convention floor.

My goal was for our national delegate team to repeat this experience in one state after another, joining forces with Obama grassroots activists everywhere to win delegates to advance Obama's march to the Magic Number.

1

Joining the Obama Team

IN EARLY 2007, the political phenomenon known as Barack Obama is gathering steam. While many are being swept up in high emotion for his presidential candidacy, I'm focused on whether he can get elected. I want to see a Democrat in the White House.

You see, my politics are Democratic. That's the way I was raised. My dad always told me—and still does—that the Democratic Party is a champion for the average man and we need to support the Party. Growing up during the Vietnam War protests, civil rights struggle, birth of the women's, consumers' and environmental movements and Watergate scandal all reinforced my father's political teachings. Ditto for my years studying at Brown University and Harvard Law School, liberal bastions of the Ivy League.

By the time I started my career as a lawyer in Washington, DC, I was ready to put my heart into Democratic campaigns for the presidency. In 1984, fresh out of school, I jumped into the presidential campaign of former astronaut and Senator John Glenn. I made myself into an expert on Democratic nominating rules and ran myself ragged to make sure Glenn qualified for all the primary ballots and had full slates of delegates available to attend the National Convention. Unfortunately, Glenn's organization and finances never achieved liftoff, and he flopped in the opening Iowa caucuses.

In 1988, I was recruited to the presidential campaign of Dick

Gephardt, then a rising young leader in the House of Representatives from St. Louis. Gephardt was putting together an all-star election team, including campaign manager Bill Carrick, who had been a top strategist for Senator Ted Kennedy, field director Donna Brazile, political director Joe Trippi, finance chair Terry McAuliffe, speechwriter Paul Begala, scheduling and advance director Jon Haber, Iowa director Steve Murphy and other outstanding staffers. Outside consultants included media consultants Bob Shrum and David Doak, pollster Ed Reilly and general counsel Bob Bauer. I took over Gephardt's national delegate operation. Gephardt won Iowa, but his lack of funding doomed his chances and he folded his tent in the following weeks.

In 1992 and 2000, I put a lot of effort into preparing Gephardt to compete again for the White House, but each time when he took a look at the political landscape, he decided to pass. In 2004, probably too many years too late, Gephardt finally decided to climb up on his saddle and make what certainly would be his last run at the presidency. I joined him, as did many of his now larger circle of aides and advisors. Sadly, Gephardt again couldn't raise the money needed to compete. Moreover, he now was too familiar to voters looking for new leadership and weakened by his support of the Iraq War—and his campaign faltered in Iowa.

I walk through my history of failed presidential campaigns to say that, by 2008, I've learned a lot about running for the presidential nomination. Now, I hope to use this learning for Senator Barack Obama. Unlike Gephardt, Obama can fund a presidential campaign and will be helped by his position on the Iraq War, not hurt. Obama's compelling life story, keen intellect and uncanny ability to communicate give him the makings of a winner—and that's what Democrats need.

* * *

Obama's strong assets for a presidential run may not matter for much, though, because there already is another Democrat in the race, Senator Hillary Clinton, who is considered a lock to win the presidential nomination. In fact, in the months leading up to the 2008 presidential race, many top Democrats would not even entertain the thought that Hillary could be denied the Democratic presidential nomination.

During a previous summer, while at a concert at the U.S. Capitol, I bumped into Steve Murphy, who managed Gephardt's 2004 campaign and now is the media advisor for Governor Bill Richardson's fledgling presidential campaign. Steve and I talked for a while, but it wasn't long before our conversation turned to the 2008 presidential race.

"So what do you think of 2008, Steve?" I asked.

"It's a total waste of time to even talk about it," he replied. "Hillary has this thing sewn up."

This attitude—that Hillary Clinton is a lock for the Democrats' presidential nomination—pretty much captured what most of political Washington was thinking before 2008.

I don't buy this view, though. I think there's room for another strong contender in 2008.

Since 1968, nearly every Democratic presidential fight has started with a large field of candidates, but quickly boiled down to a contest between two highly competitive candidates, one from the established mainstream and one from the reform wing of the Democratic Party. It's like a bowling alley where there are many candidates playing in many lanes at the outset of the nomination competition. Before long, it becomes clear that most can't compete with the leaders and we are left with two players, bowling in two lanes. In the Democratic Party, that's one player in the main lane, a favorite of the Party establishment, and one bowling just off to the left, a reformist insurgent.

In 1968, Vice President Hubert Humphrey entered the race as the mainstream liberal candidate and Eugene McCarthy and then Robert Kennedy ran anti-war challenges to Humphrey. In 1972, Ed Muskie, the 1968 vice presidential candidate, ran against anti-war candidate George McGovern. In 1976, non-traditional outsider Jimmy Carter defeated several candidates for the nomination, including Henry "Scoop" Jackson, the candidate of organized labor and the Washington establishment. In 1980, when Carter ran for re-election, he faced a stiff—but ultimately unsuccessful—

challenge from liberal icon Ted Kennedy. In 1984, former Vice President Walter Mondale almost lost the presidential nomination to reform candidate Gary Hart. In 1988, Governor Mike Dukakis became the establishment candidate and the Reverend Jesse Jackson emerged as a significant liberal challenger to Dukakis.

While the 1992 campaign didn't fit this pattern because Governor Bill Clinton was neither an establishment nor reform candidate—or maybe both—Vice President Al Gore definitely was the establishment candidate in 2000 against reformist challenger Bill Bradley. Finally, in 2004, John Kerry emerged as the establishment pick for the nomination and defeated reform upstart Howard Dean.

★   ★   ★

For 2008, Hillary Clinton is the established leader for the Democratic presidential nomination. She has earned near universal name recognition from her eight years in the White House as America's first lady. Then she won a nationally-watched race for the U.S. Senate from New York. By virtue of now serving as the senator from the financial capital in New York City, she has the capacity to raise enormous sums of money for her 2008 candidacy.

She and her husband, former President Bill Clinton, have been able to call upon many of the top tier of leaders of the Democratic Party for financial contributions, endorsements, organizational support and expert policy advice. She holds a starting position in 2007 that is on par with the commanding presidential nomination positions held by Walter Mondale in 1984 and Al Gore in 2000.

Other candidates getting in the 2008 race theoretically could compete with Hillary Clinton for the role of the establishment candidate. Senators Joe Biden and Chris Dodd are both longtime senators whose tenure in Congress makes Hillary Clinton look like a rookie by comparison. Governor Bill Richardson served as Congressman, U.S. Ambassador to the United Nations, U.S. Energy Secretary and Chairman of the Democratic Governors Association. While these three candidates have the kind of credentials that ordinarily might sustain an establishment candidacy, they can't compete in 2008, when Hillary will completely own this path to the Democratic presidential nomination.

Hillary's impressive establishment strength, though, doesn't mean that she isn't vulnerable to a reform challenge. Barack Obama's early opposition to the Iraq War, in contrast to Hillary Clinton's support of the congressional war resolution, offers him the opportunity to flank Hillary on the classic insurgent issue of war and peace. And Obama and his senior strategic advisor, David Axelrod, and the rest of their messaging team have opened Obama's campaign with a broad reform theme of "hope and change" that goes well beyond opposition to the Iraq War.

Former Senator John Edwards will try to compete to be the reform challenger to Hillary, but will not likely succeed. His anti-poverty theme won't be able to compete with Barack's anti-war appeal. Plus, the sensation surrounding Obama's quest to be the first African-American president will deny Edwards the media attention needed to survive in Obama's lane. I just don't see Edwards capturing the reform lane for himself.

The two other 2008 presidential candidates claiming the mantle of reform, Ohio Congressman Dennis Kucinich and former Alaska Senator Mike Gravel, can't mount credible campaigns that could displace Obama's reform candidacy, and won't have any role in my planning for the Democratic delegate race.

Thus, despite all the Washington chatter that Hillary Clinton is the inevitable nominee, she can be challenged, and Obama owns the reform lane to do it. But can he pull it off?

* * *

David Plouffe and I have been trading phone calls all week. It's February 2007, and I'm trying to get a read on his view of the Obama campaign plan and the role of its delegate operation. David is managing his first presidential campaign, having cut his teeth as the senior political advisor to Dick Gephardt's failed 2004 effort. David had served earlier, in the 1990s, as executive director of the Democratic Congressional Campaign Committee when Gephardt had installed Patrick Kennedy as the DCCC chairman.

David also served as an advisor in a variety of congressional and other campaigns.

At this point, David is a seasoned political strategist and manager. Unlike so many in the business, he is a quiet, focused individual who doesn't slap backs or hang out at the bar. I'm not much different. I try to understand what I need to do and work hard to get it done.

My connection with David comes from our past work together. For many of the years when I was an advisor to Gephardt, David was helping to run Gephardt's House leadership office or campaign committees. Although David hadn't arrived in Gephardt's orbit by the time of his 1988 presidential effort, David was there in 2004, when he and I collaborated closely for Gephardt's final run for office.

There's some disagreement among the small group putting together the Obama campaign team over who should run the delegate operation. Several general political operatives have been asking to handle delegates for Obama. They probably have more experience in political campaigning than I do, but lack my delegates expertise. David is worried about facing a long delegate battle against Hillary and presses the case for bringing me in.

David asks me to meet with Matt Nugen, the new political director for the campaign. Matt knows better than anyone the role of the presidential delegate director, since he served in that role for Senator Joe Lieberman's 2004 presidential effort. In fact, at times during 2003, Matt and I conspired together to find ways to contain Howard Dean's presidential juggernaut that year. After the 2004 election cycle, Matt took the position of chief of staff for the new chairman of the Democratic National Committee, the same Howard Dean.

It's Matt's job now to put together the political staff for the Obama campaign and David wants the delegate operation to be a unit within the political department. Matt and I get together at the Starbucks on Capitol Hill and hit it off just fine after being out of touch since the 2004 campaign. After various discussions about this and that, Matt offers me the job.

There is one issue that weighs on my mind. How am I going to be a dad to my kids while working in the Chicago Obama head-quarters? My wife Trish and I have four kids, all of whom attend school in Washington, DC. I can't uproot them from their classes, friends and daily routines to move to Chicago. Our oldest child, Joe, is a junior in high school, next in line is Cassie, a high school freshman, then comes Annie, a seventh grader in middle school, and last, Molly, the family mascot who is eight years old and in third grade at our neighborhood public elementary school. Trish has been close at hand for all our kids during their school years and is willing to shoulder the parenting load for both of us.

While David has assured me I can work from Washington, I'm skeptical. While a lot of people telecommute to work, they don't do it when helping run a presidential campaign.

I'll work out of Washington as much as I can for as long as I can, but I expect the campaign vortex in Chicago eventually will suck me into its abyss. This will be a sacrifice for my family, but they want me to do it. I can't thank Trish enough for bearing the burden when I'm gone. I'll do what I can from a distance.

Anyway, with some luck, the nomination will be decided quickly, and I won't be gone for long.

2

Delegate System Basics

GIVEN THAT THIS IS MY SIXTH TOUR planning for or running a Democratic presidential delegate operation, I don't need much introduction to the work at hand. It's March of 2007 and once I get settled into my workspace in Chicago, I throw myself into planning for the 2008 nomination campaign.

Most people assume that the way to win the Democratic presidential nomination is to win as many votes as possible in the primaries and caucuses. While a presidential candidate certainly does need to win votes, the reason is not to win elections. It's to earn delegates to the National Convention.

In 2008, there will be 4,415 delegates elected to the National Convention. It will take 2,208 delegates—a bare majority of the total—for a presidential candidate to reach the Magic Number and win the nomination.

It's important to know the delegate system basics to understand what lies ahead for the Democratic presidential campaign. The rules for the nominating process are written by the DNC's Rules Committee and approved by the full membership of the DNC. The basic rules aren't complicated, but it does require a few minutes of review to understand them.

There are two types of delegates, pledged and unpledged. The pledged group is by far the largest, with 3,566 delegates elected through the primaries and caucuses. Each state has been apportioned a specific number of these delegates by the DNC. The states, in turn, allocate two-thirds of their pledged delegates to their congressional districts, with the other one-third remaining as statewide delegates.

It's easier to understand how this works by looking at the pledged delegates for an individual state. In Mississippi, for example, the state is allocated 33 pledged delegates. The state has four congressional districts, and the state Democratic Party has assigned 22 of its delegates as follows:

District	Number of Delegates
District 1	5
District 2	7
District 3	5
District 4	5

Mississippi's remaining 11 pledged delegates will be elected on a statewide basis.

For all states, the votes in each congressional district will be tallied separately, as will be the votes cast statewide. Going back to the Mississippi example, there will be five "separate" elections in the state, one in each of the four congressional districts, plus one statewide. The public typically hears a great deal about the statewide election, but nothing about the congressional district voting—even though the district voting actually elects most of the delegates.

There are 3, 4, 5, 6, 7, 8 or 9 delegates apportioned to each of the congressional districts, based on Democratic voting strength. This is important, as the districts allocated the most delegates are those who vote most heavily for Democrats. And these districts, it turns out, most often are populated by African-Americans, who are among the most loyal Democratic voters in the country.

Going back to our Mississippi example, notice that District 2 has two more delegates than any other district in the state. This district is majority black. With an African-American running for president this year, the allocation of more delegates to majority black districts can produce a significant impact on the national delegate race.

DNC rules require a proportional award of delegates to any presidential candidate exceeding a threshold of 15 percent in a congressional district or statewide vote. Unlike many Republican primaries, Democratic contests never allocate delegates on a winner-take-all basis.

Each presidential candidate is allowed to approve the pool of people eligible to serve as a pledged delegate to ensure that his or her pledged delegates remain loyal when voting at the National Convention. This is necessary because the rules let all delegates—even those who are pledged—vote their conscience at the National Convention to respond to a late change in the campaign, such as the emergence of a candidate scandal. The fact that delegates aren't legally bound to their presidential candidate will be in the back of my mind throughout the 2008 nominating race. If we end up in a close race, there may be an attempt to ask delegates to disregard their presidential pledge.

This happened in 1980, when Senator Ted Kennedy, under somewhat different rules, attempted to challenge the delegate lead of President Jimmy Carter at that year's National Convention. While Carter beat back the Kennedy challenge, the fight over delegate loyalty produced a mess for Democrats that certainly didn't help achieve party unity for the general election. For 2008, I don't want any questions about the loyalty of Obama's delegates, and will do my best to make sure there are none.

★   ★   ★

The unpledged delegates to the National Convention are 849 elected officials and party leaders specially designated by DNC rules. They include 768 delegates who attend the National Convention by virtue of being a member of Congress or the DNC or of serving in another position that is designated under DNC rules. Also included are 81 delegates who are to be selected—a few in each state—to add a few extra party leader positions to round out the state delegations to the National Convention.

The unpledged delegates are free to privately or publicly commit to support any presidential candidate at any time—or not at all. With such broad discretion, they've become known as "superdelegates." The exact number of superdelegates may rise or fall as the designated elected offices or party leader positions are vacated or filled.

★ ★ ★

While the delegate math can be very important in a competitive nominating campaign, it hasn't mattered much in recent years. For the last several presidential elections, a presumptive Democratic nominee has emerged quickly after winning just a few early primaries. The winning candidate survived a brief challenge from the next strongest candidate, and then rolled on to victory after victory, with most delegates being accumulated after all other candidates were eliminated from the race. The superdelegates never came into play.

In 2008, the delegate rules and math might not matter much, or could make all the difference in the world.

3

Setting the Plan

By THE END OF THE FIRST QUARTER OF 2007, the Obama Campaign is coming together. We have moved into a beautiful space in a downtown Chicago office complex known as the Illinois Center. It's a set of several smoky black-clad office towers that look north over the Chicago River toward the historic Chicago Tribune Building and the Wrigley Building. At night, the building tops are lit up with beautiful lights that make for an inspiring sight.

Key parts of the campaign are running on all cylinders. The fundraising operation is especially impressive. Everyone in politics is expecting Hillary Clinton to lead the Democratic field in fundraising. She's had eight years in the White House, plus several years in the U.S. Senate from New York, which is a fundraising center for Democrats.

What about Barack Obama? Although he's relatively untested as a national fundraiser, he comes to this campaign with fundraising assets of his own. He has extraordinary personal appeal and Democratic donors—like other Americans—want to meet him and learn about him. Prominent fundraising chair Penny Pritzker and seasoned fundraising director Julianna Smoot are leading his fundraising effort, and by all accounts they're raising the money he needs to compete with Hillary.

When the first quarter fundraising numbers for 2007 are in, Obama has more than kept pace with Hillary. While this means Obama is going to be very competitive financially, the media still obsesses over Hillary's continuing lead in the national public opinion polls. She still is considered by most to be the "inevitable" presidential nominee of the Democratic Party.

I'm unfazed by this media consensus and concentrating on my own planning for the nominating race. I learned during my prior presidential runs that polling numbers always rise and fall during the many months before the start of the primaries. But eventually, the candidates face the voters and the delegate war begins. Now that it's clear we'll have the funding to implement a winning campaign, I'm determined that we'll have a delegate plan equal to the challenge of taking on Hillary Clinton.

★   ★   ★

My preparation for the delegate race begins the day I get to Chicago. From the outset, I don't let my analysis of the race get cluttered with any opposing candidate other than Hillary Clinton. The only other presidential candidate I think has any realistic opportunity in the coming fight is former vice presidential nominee John Edwards. Edwards is a handsome, charismatic political figure who came in second in Iowa in 2004 and at least initially can raise significant funding for a 2008 campaign. He retains a strong following in Iowa, the first state to vote in 2008, and hasn't stopped campaigning there since 2004.

But Edwards also is limited in what he brings to the contest. He's been out of office since he left the Senate and has limited political strength and organization outside Iowa. Now, Obama is the exciting new outsider and anti-war candidate, and the high profile clash between him and establishment candidate Hillary Clinton is likely to leave little political oxygen left for Edwards.

I know Edwards can argue he can win Iowa, take that momentum into New Hampshire, get through less significant Nevada, and lock up the role of frontrunner in his birth state of South Carolina. But I just don't see him winning Iowa.

Maybe my judgment on this is colored by my disappointing 2004 experience with Dick Gephardt's attempt to reprise his Iowa success from 1988, but I think it's difficult for a Democratic presidential candidate to do well in Iowa twice. Democrats in Iowa seem to expect a fresh sense of excitement from their presidential candidates with each new election cycle, and it's hard for a candidate to provide that on a second run in the state. So far, in 2007, I don't see Edwards offering Iowa voters much they haven't seen before.

Focusing just on our competition with Hillary, I bury myself in a detailed examination of the race. I research the developing calendar of primaries and caucuses to see the flow of the states. As chaotic as it may seem, every state is able to determine its own type of voting system and date for voting. The national political parties provide a few basic ground rules on how voting can occur and set a starting date and ending date to create a window of approximately four months for the primaries and caucuses.

As the states select their dates, the calendar of primaries and caucuses takes shape. For me, the question is which states likely will work for Obama and which ones will work against him? Perhaps more importantly, how might the outcome in one state influence the outcome in another?

I know from my experience in prior presidential campaigns that the voting in every state can affect the dynamic in the nominating race. Some presidential campaigns are tempted in each presidential election cycle to consider a strategy that starts at a state other than the first to vote, or that skips states that inconveniently look to be unwinnable. This is a fool's choice. Any state that isn't won, is lost—to an opposing candidate who will gain not just delegates from the win, but also momentum to compete in the subsequent primaries and caucuses.

For my analysis, I have public polling data of varying quality, but no state-specific internal polling data. I don't believe any presidential campaign does polling in states several months to a year before the primaries and caucuses begin, except perhaps for the first few states to vote. So, I'm turning over every rock I can to search for useful information on next year's voting. I consult widely within our campaign and call state and local political experts in all corners of the country to learn what they think we can expect in the primaries and caucuses.

I study local political cultures and voting histories for each region, state and congressional district. Voters in a city or suburb may vote differently from voters in a rural area. Voters in the South will vote differently from voters in the Northeast, Midwest, Mountain West or West Coast.

Some states will allow Independents to vote in the Democratic contest. Other states will let voters change their registered party affiliation at their polling place or caucus location on election day.

I boil down everything I'm learning to the following factors for the competition between Clinton and Obama:

1. Obama's strongest appeal will be among voters who are African-American, younger, reform-oriented, opposed to the Iraq War or highly educated.
2. Obama will do better when Independent (non-affiliated) voters can vote in Democratic contests.
3. Obama's geographical strength will be outside Hillary's current home region of the Northeast.
4. Hillary is going to have an advantage among voters who are older, blue-collar or Hispanic.
5. Hillary is going to be strongest not only in her home region, but also in large media-driven states, like California, where her unparalleled name recognition should give her a big boost.

These principles may seem simplistic or arbitrary, but based on everything I've learned, they ring true to me and others I've consulted. I know additional factors will come into play as we move through the primaries and caucuses, but these are the ones I'm going to use to plan our delegate strategy.

My study bores down to each of the 435 congressional districts. A volunteer data consultant, Peter Appel, who learned the mathematics of the delegate process back in the 1988 Dukakis campaign, joins our effort and produces one spreadsheet after another by cross-referencing the voting demographic factors identified above with available census data to project voting and delegate results for each state and congressional district.

I take all the data and analysis piled on my desk (and in my head) and apply it to the primaries and caucuses to plan our strategy for accumulating delegates to get to the Magic Number.

To make this task manageable, I break the calendar into three parts: the early voting states, Super Tuesday, and the states voting after Super Tuesday.

$$\star \quad \star \quad \star$$

The Early Voting States

Our path through the primaries and caucuses starts with Iowa. It's hard to see how we can go forward without doing well in this state, which almost certainly means winning it. Obama has tremendous potential in Iowa, given the thirst of Democrats there for inspiring candidates who articulate an agenda for change and reform. It also helps a lot that he was an early opponent to the Iraq War, which is unpopular among Iowa Democrats.

Our campaign manager, David Plouffe, knows Iowa well and is going to do everything in his power to keep us focused on succeeding in the state. While Edwards likely will maintain significant support all the way to the state's caucuses, I believe in the end, Iowa Democrats will hand victory to one of the two marquis candidates of this election cycle, Barack Obama or Hillary Clinton.

Of course, winning Iowa is no guarantee of achieving the presidential nomination, especially given that we are running against the political powerhouse of Hillary and Bill Clinton. Defeating them would be the political equivalent of climbing Mount Everest, so besting Hillary in a single state—even first-to-vote Iowa—is not going to knock her out of the 2008 presidential race.

If Obama were to win Iowa and slingshot from there to a victory in New Hampshire, that could be a different story. That could knock Hillary out of the race. There is clear precedent for a strong finish in Iowa carrying a candidate to victory in the New Hampshire primary. And since Hillary is not from New England, she cannot count on New Hampshire to give her a rebound from an Iowa loss, as occurred in prior primaries for New Hampshire neighbors Massachusetts Governor Mike Dukakis and former

Senator Paul Tsongas. An Obama win in Iowa could beget a win in New Hampshire.

But I'm not convinced that even a staggered Hillary Clinton would fold on the basis of losses in Iowa and New Hampshire. Rather, I think she'd try to make a comeback—the type of move for which Bill Clinton is famous—in Nevada.

Nevada will be holding important early Democratic caucuses for the first time. The state has a unique mix of rugged Western sensibility and Las Vegas culture that could turn its caucuses into more of a professional wrestling match—or even pay-per-view chain-link cage brawl—than a high-minded competition for the presidency.

Based on Hillary's already obvious appeal to Hispanic voters, she should be able to rally support from the large Hispanic community in Las Vegas, while her husband helps win over the gaming and resort industries and Las Vegas media machine. Given that roughly 75% of the Nevada's population lives in the Las Vegas metropolitan area, Hillary has ample reason to believe she can succeed in the state regardless of the earlier verdicts in Iowa and New Hampshire.

If we're able to get through Nevada with our momentum reasonably intact, we will come to South Carolina, the second jewel of the 2008 nominating calendar for Barack Obama—behind Iowa. South Carolina has a large Democratic African-American voting constituency that can provide a strong foundation for Obama in the state. Blacks comprise about 30 percent of the South Carolina population and can comprise 50 percent or more of the Democratic presidential primary vote in South Carolina.

Early polls show Hillary to be popular among African-Americans, but we in the Obama campaign believe Barack will more than hold his own with this group once the voting begins. African-Americans are as independent-thinking as any voters, but respect for Obama's potential and pride in his candidacy can draw them behind him. South Carolina can deliver Obama the strong win he needs to succeed in the massive Super Tuesday voting the next week.

★   ★   ★

Super Tuesday

To say the range of state contests the next week offers a unique challenge to the presidential campaigns would be a major understatement. The next Tuesday is known as Super Tuesday, because it includes voting in 23 states and U.S. territories. This is the largest number of states holding nominating contests on one day in our country's history.

Why do so many states hold their primary or caucus on Super Tuesday? States simply want to vote on the earliest allowable date to have maximum influence over the selection of the presidential nominee. The states know that in recent years only the earliest nominating contests have had much impact in selecting the Democratic nominee. Since Super Tuesday is the first allowable day for voting for all states except the four approved early states, this is the date a lot of states choose for their primary or caucus.

This desire to influence the nomination through holding an early voting contest has moved other states, principally Florida and Michigan, to talk about leapfrogging ahead of the Super Tuesday contests in violation of national party rules. Florida already is considering legislation to that end. But the DNC is discouraging this potentially explosive threat to the nominating calendar, and at this early point in 2007, the jury remains out on whether Florida, Michigan or any other state will jump ahead of the national party's starting gun.

If the Democratic nomination race is still closely contested when the candidates get to Super Tuesday, we could see a titanic battle between Hillary Clinton and Barack Obama, the political equivalent of Armageddon Day. The race will change from being about who can win a particular state to who can master a wide range of voting across the nation.

Sixteen primaries and seven caucuses will vote on Super Tuesday, allocating 1,681 pledged delegates. These primaries and caucuses extend from the Atlantic to the Pacific and from Canada to Mexico, and even to the U.S. territory of American Samoa over seven thousand miles away. This will be one very long day of voting.

What will be considered a "win" on this huge voting day and what campaign strategies will offer the best chance for victory?

To begin to understand the magnitude of Super Tuesday, it's best to view these states and their pledged delegates according to the following regional breakdown:

Super Tuesday Delegates Grouped by Region

West		Midwest		Northeast	
Alaska	13	Illinois	153	Connecticut	48
Arizona	56	Kansas	32	Delaware	15
California	370	Minnesota	72	Massachusetts	93
Colorado	55	Missouri	72	New Jersey	107
Idaho	18	N. Dakota	13	New York	232
New Mexico	26	Oklahoma	38	**Total**	**495**
Utah	23	**Total**	**380**		
Total	**561**				

South		U.S. Territory	
Alabama	52	American Samoa	3
Arkansas	35	**Total**	**3**
Georgia	87		
Tennessee	68		
Total	**242**		

If Obama is not in strong shape coming into these states—which include Hillary-leaning mega-states New York, New Jersey and California—he risks an electoral defeat that could knock him out of the race. Of course, we're hoping Obama will get a strong boost from South Carolina going into Super Tuesday. But what should be our plan for surviving Super Tuesday, and can we position Obama to win in the contests to follow this big day of voting?

★   ★   ★

One ace up our sleeve for Super Tuesday is that six caucuses will vote on this day. States that use a caucus system instead of a primary to allocate delegates have a history of being dominated by grassroots activists who favor reform candidates over establishment ones. This may seem counter-intuitive because seasoned party regulars should be more skilled at participating in their own caucus systems than "civilian" activists, but Democratic caucuses simply get overrun by highly motivated reformers during election years when a presidential candidate activates this support.

I know caucuses can be dominated by reform activists because I personally observed them doing so in earlier presidential elections. Reform candidates Jerry Brown in 1992, Jesse Jackson in 1988 and Gary Hart in 1984 all found some of their greatest success in caucus states. The chart below shows caucus states where reform candidates out performed establishment opponents—even though in some cases the reform candidates had no chance to win the nomination when dominating caucus contests.

Reform Candidate Success in Past Caucus States

1992   Jerry Brown over Bill Clinton

Alaska	Utah
Maine	Vermont
Nevada	Washington

1988   Jesse Jackson over Mike Dukakis

Alaska	South Carolina
Delaware	Texas
Michigan	Vermont

1984   Gary Hart over Walter Mondale

Alaska	Montana	Utah
Arizona	Nevada	Vermont
Colorado	North Dakota	Washington
Idaho	Oklahoma	Wyoming
Maine	South Carolina	

I am convinced we have a candidate in Barack Obama who can achieve—or eclipse—this past level of reform candidate success in the caucus states. Obama has a clear message of hope and change that motivates activist voters. Many Obama grassroots supporters already are organizing their own Obama support groups, providing a foundation for our efforts to win the caucus states.

In order to assure caucus state success for Obama, I want us to go farther than past reform candidates to prepare for the caucus contests. Candidates Jerry Brown, Jesse Jackson and Gary Hart often seemed to struggle to make their way through the primaries and caucuses. Their candidacies were terribly underfunded and lacked strong organization for many of the voting contests. We can do better—and with Hillary as our opponent—we must do better.

Of course, many of our supporters likely will be participating in a presidential caucus for the first time, no different than the supporters of Brown, Jackson and Hart. In fact, I expect that many of our grassroots supporters will have little idea how a caucus operates or what challenges will arise.

But our national delegate operation will have the luxury of time, some money and a clear plan to prepare for these caucus contests. We can put in place a caucus strategy and organizing structure for each of them that can give us an advantage over Hillary once the caucus state voting arrives. No presidential campaign has prepared in this way this early in a presidential cycle. But we can do it.

★   ★   ★

With 23 states holding a primary or caucus on Super Tuesday, how will all this voting come together? I believe victory on Super Tuesday likely will be measured in multiple ways, not in one dimension.

If we're in a position of strength coming out of South Carolina, I foresee the media and public focusing on the following three metrics to assess this national voting day:

1. Who has won the most states?
2. Who, at the end of the day, is leading in the national delegate count?
3. Who has won the marquis contests outside of their home region, principally California?

I have no doubt that different political journalists, analysts and opinion leaders will focus on different combinations of these three measurements—and maybe others—but, to me, these will be the keys to winning Super Tuesday. Our goal should be to try to win all three of them.

Let's start with the first of the three metrics, winning the most states on Super Tuesday. This metric is important for a variety of reasons. First, if either candidate is able to win substantially more Super Tuesday contests than the other, there's a good chance the nominating race will be effectively over. If that doesn't happen, the number and breadth of each candidate's election wins will show the strength he or she can bring to the general election.

Seeing is believing and, especially for Barack Obama, winning a broad range of state contests on Super Tuesday will be the best way to convince voters and opinion leaders he can win the states he'll need to prevail in November of 2008. This is particularly important since, as a candidate of color, he inevitably will face doubts by some as to whether he can build a winning coalition that includes white voters and reaches into multiple regions.

Winning the most states also would provide a compelling picture of victory for the media, who can be expected to cover the Super Tuesday voting as a national primary day. I can see them depicting the day's voting results in two types of visual displays. One will be a graphic of Obama's state wins shown alongside the list of Hillary state wins. We'll want a longer Obama list.

A different graphic will show all state wins depicted on a national electoral map, with a specific color, personal portrait or unique emblem used to designate the winning presidential candidate for each state. The TV networks will develop splashy, hi-tech national maps for their Super Tuesday election coverage. Similar to a fall general election, we'll want to see Obama shown winning the most states spreading across several regions.

So, with 23 nominating contests around the country, how do we win more states than Hillary, and in a wide range of regions?

Obama Base States

Based on the strengths and weaknesses of Obama and Hillary, Obama should be able to do well in ten Super Tuesday states that will elect 567 pledged delegates. These Obama "Base States" include two states in Obama's home region, Illinois and Missouri. Then, there are two states, Georgia and Alabama, which have high percentages of African-American voters, which Obama can win if he pulls in at least a modicum of white voters. Finally, we have the six Western and Midwestern states that hold caucuses that we can target to win with Obama's strong network of grassroots activists.

All of the Obama Base States made their own decisions to hold their contest on Super Tuesday. Rather than leave this to chance, I called senior Democrats in a number of these states to consider scheduling their voting on Super Tuesday. These date selections are made by state legislative leaders, governors, secretaries of state or party leaders—or some combination of them. My calls might or might not have had an impact with some of these leaders, but it's hard to say how most of these decisions came together.

Here are the ten Obama Base States with their total of 567 pledged delegates:

Home Region		High % Black		Caucus System	
Illinois	153	Georgia	87	Minnesota	72
Missouri	72	Alabama	52	Colorado	55
Total	**225**	**Total**	**139**	Kansas	32
				Idaho	18
				Alaska	13
				North Dakota	13
				Total	**203**

Competitive States

On Super Tuesday, there will be an additional six states with a total of 558 delegates that should be within our reach, but are far from a chip shot for Obama. I consider these states to be competitive based on their voting history and demographics. These "Competitive States" are all states outside the Northeastern region, where Hillary will have her strongest pull.

California is by far the most important of these states. While the Clinton brand is quite valuable in California, I believe Obama's freshness as a new candidate and his reform appeal makes him potentially competitive here. Of course, this state starts as Hillary's to lose, given her high name recognition and the large number of Hispanic voters sympathetic to her candidacy, but I feel we could have a shot here.

Arizona falls into the same category as California, with reform Democratic voters who might support Obama, particularly in the Tucson area, offset by the large Hispanic vote that trends toward Hillary.

Oklahoma and Tennessee are relatively conservative states that might not vote for New York Senator Hillary Clinton, though the lack of large African-American populations makes them questionable for Obama. Utah, and its Western values, seems like it should favor Obama over Clinton, but I'm not particularly comfortable predicting the vote in this heavily Republican state.

Here are the six Competitive States and their 558 delegates:

California	370
Arizona	56
Oklahoma	38
Tennessee	68
Utah	23
American Samoa	3
Total	**558**

Hillary Base States

The last major basket of Super Tuesday states are the six states with 530 delegates that Hillary should win. These are Hillary's Base States and include three in her home region: her state of New York, New Jersey, which shares the New York City metropolitan area, and contiguous Connecticut. Massachusetts and Delaware are in her Northeastern region, though Delaware has a particularly significant African-American population in Wilmington and thus is more marginal in her basket.

The last of Hillary's Base States is her husband's home state of Arkansas, where Hillary worked in a major law firm before serving as the state's first lady. While it is possible that two of Hillary's Base States, Connecticut and Delaware, could vote for their favorite sons, Senators Chris Dodd and Joe Biden, I expect both of these candidates to be out of the race by Super Tuesday.

Here are the six Hillary Base States and their 530 delegates:

New York	232
New Jersey	107
Massachusetts	93
Connecticut	48
Delaware	15
Arkansas	35
Total	**530**

★   ★   ★

The second key metric for winning Super Tuesday is leading in the national count of pledged delegates. This will be a close call under the best of scenarios. If we win Iowa and South Carolina and hold our own in New Hampshire and Nevada, we should head into Super Tuesday with a small pledged delegate lead.

During Super Tuesday itself, we'll have the ten Obama Base States and their 567 pledged delegates versus the 530 delegates in the six Clinton Base States, giving us a modest potential advantage of 37 delegates in our Base States. There also are the six Competitive States on Super Tuesday, where 558 pledged delegates will be up for grabs. Among these states, I expect Hillary's greater strength in California to offset whatever modest advantage we might have from our larger pool of Base State delegates. Of course, neither candidate can win all the delegates in any state.

★ ★ ★

I consult with our numbers guru, Peter Appel, on the delegate math. The number of delegates apportioned to a district affects the calculation of what percentage of the vote a candidate must win to earn delegates. This math isn't overly complicated. In the chart below, the column on the left side of the chart is for how many delegates are available to be won in the district. The row across the top is for how many delegates are won based on the vote percentage shown where each column and row intersect.

Delegate Math Chart

Vote Percentage Thresholds for Achieving Delegates

	1	2	3	4	5	6	7	8	9
3	16.7	50.1	83.4						
4	15.0	37.6	62.6	85.1					
5	15.0	30.1	50.1	70.1	85.1				
6	15.0	25.1	41.7	58.4	75.1	85.1			
7	15.0	21.5	35.8	50.1	64.3	78.6	85.1		
8	15.0	18.8	31.3	43.8	56.3	68.8	81.3	85.1	
9	15.0	16.7	27.8	38.9	50.1	61.2	72.3	83.4	85.1

For example, in a congressional district with four delegates, find the number 4 in the column on the left and follow the row as it goes off to the right. For each vote percentage, the candidate wins another delegate. Upon winning 15 percent of the vote (the minimum required under DNC rules), the candidate wins the first delegate, a vote percentage of 37.6% wins the second delegate, 62.6% wins the third delegate, and 85.1% wins the fourth delegate.

For a presidential campaign, the key to using the information in the Delegate Math Chart is to estimate the percentage of votes likely to be achieved in each congressional district and to match the candidate's percentage with the closest delegate threshold. If the expected election result is just below or above this closest delegate threshold, the presidential campaign should target that district—to either win the next available delegate if it looks to be within reach, or hold the last delegate that appears to be at risk. If the candidate's likely vote estimate for the district is far from the closest delegate threshold, the presidential campaign shouldn't waste any effort, unless merited for the statewide contest.

There are some interesting rules of thumb to glean from the Delegate Math Chart for different sizes of delegate districts. In the 5-delegate districts, which are very common, the focus should be on whether the candidate can achieve a vote total close to the 50% mark. If yes, go for the fifth delegate. If no, in nearly all cases, assume a 2-delegate win and move on. For 4-delegate districts, which also are common, it's important to determine whether the 37.6% delegate threshold is likely to be in play. If yes, play hard in the district to get the 2 to 2 split. If no, focus elsewhere for primary election day. In a 3-delegate district, which is much less common, a candidate only needs to know if the vote in the district will be close to an even split. If so, the candidate should fight for the third delegate. Otherwise, the other thresholds are so far away that there's nothing left to fight for in the district. The other district sizes also each have a rule of thumb for election planning.

*   *   *

Applying this delegate targeting approach to Super Tuesday, Obama should have a good chance to win substantial numbers of delegates in his Base States, the Competitive States, and even Hillary's Base States. For weeks, I've been running through my analysis of every Super Tuesday state and congressional district to look for delegates we reasonably can hope to win for Obama.

Opportunities in two of Hillary's Base States, New York and New Jersey, catch my eye. In New York, I see that 23 of the state's 29 congressional districts—all located outside New York City—each elect five delegates. Given Hillary's home state advantage, I have no doubt she'll win the majority of the vote in all these districts. But, as long as Barack obtains 30.1% or more of the vote in these districts, he'll take two delegates in each district—per the

Delegate Math Chart. This means he can lose all 23 of New York's 5-delegate districts by nearly 40 percentage points, and still win 46 of the 115 delegates at stake in these districts. We don't need to contest these 5-delegate districts to win these 46 delegates.

It would be far better to focus our New York efforts on the districts in the New York City area, where all of the state's remaining districts—each with 6 delegates—are located. These districts tend to be more reform-oriented, and some of them are majority African-American. Barack should be able to obtain a 3 to 3 delegate split in each of them—if he can capture 41.7% of the vote in these Big Apple districts. He can lose by 16 percentage points in these districts, and Hillary won't gain one delegate on him in them. Overall, Hillary's advantage among New York's district delegates should be just the 23 extra delegates she's likely to win in the 5-delegate districts. This wouldn't be much of a gain from her home state.

Similar results should be possible in Hillary's other "home" state of New Jersey. Ten of the state's 20 delegate districts elect 3 delegates each, meaning that Hillary will win only one extra delegate in each of these districts as long as Obama obtains just 16.7% of the vote. In the remaining 10 districts, 4 delegates are to be elected, and Barack will gain an even 2 to 2 split of the delegates if he wins 37.6% of the vote. In other words, he just needs to lose by no more than 24 percentage points in order to gain an even split of the delegates in each 4-delegate district. This should be achievable and would leave Hillary with just a 10-delegate margin from New Jersey's district delegates—not bad for Obama in a state that shares the New York City media market.

The examples of New York and New Jersey provide a taste of what proportional representation will produce in terms of delegate accumulation in all the states voting on Super Tuesday. I've studied all the Super Tuesday states and districts and believe Obama can achieve something of a national draw in the day's delegate competition by focusing on his Base States, the Competitive States and those areas within Hillary's Base States where we can increase his delegate yield. We might even win the day in delegates—and this important Super Tuesday metric—if we have enough momentum going into the day's voting.

* * *

The third key metric we need to focus on for Super Tuesday is winning the marquis Super Tuesday contests that are not considered a home state for either candidate. The media will want to show not only who has won the biggest pile of states, but also who has won the most important states. Success in key Super Tuesday states will be a huge topic of discussion, and winning these marquis states will be of great benefit in being judged the winner of this major voting day.

Since Illinois is Obama's home state and both New York and New Jersey are considered home for Hillary, the media will look at other states for this metric. First and foremost, the attention will be on California, which closes its polls at 11 pm Eastern, concluding the important voting on Super Tuesday.

While a consensus of which candidate is doing better in the nationwide voting will develop before the California results come in, until California is called by the networks, the media is unlikely to anoint the winner of Super Tuesday.

While California is far and away the top marquis state on Super Tuesday, other important states vote that day. There are Georgia and Tennessee, whose results will be viewed as indicative of each candidate's appeal in the South. The primary in Missouri is a national political bellwether. The Colorado and Minnesota caucuses will indicate candidate appeal in the Mountain states and upper Midwest. The primary in Arizona will show the voting tendencies of its large Hispanic population.

While all of these states will be well covered by the media on election night, they will pale in significance compared to California, which is why the third key metric is mostly just about winning California.

* * *

The States Voting After Super Tuesday

Once the voting on Super Tuesday is finished, if Hillary has prevailed on even just one of the three key Super Tuesday metrics, she probably will have the staying power to fight on to other primaries and caucuses. The Clintons are political survivors. They know that anything can, and will, happen in politics, if they can hang on to play for the time to turn around their political fortunes.

Also, because Barack Obama is relatively new to the national scene and in his first national political race, there is a greater chance for information to develop that could undermine his candidacy—and the Clintons know it. Unless we win all three metrics, I expect the Clintons to soldier on in the nominating race, waiting, hoping, for a chance to rebound against Obama.

So what happens if titanic Super Tuesday doesn't end the nominating race? The competition will begin to stretch out as each of the two mega-candidates works to assemble a majority of the delegates to win the nomination at the National Convention, while still looking for a knockout punch to end the nominating race.

The simple math is that if Barack and Hillary split the 1819 pledged delegates elected through Super Tuesday—as I expect they roughly will—then both candidates still would be over 1,000 delegates short of a nominating majority, leaving a long way to go before either can claim victory.

We are fortunate, though, to have an excellent opportunity to take control of the race during the period immediately following Super Tuesday. Eleven February contests roll out during a two-week period beginning after Super Tuesday that offer Obama the chance for a long string of wins that could comprise a knockout blow against Hillary.

On Saturday, February 9th, Louisiana will hold a primary, while Washington, Nebraska and U.S. Virgin Island Democrats will meet in caucuses. Louisiana has a large African-American population that should provide a strong base for victory there. Washington, and Seattle in particular, have a strong strain of anti-war activism that can sustain a significant Obama win.

Nebraska holds fewer clear advantages to either candidate, but we should be able to fire up the kind of activist Democrats who can dominate this type of low-turnout nominating contest.

The U.S. Virgin Islands, with its nearly total African-American population, likely will go all-out for Obama.

The next day, February 10ᵗʰ, will feature a single Sunday contest in Maine, the only caucus state east of the Mississippi River. Given Maine's location in Hillary's Northeastern region, it's not entirely clear to me who will have the advantage in the caucus state. Normally, Maine gets so swamped by the media attention associated with New Hampshire's primary that its caucuses follow New Hampshire's lead in presidential voting. This is a tough call, but I'm going to project it for Hillary.

Hard on the heels of this bundle of weekend contests will be the Tuesday, February 12ᵗʰ "Potomac Primaries" in the District of Columbia, Maryland, Virginia, plus a small contest for overseas Democrats known as "Democrats Abroad." Given its large number of African-American and upscale white voters, DC should be strong for Obama. Maryland, with its large black population in Baltimore and Prince George's County and well-healed white suburbs in lower Montgomery County, should be another easy Obama win. Virginia could be more of a challenge, but the combination of the state's African-American communities plus the melting pot liberalism of northern Virginia provides a strong foundation for an Obama victory here, too.

The post-Super Tuesday period winds up on Tuesday, February 19ᵗʰ, with the traditionally important Wisconsin primary, the Hawaii caucuses and a Washington State beauty contest primary. Wisconsin, the home of Bob LaFollette, prairie populism and the liberal University of Wisconsin in Madison, is tailor made for Barack Obama, especially when you add in the large African-American population in Milwaukee. Hawaii is Obama's birth state, so while some of the Democratic Party establishment might support Hillary Clinton, we can't lose there. Finally, while the Washington primary will not be used to allocate that state's delegates, which are chosen through a parallel caucus system, it can be a win for Obama that contributes to the political momentum created by his other wins during this period.

These eleven nominating contests during the two-week period that follows Super Tuesday offer Obama what may be the best opportunity to take control of the nominating race. He can beat Hillary in all eleven of them!

Any ordinary presidential candidate who lost eleven straight contests would give up the nominating race, but this might not apply to resilient Hillary.

If Hillary were to survive these eleven likely pro-Obama states, she and Obama will continue competing into the spring. A major day of voting will occur on March 4th, when voters in four states will cast ballots, including in the major states of Texas and Ohio. Less significant contests will be held in the New England states of Rhode Island and Vermont.

If Obama could sweep both Ohio and Texas on March 4th after running the table during the post-Super Tuesday period, he probably could sew up the nomination. Splitting these contests, though, likely wouldn't be sufficient to force Hillary to leave the race.

If the March 4th voting doesn't end the nomination race, we'll likely have to fight all the way through the last primaries.

After a primary in Mississippi, the candidates will campaign for six weeks for the Pennsylvania primary scheduled for April 22nd. Hillary should have real strength here. She was born in Scranton and is supported by powerful Governor Ed Rendell and most of the state Democratic establishment. The state has a substantial white blue-collar vote that's likely to support her. While a win here for Obama theoretically could end the nominating race, I'm skeptical the race will end before June if it's still going after the Ohio and Texas primaries.

After Pennsylvania, there will be five midsize primaries in May, including Indiana, North Carolina, West Virginia, Kentucky and Oregon, but the mix of regions makes these states unlikely to lean heavily as a group toward one candidate. Early June offers no other major primaries for closing out the race, and these contests should end with more a whimper than a bang.

★ ★ ★

If the primaries and caucuses have not produced a significant advantage for either candidate, we will be forced into a long struggle to take and hold the lead in the national delegate count. This delegate race from hell hasn't been seen in decades in Democratic presidential politics.

We'll do everything we can to maximize our yield of delegates by targeting states and individual congressional districts. We'll also target every opportunity created in the national and state party rules to win delegates apart from those awarded in the primaries and caucuses. One wrinkle, in particular, that I'll focus on will be the 81 "add-on" superdelegates to be selected—no more than a handful in any one state—at the discretion of party leaders, state conventions or other party groups without regard to the primary or caucus results.

Strategically, this leaves us with the remaining 768 known superdelegates, most of who are members of the DNC or Congress. We'll have to convince enough of these superdelegates to join with the pledged delegates for Obama to create a nominating majority at the National Convention.

A theoretical even split of the 3,566 pledged delegates between Obama and Hillary would provide only 1,783 delegates to each candidate, well short of the 2,208 needed for a nominating majority. If an additional candidate breaks the 15% threshold to win pledged delegates, it will be even more difficult for the top two candidates to reach the 2,208 delegate nominating goal. The battle for superdelegates in this scenario will reach its zenith as the primaries and caucuses end and the delegate leader seeks their support to achieve a majority for the National Convention.

One of my biggest concerns is that, if we're unable to end the nominating race at our few key opportunities during the primaries, Hillary will stay in the race all the way to the National Convention and make it difficult for Obama to unify Democrats for the general election.

Obama will need a big enough pledged delegate lead by the end of the primaries that he can obtain sufficient superdelegate support to reach the Magic Number. Otherwise, the race will go to the National Convention in Denver.

★   ★   ★

My study of the 2008 nominating calendar runs for many weeks. By mid-summer, I've got lists, maps and charts festooned all around my desk and nearby walls, making my area a curiosity for some of our staff, especially those who've never experienced a presidential nominating campaign.

Steve Hildebrand, or "Hilde," our deputy campaign manager, asks me what my analysis is showing. We hold a series of conversations during which I lay out my views on the nominating race.

Hilde wants to get as broad a range of input as possible about our prospects and convenes a series of staff meetings with leaders from each of our political and field components. Perhaps a dozen people join each meeting, where staffers speak up and give their views in terms of our political, field, or constituency group strength. I set out what I believe we can accomplish in each state, including whether we'll win the state and how many delegates we can hope to obtain. I identify which parts of each state are critical to the delegate outcome, including which congressional districts deserve our greatest attention. These meetings are routinely collegial, as we share information and opinions on how to best craft our campaign plan.

By the end of summer, our meetings are finished and Hilde is finalizing our approach for the primaries and caucuses. We have a solid plan to pursue — as long as things go as expected.

4

Florida Jumps the Gun

AT THE VERY TIME I'M SETTING UP SHOP at the Obama headquarters in Chicago, a storm is quietly starting to brew in the State Capitol in Tallahassee, Florida. I'm hearing that a young Democratic state senator, Jeremy Ring from Broward County, has developed a plan, along with some Republican state legislators, to jump the state's presidential primary ahead of nearly all the other states in the country. The goal is to gain more attention for Florida in the nominating races of both political parties.

Scheduling the Florida primary this early, however, would violate the nominating rules of both national parties. These rules protect the right of Iowa and New Hampshire to hold the first nomination contests. Democratic National Committee rules also enable Nevada and South Carolina to hold the first contests in their regions. These rules are intended to allow the presidential candidates to have maximum personal contact with the voters in these smaller states before the national nominating race expands to include the rest of the country.

Florida's attempt to break the Democratic and Republican primary timing rules could radically change the dynamic of the Democratic nomination race. The rules for the timing of the primaries creates a specific order of voting leading into Super Tuesday, and a move by Florida to the front of the primary calendar would disrupt this order and alter the crucial path to Super Tuesday. Moreover, if other states decide to follow Florida's example and leapfrog to the start of the primaries, the entire nominating process could be thrown into chaos.

Publicly, a number of Florida's elected leaders explain their interest in moving the state's primary date forward as something of a protest against the special status accorded under national party rules to the approved early voting states. The Floridians argue that it's unfair for these states to be allowed to go early and potentially dictate the course of the nomination race, while large states like Florida that are critical to the general election outcome are required to vote later.

★   ★   ★

While Florida isn't the only state to complain about Iowa and New Hampshire always voting first, it's no accident that these two states have this privilege. New Hampshire's presidential primary became first-in-the-nation in 1920. After three decades of relative obscurity, the New Hampshire primary made its first major mark on the national nominating process in 1952. GOP candidate Dwight Eisenhower vanquished Ohio Senator Robert Taft in that year's New Hampshire primary, even though Taft was so highly regarded by his party's voters that he was known as "Mr. Republican." That same year, in the Democratic race, populist Tennessee Senator Estes Kefauver defeated incumbent President Harry Truman in the New Hampshire primary, driving President Truman right out of the presidential race.

Years later, in 1968, anti-Vietnam War candidate Eugene McCarthy stunned President Lyndon Johnson in the New Hampshire Primary by coming within a few percentage points of him, convincing Johnson that the nation would not elect him to another term. Four years after that, in 1972, Democratic frontrunner Senator Ed Muskie's presidential effort collapsed while campaigning in New Hampshire when—only five days before the primary—he became emotional on TV while responding to disparaging depictions of his wife by the state's leading newspaper.

Iowa also has a special history of early presidential voting. Iowa began using a caucus system as early as 1800, way before the

Iowa Territory even became a state. In fact, ever since the time of George Washington, Iowa has used a caucus system in every election cycle except one (and that was almost 100 years ago).

The importance of Iowa's caucuses grew after the tumultuous 1968 National Convention led the Democratic Party to reform its presidential process. Among the changes was a new requirement that delegates be chosen during the year of the election, to prevent party bosses from picking them before the public knew who would be running. Iowa responded by scheduling their 1972 precinct caucuses for January 24th, ahead of that year's New Hampshire Primary. George McGovern won a second place finish in these caucuses, but it was four years later, in 1976, that Iowa really made its mark on the presidential nominating process. That year, little-known Jimmy Carter used a very focused Iowa campaign to place first among much better known Democrats in the state, going on to win both the presidential nomination and the White House itself. Ever since, no one has questioned Iowa's importance as a make-or-break early contest for the presidential nomination.

In order to guard the tradition of their early contests, both Iowa and New Hampshire have modified their election laws to guarantee their early position in the nominating process. Iowa's election law says the state must hold its caucuses at least eight days before any other contest in the country. New Hampshire state law directs the state's secretary of state to set the date of its primary on any day that is at least eight days earlier than that of any similar election. Both national political parties have concluded over the years that it's better to honor these state laws and early voting traditions, rather than try to share this privilege with other states.

Iowa and New Hampshire voters do, in fact, seem to take seriously their responsibility as early vetters of the presidential candidates. Many voters study the issues, open their homes and businesses to the candidates, organize early and intensively for their preferred candidate, and turn out to vote on election day. While it's true that the political class in Iowa and New Hampshire sometimes take advantage of their privileged early status to demand fundraising assistance and consulting agreements for their members, both national parties have codified the right of these two states to vote early in national party rules.

Leaders in other states have not been happy with Iowa and New Hampshire always voting first. They say their states have the same right to an early voice in the presidential race. Many Democrats also say that Iowa and New Hampshire aren't sufficiently diverse racially or ethnically to merit voting first every presidential election year.

The DNC has not ignored these complaints. In 2006, the DNC responded by adding two other states, Nevada and South Carolina, to the front of the presidential nominating calendar. Nevada is a Western state with a substantial Hispanic population and organized labor presence. South Carolina is a Southern state with a large African-American population and an early voting history of its own.

* * *

Neither the Iowa and New Hampshire early voting tradition nor the addition of Nevada and South Carolina to the front of the voting appears to have had any bearing on the movement in Florida to leapfrog to the start of the primaries. Florida's leaders simply want to vote early also, and don't seem to feel constrained by national party rules to the contrary.

The wheels of Florida state government start to roll almost as soon as the plan to advance the primary date is developed.

On January 11, 2007, the Elections Committee of the Florida House of Representatives holds a hearing on the idea of an early primary. Two weeks later, House Republicans introduce legislation co-sponsored by seven Democrats to move up the primary. Every Democrat and Republican on two different House committees promptly votes to approve the legislation. In March, the Florida House approves the legislation by a vote of 115-1, with every Democrat in the Florida House, except one, voting for the legislation.

In the Florida Senate, parallel legislation to advance the primary date is introduced. The Republican Elections Committee

Chairman engineers a unanimous committee vote to merge the primary legislation into his own elections legislation, putting the primary date change on a fast track toward Senate approval. In April, the full Florida Senate takes up the merged elections legislation. Senate Democratic leaders offer a "late-filed" amendment to keep the primary on a later date, but do not even ask for debate on their amendment. Senators openly laugh in the chamber when the amendment is put to a vote. The amendment immediately is defeated by a voice vote, and the elections legislation—after being merged with other legislation—passes the Senate by a vote of 37-2, with no Democrats voting in opposition.

The Florida House then takes up the Senate legislation for final approval. House Democratic leaders, already having voted for the early primary, introduce their own last-minute amendment to keep the primary on a later date, but also don't ask to debate the amendment. The amendment is immediately defeated by voice vote and one of its sponsors explains to his colleagues that he offered it only to create a record to show to the national Democratic Party. The House immediately votes 118-0 for the legislation—with every Democrat in support—sending it to the Governor for his signature.

Florida's primary is advanced to January 29, 2008, three days after South Carolina will be voting.

*   *   *

As the Florida Legislature works to move up the state's primary, alarm bells go off at the Democratic National Committee headquarters in Washington. The danger to the DNC and its chairman, Howard Dean, is immediately clear. Florida's effort to leapfrog the other states could trigger a stampede of states seeking to increase their own influence, possibly leading to a breakdown of the presidential nominating system.

No national party chair wants the presidential nominating system to collapse on his or her watch, so Dean's staff moves into overdrive. Upon seeing the press reports on what is developing in Florida, DNC leaders contact Florida Democrats. Dean warns them that if they support the move of their state primary into January, they'll face tough sanctions against the state's delegation to the Democratic National Convention.

There are two major penalties if Florida schedules its primary earlier than allowed under the rules. First, Florida automatically would lose half its pledged delegates and all its superdelegates. Second, any presidential candidate who campaigns in the state would not be able to receive any delegates from Florida. Democratic rules, moreover, authorize additional steps to enforce the primary timing rule, including the possible elimination of all the state's pledged delegates.

Florida's effort to catapult itself to the front of the primary schedule also violates national Republican Party rules, which require an automatic loss of half the state's delegates to the Republican National Convention. Under Republican rules, though, presidential candidates are not prohibited from campaigning for the state's remaining delegates, and the RNC has no authority to take away more than half the state's delegates.

DNC rules recognize that, in some situations, Democrats simply cannot influence the date selected for their state's presidential primary because the Republicans have complete control of the state government. In such a case, Democrats in the state will not be penalized for a primary date that violates DNC rules, as long as state Democrats show they have taken provable positive steps to schedule the primary on an allowable date.

The Florida Democratic Party believes they can show they took "provable positive steps" to set an allowable primary date, but that they were thwarted by state Republicans. Florida Democrats will highlight both the state party's public communications to legislators requesting a later primary, and also the legislative amendments for a later primary that were proposed by Democrats late in the process. But this telling of the tale does not square with state Democratic support for the legislation as it made its way to enactment.

Rumors emanating from Florida indicate that state Democratic leaders joined Republican leaders in privately giving the "green light" to legislators to advance the primary date into January, though it's impossible to confirm what would be confidential conversations among state leaders.

After the January primary legislation is signed into law, the DNC requests that Florida Democrats ignore the early primary and instead hold a separate caucus later in the calendar to choose their delegates. The Florida Democratic State Executive Committee meets, but is not swayed by the DNC. The Executive Committee votes unanimously to stick with the new early primary.

*   *   *

Hearing about these developments in Florida, I turn my attention to what is really going on in Florida and what it might mean for our campaign. I get on the phone with the DNC staff and Obama supporters in Florida to ask, "What the hell is going on down there?" There are a lot of problems for the national Democratic Party with Florida moving its primary into January, but I'm concerned about the potential effect on our campaign.

A January 29th Florida primary could completely blow up Obama's winning path to the presidential nomination. This path requires him to win in Iowa, get through New Hampshire and Nevada and emerge, the week before Super Tuesday, as a leading candidate in South Carolina, whose large African-American population can carry him to a major victory one week before Super Tuesday. Moving the Florida primary to three days after South Carolina's primary would block this strategy, as the election outcome in massive Florida would surely overshadow the results from smaller South Carolina.

I can't help but suspect that Clinton supporters are playing some role behind the scene in seeking the early date for the Florida Primary. Hillary has more than enough reason to want an early showdown in Florida. Right now, all the polls in Florida show Hillary holding a commanding lead among Democrats in the state, and moving the primary to January 29th could offer her a second, alternative path to the nomination if we win Iowa's caucuses. She could use Florida to trump our path to the nomination through South Carolina.

I don't have an intelligence operation for tracking Clinton influence in Florida. I have no idea what her people might be doing in the state and have to assume they're maneuvering to push the primary to the front of the nominating calendar.

I've seen frontrunners steer the national nominating process before. Back in 1984, when I was working on my first Democratic presidential campaign for Senator John Glenn, I watched as former Vice President Walter Mondale's supporters used their candidate's quasi-incumbency to dominate the Democratic Party's institutional machinery, including the process for writing the nominating rules. Outsider candidates like mine couldn't compete in the inside game for the nomination.

Now, we're facing a former president and a former first lady, who are among the smartest politicians of our generation, and they can only benefit from an early Florida primary. I'm concerned about our vulnerability in this situation and am convinced we need to make sure no DNC rules are skirted in the timing of Florida's primary.

I understand that any effort by the national party to discipline Florida for the violation of the primary timing rules can be painful to the state's voters and activists. I grew up in Broward County, Florida and my parents, relatives and friends still live in Broward. I understand Floridians' desire to have greater influence in the presidential primaries.

But I also know that at this point Florida is the only state that has chosen to violate the national party's primary timing rules. This action could easily trigger other states to jump the gun and lead to a complete breakdown of the presidential nominating process. All Democrats everywhere will suffer if we don't have a functional, orderly and respected system for selecting our presidential nominee. Florida leaders have created a terrible dilemma for our national Democratic Party, which will have to figure out how to protect its 2008 nominating process.

Concerned about the machinations in Florida, I talk to Plouffe about the serious problem developing in the state. We discuss what could happen if Florida jumps ahead of the approved start of the primary season. David immediately agrees that we can't stand by and watch Florida or any other state violate party rules to the detriment of South Carolina's important—and DNC-sanctioned—place in the nominating calendar.

For the next year, our mantra will not change: the DNC has to stand firm against any attack on the nominating calendar. The Democratic Party has a single set of rules for all states and presidential candidates, and the DNC must apply and enforce these rules uniformly throughout the country.

★   ★   ★

The DNC understands it has to defend its rules against Florida's attack. Throughout the Florida Legislature's consideration of the early primary legislation, DNC Chair Howard Dean and his senior staff have been telling Florida Democrats they are in danger of being penalized if they don't take serious steps to hinder passage of the legislation.

One of our top Florida supporters, Tallahassee City Commissioner and DNC Member Allan Katz, is very close to Howard Dean. He explains to Dean and his staff the nuances of what is happening in the state. After numerous conference calls and emails to Florida party leaders, DNC officials conclude that the Florida Democratic Party is making only half-hearted efforts, at best, to conform their primary to DNC rules.

When the January primary becomes law, the DNC tells the state Democratic Party they must develop an alternative voting process that complies with the national party's primary timing rule. This typically means that the state party has to set up its own statewide caucus system to allocate Florida's delegates to the competing presidential candidates. In this scenario, the state-run primary would be ignored by Florida Democrats.

Running caucuses in a state as large as Florida would be difficult for any state party organization. Florida Democrats, though, are especially ill-equipped to run a caucus system, which requires a skilled staff and a boatload of money. The Florida Democratic Party has few employees—none with experience running presidential caucuses—and no funds available to implement a caucus.

This is no secret to the DNC. If they really want the Florida state party to institute a statewide caucus system, the DNC will have to help Florida create a feasible caucus plan and find the needed funding.

"Give us a proposal for a caucus system, along with a cost estimate," the DNC tells the Florida Democratic Party. "We'll go to supportive labor unions and others to help raise the money you'll need to pay for it."

The state party hires a consultant to develop the plan. Florida DNC Member Allan Katz advises that the plan be affordable, with a limited number of caucus sites. Instead, the plan that surfaces is "gold-plated" and would cost a whopping $8-10 million.

The DNC has been told by its own experts that a down-and-dirty caucus system would cost in the neighborhood of $800,000, and asks the state party to produce a more affordable plan. The state party offers nothing else, leaving in place the rule-breaking early primary. Florida Democrats, in effect, are challenging the DNC's willingness to enforce its rules against the state.

This is a fateful decision by the Florida Democratic Party. From this point forward, they will be in direct confrontation with the national Democratic Party. The DNC's only option now is to bring the hammer down on Florida Democrats and bar them from the National Convention.

Imposing severe penalties on a major state is not an easy thing for a national party organization to do. In fact, Plouffe and I are worried that the DNC may flinch from the challenge. For months, the DNC has been unable to obtain real cooperation from the Florida Democratic Party or to impede the state legislature's advance of the primary into January. Now, after the DNC has offered to help pay for the state party to conduct an alternative delegate selection process, the state party is toying with the DNC by proposing a state caucus plan the DNC could never fund.

* * *

As far as I'm concerned, we've now passed the point where we can continue to watch this disaster unfold from the sidelines.

We need to get involved and encourage the DNC to defend its rules from Florida's frontal attack.

I tell Plouffe: "We're at a pivotal moment and the DNC leadership needs to stand its ground to prevent the nominating system from breaking down. We can talk to them all we want about this, but to me, they have to feel the danger in their bones."

"No question about that," says David.

"Well, one thing that will get the DNC's attention," I continue, "is if other states start moving legislation to advance their own primaries into January along with Florida."

"Are other states ready to do that?" David asks.

"Maybe, but we can't afford to wait to find out. If too much time goes by, the DNC could lose control of the situation," I tell David.

I hit the phones and within 48 hours, various pieces are moving into place. Media reports begin to bubble up from different corners of the country about possible primary date changes.

Then the story cracks wide open in Cincinnati, Ohio. State Senator Eric Kearney, incensed at Florida's threat to break national Democratic rules, has introduced legislation to move the Ohio primary into January to keep pace with Florida. This is big news for Cincinnati's major newspaper, The Enquirer, which puts the story across the top of its front page.

The same day the story runs, Plouffe gets a call from senior DNC staff. They want David and me to get on a conference call with them. They're agitated.

"Did you see today's story from Ohio?" they ask. "It says there's new legislation for Ohio to move its primary into January. The primary calendar could implode."

I see a smile peeking out from David's typical poker face, and I signal him that I'll respond.

"Yeah, we saw the Ohio report," I say. "You're playing with fire if you don't defend your rules."

As it turns out—unknown to me—Obama is visiting Cincinnati that day and sees The Enquirer headline on the early primary legislation. This timing is unfortunate. When Barack reads the story, he unloads on Kearney.

Soon, my phone is ringing.

"Damn it, Jeff," Kearney says. "Barack is in town and just gave me hell for the legislation to move up Ohio's primary. He thinks I'm putting the nominating system at risk in the middle of his presidential campaign—and he's pissed."

"Don't worry about it," I assure him. "We'll make sure he knows you're standing up for the DNC and its rules, not undermining them."

★   ★   ★

The talk at the DNC is hardening on Florida and the leadership there is firming up its commitment to sanction any state party that violates the primary timing rule. DNC rules mandate that a state is to lose half its delegates if it schedules its primary or caucus earlier than permitted. Moreover, both outside advisors and DNC staffers are coming around to the conclusion that—in order to put even sharper teeth into this penalty—all delegates, not just half, will be eliminated for any state violating the timing rules. DNC leaders warn Florida Democrats that there will be no tolerance for an early primary in their state and that they have to find a way to stay within party rules.

The Florida Democratic Party responds to this warning by trying to negotiate a lower level of the penalty to be enforced against the state's delegation to the National Convention. Rather than the 50 percent penalty specified in the rules, they ask for a reduction of only 25 percent, suggesting that they're looking for a penalty with which they can live.

This is a mistake. This isn't like haggling over the price of a used car. They're toying with the DNC again, and the DNC is still in no mood for games.

There is no bargaining by DNC leaders. The rules authorize them to increase the penalty on Florida, and if the state party does not relent, the DNC will hit the state with the maximum penalty—a complete loss of delegates.

The DNC's Rules Committee, which has jurisdiction over the national nominating rules, schedules a meeting to review the Florida situation. The Florida Democratic Party will send representatives to the meeting to argue that they had no role in scheduling the early presidential primary and that all of the decisions were made by the Republican Legislature, Governor and state party. The Rules Committee has numerous Clinton loyalists among its members who might resist reducing the size of Florida's delegation to the National Convention.

In anticipation of a DNC showdown against the Florida Democratic Party, I ask former Iran-Contra prosecutor John Nields and fellow lawyers Curtis LeGeyt and Jordan Usdan to investigate exactly how the Florida primary legislation was enacted. John and his team comb through the obscure records of the Florida Legislature, tracking down the details of every committee hearing and meeting, every vote and every speech made in connection with the legislation. They produce an authoritative legal report on what they found.

I study the legal report and personally listen to every tape of the committee hearings, meetings and floor speeches to verify every aspect of the legislative proceedings. The materials leave no doubt as to Democratic involvement in the advance of the early primary legislation through the Florida Legislature.

Recognizing the potential value of the thoroughly-researched legal report to the deliberations of the DNC Rules Committee, I forward it to the DNC staff. The report includes Internet links to the Florida Legislature's website for each of the meetings, hearings and speeches that advanced the early primary legislation. It's a powerful tool for understanding what happened in the state.

After the DNC staff reviews the report, they ask me, "Do you care if we use this information for our hearing on the Florida legislation?"

"Knock yourself out," I reply. "It's your rules and hearing, and this whole situation is your problem to resolve."

When the Rules Committee meeting convenes, representatives from Florida give their version of events, which is that the responsibility for the early primary legislation lies solely with state Republicans. As the testimony continues, the DNC staff works their way around the room distributing a document to each of the members of the Rules Committee in advance of questions to the Florida representatives.

I'm sitting in the audience and wave to one of the staffers to ask for a copy of the document. As I flip through the pages, I realize it's virtually identical to the legal report I provided to the DNC staff. In fact, I can't find anything in there that wasn't in the report.

At first I'm not sure how I feel about the staff distributing the document. I initially figure this is okay, since I know firsthand that the information being provided is 100% accurate. As the Committee's debate ensues, I see one member after another scanning through the pages of the report.

Immediately, the members are quoting liberally from the document to grill the Florida representatives on exactly what happened during consideration by the Florida Legislature.

The Floridians don't appear to be prepared. They seem to have limited information about what happened at each step of the legislative process. All they seem to be able to say is what is written in their prepared talking points, which is that the Republicans are responsible for the early primary legislation.

As the discussion moves along, the Committee members are more convinced than ever about the need to take strong enforcement action against Florida. Harold Ickes, the senior advisor to the Clinton campaign and longtime Democratic Party rules expert, asks to be recognized to speak in connection with the document just distributed by the DNC staff.

"Shit," I say to myself. "I wonder what Harold is going to say about the document, or where it came from."

My breathing slows down as I wait for Harold to unload.

Harold says he has reviewed the document and wants to make a motion.

Now my breathing stops, wondering how he may attack the document.

Rather than raise hell about the provenance of the document, Harold praises it as providing an excellent record of the history of the early primary legislation. Apparently, as far as he is concerned, the document eliminates any possibility that Florida deserves leniency from the national Democratic Party. Of course, he's right.

To my utter surprise, he asks that the Rules Committee adopt the document as an exhibit to their proceeding. When no other Committee member objects, the presiding chair grants Harold's request.

And with that, the detailed report painstakingly developed by my team of lawyers provides the critical record on Democratic involvement in the enactment of the early Florida primary.

The Rules Committee moves promptly to a vote on the ultimate penalty for Florida's violation of the national party's primary timing rule. With little further debate, the question is brought to a vote. The entire 30-member Rules Committee, except for its one Florida member and the abstaining co-chairs, votes to strip Florida of all its delegates to the National Convention. All the members of the Rules Committee who have endorsed Hillary Clinton join in the vote to eliminate Florida's delegates.

I'm relieved that the vote is over and I'm impressed by the integrity shown by all the Committee members, particularly the Clinton supporters, including Harold. They have taken the high road and acted to enforce the rules of the DNC to protect the national Democratic Party and its millions of members across the country.

When the vote is taken, the Rules Committee defers the effective date of the penalty for 30 days to give Florida Democrats one last chance to avoid losing its delegates. Immediately following the Rules Committee vote, though, the Florida Democratic Party chair walks out of the meeting room. Before the assembled Florida and national press, she says that while she will consult with state Democrats on her next step, she expects all the presidential candidates to ignore the national party's edict and to compete vigorously in the Sunshine State's early primary.

This expectation, however, is at odds with one more aspect of the Rules Committee's decision. Concurrent with the decision to strip Florida of its delegates, DNC rules mandate that any presidential candidate who campaigns in Florida will be ineligible to receive any delegates from the state.

While this may seem meaningless since the state now will have no delegates, it provides notice to all the presidential candidates that campaigning in the state is a violation of the rules that has a separate penalty specifically applicable to them.

The Florida Democratic Party takes no remedial action before the 30-day delay in implementation of its penalty expires and the state loses all its delegates. Soon thereafter, the DNC adjusts its official list of state delegations to the Democratic National Convention to show that Florida will have no delegates.

This change reduces the national total of pledged delegates by 185 and unpledged delegates by 25. Now, there are 3381 pledged delegates and 824 superdelegates, for a total of 4,205 delegates to the National Convention. The all-important Magic Number drops from 2,208 to 2,103.

Florida's threat to the approved sequence of state primaries and caucuses still might not be behind us. Florida Democrats remain unbowed by the DNC penalty and continue to insist publicly that their primary will go forward and play an early, leading role in selecting the Democratic presidential nominee. Florida Republicans, who have lost only half their national convention delegates due to the early timing of the state's primary, are echoing the Democrats' defiance of national party rules.

If Florida Democrats and Republicans have their way, their state—not South Carolina—will have the last say before the voting on Super Tuesday.

5

Michigan Takes On New Hampshire

ONE OF THE REASONS that Florida's move to break the DNC's primary timing rule is so dangerous is that it could trigger other states to jump to even earlier primary dates and reduce the nominating process to chaos. For the DNC and for our campaign, which has to thread a needle to win the presidential nomination over Hillary Clinton, this would be a nightmare. As far as Plouffe and I are concerned, we need certainty in the primary schedule so we can plan and prepare for what certainly will be a difficult battle against a nearly invincible competitor.

Unfortunately, it isn't long before it becomes clear that Florida's decision to violate DNC and RNC presidential primary rules is leading another state to challenge the approved primary calendar. Michigan Senator Carl Levin has long believed it's unfair to the rest of the country for New Hampshire and Iowa to always hold the first primary and caucus. He feels that Michigan and other industrial states that are suffering from a decline in manufacturing should have the same opportunity to have an early voice in the nominating process. I'm sympathetic to the need for industrial states to have an early voice in the presidential process, but don't want to see the 2008 primary calendar, which already is set, disrupted.

Through the years, Senator Levin has regularly recruited other leading Michigan Democrats to his opposition to the monopoly that Iowa and New Hampshire have on first-in-the-nation voting. One of those who joined his cause early was Debbie Dingell, the wife of the dean of the Michigan congressional delegation, John Dingell, and a power in her own right in the Michigan political world. For many years, Debbie headed the charitable foundation of General Motors, which is an important pillar of the nonprofit community in Michigan.

When Levin and Dingell see the Florida Legislature moving forward to challenge the approved early voting states, they decide Michigan should join the fray. Their opening occurs when Iowa, New Hampshire, Nevada and South Carolina—with the tacit support of the DNC leadership—move their primary and caucus dates earlier to stay in front of the January primary date in Florida. While these states are advancing their voting dates only to preserve the early role granted them by the DNC, Levin and Dingell cast these moves as justifying Michigan's own move of its primary to the start of the nominating process.

Levin and Dingell find an ally in their effort to advance Michigan's primary in Governor Jennifer Granholm, who is the senior Michigan Democrat supporting Hillary Clinton. These top Michigan Democrats quickly engage with their senior Republican counterparts to develop a plan to move Michigan's primary to the front of the national primary voting.

Michigan Republican leaders are eager to move the state's primary to the start of the election calendar perhaps partly to give a boost to GOP presidential candidate Mitt Romney, whose father served as the state's governor during the 1960s. No leader in the state, Democratic or Republican, seems to have an interest in opposing an early Michigan primary.

* * *

As Michigan's interest in an early primary has been growing, I've become increasingly concerned about the potential for the state to impact the approved sequence of early state voting. Once

Florida enacts its move to a January primary date, my nervousness about both states evolves into total alarm.

If both of these states hold early contests, I'm not sure that even the DNC's penalties will prevent the early state voting order from being disrupted. I begin brainstorming for a more potent approach to protecting the approved early presidential nominating calendar.

Over a period of several nights in early June 2007, after finishing my day-to-day work, I focus on little else as I gaze out our windows at the beautifully illuminated Wrigley and Chicago Tribune buildings. It's during these late nights when I realize that, rather than look for a new way to defend DNC rules, maybe I should look to one of my past presidential campaigns.

In fact, the answer to the current threat to the early voting calendar was developed years ago. I remember that New Hampshire, when it was threatened by the encroachment of another state's early primary, demanded that the presidential candidates boycott the offending primary. The candidates, always fearful of alienating New Hampshire voters, routinely crumbled in the face of this demand and agreed to the boycott.

If this worked for New Hampshire back then, why wouldn't it work for the approved early states now? While South Carolina alone might not have the clout to convince the presidential candidates to stay out of major-state Florida, all the early primary states together might be able to pull it off.

The decision of Florida Democrats to defy the DNC and use the rule-breaking January 29th primary enacted by the Florida Legislature amounted to a crossing of the Rubicon that led DNC Chairman Dean to tell a New Hampshire crowd that Florida's move means "their primary essentially won't count." I'm heartened to see that Dean is willing to stand up to Florida, but DNC penalties alone might not keep Florida from blowing up our one path to the nomination. I'm convinced getting all the candidates to boycott Florida—and any other state that chooses to jump the starting gun—is what's needed to support Dean and the DNC.

I call my longtime friend, Bill Carrick, who was the executive director of the South Carolina Democratic Party many years ago, to confirm my candidate boycott plan isn't crazy. Bill is now a top Democratic strategist located in Los Angeles. He and I met in 1987, when he was the campaign manager for Dick Gephardt's 1988 presidential campaign and brought me in to run Gephardt's delegate operation. Bill is an expert himself on the presidential nominating process, having worked as a top aide to Senator Ted Kennedy in his 1980 national convention fight with President Jimmy Carter.

Bill responds to my idea immediately: "I think getting the early 4 together on a pledge is an excellent move...the political cost and possible bad early state press are much more serious to the campaigns than the loss of potential delegates."

I send a note to Plouffe suggesting we move forward to launch the early states demand for a boycott and he instantly responds in his typical understated way: "I agree with that. They should, and I think it would be effective."

Within minutes, Bill floats the idea to leading South Carolina Democrat Don Fowler. Don, his wife Carol, who is chair of the South Carolina Democratic Party, and other state Democrats are struggling to find a way to protect their state's approved early primary from being overshadowed by Florida's new January contest. Don is interested in the concept and says he'll discuss it with Carol.

Over the ensuing weeks, it becomes clear that for whatever reason South Carolina isn't moving quickly to request the presidential candidate boycott pledge. It will take a stronger push from our Campaign's political operation if the approved early states are to get off the dime.

I reach the end of my rope on this dithering when I get wind that Michigan Democrats themselves are preparing a letter to the presidential candidates requesting a pledge to campaign in Michigan's primary even if it is held in January in violation of DNC rules.

I head straight to Plouffe's office and hit the ceiling.

"Michigan is about to beat the early states to the punch by issuing its own letter to the presidential candidates," I complain to David. "There is no way we can let this happen."

"I know, I know," David says. "I'll talk to Hilde. He's got the lead for us in the early states, so he's the best person to do this. We'll get it done."

Hilde (Deputy Campaign Manager Steve Hildebrand) immediately begins calling into the early states to urge them to defend their early voting dates. Finally, they get the message, and they're ready to act immediately.

Hilde sends me a note to say the state Democratic chairs of Iowa, New Hampshire, Nevada and South Carolina all agree to demand the boycott pledge from the presidential candidates.

"Hallelujah!" I say to myself. "Hilde did it."

With the early states now set to demand the pledge, I want to make sure the other Democratic candidates accept it. All of them other than Hillary should accept the pledge since, like Barack, they need to overtake Hillary in the small, approved early states to have any chance of winning the nomination. Allowing large, media-intensive states like Florida and Michigan to crash into the early voting period would make it almost impossible for this strategy to succeed. Also, with Florida likely an easy win for Hillary, the other campaigns should have no reluctance to back the DNC in its defense of the early primary calendar.

I make the rounds to each of the competing Democratic campaigns, except for that of Hillary, to give the others a heads-up about the coming boycott demand from the approved early states. In some cases, I get on the phone with my contacts at the other campaigns. In the case of Bill Richardson's campaign, I take the opportunity to have lunch with my longtime friend, Steve Murphy, who worked with me on both of the Gephardt presidential campaigns and now is Richardson's media consultant. Steve thinks the idea is a good one and says he'll raise it internally with the Richardson team.

As the summer of 2007 ends, when the approved early states finally issue their joint boycott demand to the presidential candidates, Governor Richardson jumps to be the first candidate to accept the pledge. He announces his acceptance early on a Friday afternoon. One by one, the other presidential candidates follow suit as the day goes on.

Plouffe holds our acceptance until Saturday morning to heighten media interest in whether we're going to accept.

By Saturday afternoon, only Hillary still has not said if she'll make the boycott pledge. Will she close the door to campaigning in Florida, even if she may come to need the state to re-energize her candidacy if she stumbles in Iowa? She's leading comfortably in the national polling now, so she might accept the pledge.

Then, we get our answer. In a pivotal moment in the 2008 presidential campaign, Hillary issues a news release Saturday evening to announce that she will stand with the approved early states of Iowa, New Hampshire, Nevada and South Carolina. She pledges not to campaign in any state that breaks national party rules to encroach on the approved early states. Finally, I'm feeling relieved.

⋆　⋆　⋆

Although the early states have won the loyalty of the presidential candidates in defending the early state voting, Michigan's Democratic and Republican leaders decide to plow forward in adopting an early January primary. The only live question is when in January the primary will be held. Senator Levin reportedly wants a date that will directly challenge New Hampshire's ability to hold the first primary in the nation. A good date to accomplish Levin's purpose would be near the very start of January, so New Hampshire would have no room for its primary after the Christmas and New Year's holidays.

On the other hand, Hillary would benefit more from a date in mid-January when the state could hand her a victory in the event she stumbles in Iowa or New Hampshire. I can't confirm any of the in-state discussions surrounding Michigan's choice of a January primary date, but I eventually learn that the date will be January 15th.

I'm concerned for several reasons about how this date will affect Obama. First, while he could be competitive against Hillary in a Michigan primary, the reality is that our campaign is organized to win in Iowa and South Carolina to have momentum going into

Super Tuesday. A state as large as Michigan voting in mid-January could upend everything we've been counting on and ruin our path from Iowa to South Carolina.

Equally important, a successful effort by Michigan to break into the January voting would lend strength to Florida's continuing effort to vote on January 29th and quite possibly entice even more states to leapfrog to the front of the primary calendar. If Michigan gets away with this rules violation, the DNC will be in a weaker position to deal with Florida and prevent other states from violating the primary timing rule.

But there is nothing we can do to prevent Michigan from moving its primary forward. In September 2007, just days after the DNC's stiff penalty becomes effective against Florida due to its rules violation, the Michigan Legislature enacts its own legislation for a January primary. A new assault on the early 2008 presidential primary schedule is underway.

★   ★   ★

I have no doubt that Michigan's decision to violate the DNC's primary timing rule will result in the DNC stripping the state of its delegates. The DNC's imposition of this penalty on Florida requires the same action against Michigan. In fact, the rules violation in Michigan is even more egregious than it was in Florida, where that state's Democrats could try to blame Republicans, who control the state government, for the early primary date.

In Michigan, top state Democrats were front and center in pushing for the early primary date, and both the House of Representatives and Governor's office are controlled by the Democrats. With even the Clinton supporters on the DNC Rules Committee voting to strip Florida of its delegates, there is no reason to believe the Committee won't enforce the same penalty against Michigan.

Still, I want the Obama campaign to do everything possible to make clear that it will not participate in the early Michigan primary. The refusal by the presidential candidates to participate in Michigan and Florida is key to defending the DNC's approved early calendar. While all the candidates have pledged not to participate in these contests, I'm concerned that Hillary may revisit her pledge and use Michigan and Florida to gain victories—even if not delegates—if it looks like Obama is gaining traction in Iowa.

In the mid-fall of 2007, I decide to pull a copy of the election law in Michigan and Florida to see if there are any provisions in the law that can help contain the situation. I find an obscure provision in Michigan that sets the rules for determining which candidate names are placed on the presidential primary ballot. Michigan's highest election official, the Secretary of State, is to compile a list of the bona fide candidates running for president from each political party. What I want to determine is whether the law includes another, even more obscure, provision that addresses not how presidential candidates get on the ballot, but how they can get off.

Then, I find the answer. Michigan law—unlike that in Florida—allows any presidential candidate whose name is placed on the ballot list by the Secretary of State to remove the candidate's name from the list. All that a candidate must do is file an affidavit asking not to be placed on the ballot, in which case the secretary of state cannot do so, with no questions asked. I confirm my reading of Michigan law with Detroit attorney Curtis Blessing, who has been pinging me with updates about litigation in the state challenging various provisions in the early primary law.

If Obama employs this procedure to remove his name from the Michigan primary ballot, Hillary won't be able to get any mileage out of the primary if circumstances change and she decides to renege on her pledge to boycott the early primary. If Obama is not on the ballot, the press corps won't be able to read any significance into the voting results, whether or not Hillary campaigns for the primary. This would end any chance that the early Michigan primary somehow could upend the early presidential nominating process.

All that's required to make this happen is for the presidential candidates to publicly withdraw from Michigan's primary. However, this might be easier said than done.

Michigan is a key battleground state in the general election, and the Democratic nominee must win the state. This applies to

Obama, as well as to every other Democrat who wants to be President. Publicly refusing to participate in the state's primary could alienate voters and endanger a candidate's prospects for the general election. As a result, it's a dicey proposition.

Contemplating the risks involved if I have Obama opt out of the Michigan Primary, it comes to me that I've dealt with exactly this kind of situation before. Back in 2004, when Howard Dean was surging ahead of my candidate for the presidential nomination, Dick Gephardt, Dean's campaign decided they would try—with their allies in the District of Columbia—to maneuver around Gephardt's strength in the Iowa caucuses by moving the District of Columbia primary in front of Iowa's contest. This would violate the 2004 national Democratic Party rules, but DC Democrats viewed it as a necessary protest of their lack of congressional representation, which is a big issue for DC voters.

I found that District of Columbia election law had a provision similar to what I'm seeing now in Michigan, which allowed presidential candidates to get off the ballot at their request. The question I faced in 2004 was how to use this provision without endangering Gephardt's support among DC voters.

My answer, then, was to seek strength in numbers and coordinate with the other Dean opponents to pull out of the DC Primary together. I was able to achieve this unity and most of the candidates removed their names from the DC primary ballot, which ended the threat to Iowa's opening caucuses.

I see no reason why the 2004 DC Primary model won't work for Michigan in 2008. The key will be to convince a critical mass of the 2008 Democratic candidates to submit the necessary paperwork to remove their names from the Michigan primary ballot.

This will require a reprise of our roundup of the candidates a couple months ago for the approved early states' boycott pledge. So, I'm back on the phone with all the Democratic campaigns, except for Hillary's campaign. I decide to make another trip to see Steve Murphy, my former Gephardt colleague at the Richardson campaign.

We reconvene for lunch near his office in Alexandria, Virginia and I tell Steve about the Michigan election law provision I found and slide a copy of the affidavit to get off the Michigan ballot across the table. As with the early states' boycott pledge, he agrees that filing the affidavit would be in Richardson's best interest. If Richardson is to have any chance in 2008, he's going to have to exceed expectations in Iowa, pick up steam in New Hampshire and hold on until Super Tuesday. An unauthorized primary in Michigan in mid-January, which would be too expensive for Richardson to contest, could ruin any chance he might have of winning the nomination.

Steve will talk to his campaign to get their approval, but says, "Jeff, I'll bet you the price of lunch that Hillary will never file this affidavit. She won't repeat her signing of the pledge to boycott the outlaw early states."

"You may well be right," I say to Steve, "but I'll take the bet. She went along with us once and I'm hoping she'll do it again."

As for the other Democratic candidates, I'm having trouble getting them to move on filing the affidavit, even as the Michigan filing deadline gets closer. Joe Biden's folks are taking their time. Dennis Kucinich's staff wants to file the affidavit, but aren't allowed to decide the issue without their candidate's personal involvement. Someone in the Edwards campaign apparently suspects I'm pulling a trick where they'll withdraw and we won't. Chris Dodd's campaign is having trouble making up its mind. I don't even bother communicating with Mike Gravel's campaign.

Finally, Biden signs on. Bill Richardson files his affidavit with little drama. The Kucinich staff struggles to get their candidate, who is always on the move, to approve and sign the required paperwork. Eventually, they get his approval to file, but are unable to get the document in front of him for his signature. With time running out, his staff, against my advice, signs the document for him and delivers it to the Secretary of State's office just before the deadline.

Unfortunately for the Kucinich campaign, the Secretary of State is a stickler for details and rejects the filing because the candidate didn't sign it himself. The Kucinich staff protests, but gets nowhere. As a result, Kucinich's name will be printed on the ballot despite him wanting it off.

Mid-morning on the last legal day for filing, October 9th, we get a phone call from the Dodd campaign. They want to hear again what they need to do to get the document filed. I can't believe it. After all this time, they're asking for this basic information just hours before it has to be filed in Michigan? At the end of the day, there is no Dodd filing. His campaign issues a statement that they're staying on the Michigan primary ballot.

The Edwards campaign knows from the start that filing the affidavit is the right thing to do, but they have extra reason to handle this carefully. Michigan is potentially a strong state for Edwards given his working class message. Also, their campaign manager, David Bonior, served for many years in Congress from the state, and he is reluctant to undermine his state's presidential primary. The Edwards staff has to work hard to convince Bonior to let them file the affidavit. Eventually they get his assent.

They call to give me the news, saying: "We'll do it, but only if you arrange for your courier to meet ours in Lansing, so they can make the filing together."

"Sure," I say. After all, why do I care how we physically make the filing?

With regard to my candidate's affidavit, usually when I need Barack to sign this kind of document, I arrange to meet him myself and explain what we're doing. In this case, he's on the road and I don't have time to wait for him to get back to Chicago, so I arrange for another campaign staffer traveling with him to get it signed, notarized and immediately delivered back to me. Barack has never signed an affidavit to pull his name off an election ballot, which is a pretty unusual filing for any candidate to make. So, when I receive the affidavit back, I call the staffer who gave Barack the document to see if he had questions.

"Hey, thanks for getting that form completed and back in my hands. It was a big help," I say. "By the way, did Barack hesitate to sign it?"

"Nope," the staffer replied. "He knew the affidavit was from you and signed it without saying a word."

Plouffe and I decide to tell the Clinton campaign the day before the deadline for the affidavit about our intent to withdraw from the ballot, and that we expect the other major campaigns to do the same. As far as we're all concerned, the January Michigan primary is being held in direct violation of national party rules and we're not going to do anything to legitimize it. We also believe that New Hampshire Democrats will appreciate the candidates taking their name off the Michigan ballot. Of course, Hillary can do whatever she wants.

Early that night, on the eve of the filing deadline, David tells me he has heard a rumor.

"I just got off the phone," he says, "and was told—not officially—that Hillary is going to file the affidavit to get off the Michigan ballot."

"Wow!" I respond. "I guess she really doesn't want to be the skunk at the picnic in New Hampshire."

This is somewhat of a surprise for us, because we haven't been counting on her to remove her name from the Michigan ballot. Having just the other major candidates get off the ballot would probably provide the result for which I'm looking. Having Hillary join in would be icing on the cake.

Of course, her getting off the Michigan ballot would be consistent with her decision earlier to sign the pledge to the approved early states not to campaign in any state busting to the front of the calendar. Why be on the ballot if the primary doesn't count?

Later in the night, though, we get new indications from Hillary's campaign. It now seems that her organization—perhaps Hillary herself—has second thoughts about filing the affidavit tomorrow. Of course, I can see the logic of her deciding not to file the affidavit. The crucial Iowa caucuses are not that far away and Hillary is still riding high in the national polls, so she doesn't have to do anything that doesn't serve her purposes, such as filing the affidavit.

The next morning, the Clinton campaign makes clear that Hillary believes Michigan voters should have their chance to vote regardless of whether the state has any delegates to the National Convention. She is not taking her name off the ballot.

"Damn!" I say to myself. "I'm going to be buying lunch for Steve Murphy."

I get Barack's signed affidavit to my courier in Michigan for its submission to the Secretary of State. The courier goes to the filing office in Lansing where, by prior arrangement, the Edwards courier arrives at the exact same time.

The couriers acknowledge each other and walk into the elections office together. Each pulls out an executed candidate affidavit and places it on the official counter—together—for filing. When the elections office staff come to the counter to look at the documents, they can't believe their eyes. Two of the leading Democrats are pulling out of the state's presidential primary.

When all the filings are compiled, the Michigan Secretary of State announces to the public that the Michigan presidential primary will be a contest among Hillary Clinton, Dennis Kucinich, Chris Dodd and Mike Gravel. Because of the affidavits filed by Obama, Richardson, Edwards and Biden, their names will not be on the Michigan primary ballot. Hillary will not be able to defeat a major presidential candidate during the January 15th contest.

The Washington Post reports that when all the top tier challengers to Hillary took their name off the Michigan primary ballot, "Michigan's hope for nominating clout all but evaporated."

Hillary faces a brief period of criticism in New Hampshire for not removing her name from the Michigan primary ballot. On the New Hampshire public radio call-in show "The Exchange," she explains her Michigan decision by saying, "it's clear this election they're having is not going to count for anything."

★   ★   ★

Michigan Democrats are stunned by the action of Hillary's major opponents and determined to force them to participate in the early presidential primary whether they like it or not. Michigan leaders quickly develop a new strategy that would require all of the candidates whose name was removed from the ballot to have their name placed back on the ballot.

The key to this effort is enacting new legislation to revise the Secretary of State's process for selecting the candidates for the presidential primary ballot. The legislation would require the Secretary of State to re-issue the original ballot list for the 2008 primary, but this time the presidential candidates would be denied the right to remove their names from the list unless they swear they are not a candidate for president.

While some other states don't allow a presidential candidate to choose to stay off the primary ballot, I question whether it's ever fair to force a candidate to compete in an election against his or her will.

More importantly, at this time, in this presidential election, the candidates withdrew their names from Michigan's primary ballot for a valid reason. The primary was scheduled in violation of national party rules, and non-participation is required by these same rules.

Also, it's unfair to change the rules for the 2008 primary in the middle of the process. The election laws were set in advance and several of the candidates already exercised their legal right not to participate. State legislators shouldn't change the law now to reverse this use of rights—especially since those candidates who decided to keep their name off the ballot could be subjected to voter disapproval for doing so. It's not lost on me that, unlike Barack, Hillary couldn't suffer this fate from the legislation.

Of course, the reality is that we're now in a fight with senior Michigan Democrats who are insisting that all the Democratic presidential candidates be put on the ballot for Michigan's challenge to the early New Hampshire primary. Like all the other major Democratic candidates other than Hillary, we made our decision to stay off the ballot and have to oppose the legislation to protect our candidates from being hurt.

★   ★   ★

But how can we survive a fight in the Michigan Legislature? I didn't even consider opposing the enactment of the law that advanced the Michigan primary to January 15th, since it seemed impossible to affect the debate on that legislation. Now we're facing a fight with the Governor, senior U.S. Senator, and a legion of their allies. Even worse, I'm receiving word that Democratic leaders backing the legislation are reaching out to state Republicans to join in the effort to amend the ballot law.

Due to our boycott of Michigan's early primary, we're limited in what we can bring to a political fight in the state. We have no organizational presence in the state. No office, no staff, nothing that could be used as a beachhead to get us started in opposing the ballot legislation. We do have a core group of supporters in the Legislature, including Detroit-area state senators Buzz Thomas and Tupac Hunter, but they've been hamstrung in leading any effort on Obama's behalf by our absence from the state.

If Obama's name is forced onto the primary ballot, the voters may punish him for having supported the DNC's boycott of the primary. The DNC's actions against the early Michigan primary have been under constant criticism from state leaders, so this is not a far-fetched fear. There is no turning away from this fight.

I get on the phone with our top political supporters in the state, a group of very committed elected leaders, some of whom are members of the Michigan Legislature. It quickly becomes clear that we have to reach beyond this core group to other political players who might provide the critical mass needed to stop the Legislature from steamrolling over us.

A unique aspect of Michigan's politics is the extraordinary influence of the United Auto Workers within the Democratic Party. If we can ally with them, we just might have a chance.

It helps that the campaign of John Edwards is aligned with us in opposing the primary ballot legislation. With former Michigan Congressman David Bonior at the helm of the Edwards Campaign, they have a special relationship with the UAW. The union has had a long and close relationship with Bonior from his days as a strong supporter of organized labor in the U.S. House of Representatives.

I jump on the phone with UAW political director Dick Long, who I got to know when I was a senior advisor to the Gephardt presidential campaign. Dick is a senior member of the UAW's leadership and someone I can trust.

"I need your help to fight the new legislation being pushed to force Obama, Edwards and the others onto the primary ballot," I tell Dick. "We're trying to run a national campaign according to the DNC's rules and we shouldn't be pulled into Michigan's fight against New Hampshire's early primary."

Dick, true to form, responds carefully, "Well, the UAW is not interested in this legislation ourselves. We don't see the point in forcing people to be in an election if they don't want to be on the ballot. You guys made your choice to stay off the ballot and you'll have to live with it. We're all good Democrats and you don't deserve to be treated like this. I'll make a few calls and see what I can do."

When the UAW makes a few calls in a political fight in Michigan, the political calculus of the fight changes. Up to this point, the state's Democratic and Republican leadership has been able to move the legislation through every step of the legislative process and requires only one more vote in the Michigan House of Representatives to change the law to force the candidates on the ballot.

It's now late November 2007 and time is running out for the House to take this vote. I'm on the phone with our allies in the House, sweating every detail of every step they're taking. I'm pacing back and forth along our bank of office windows facing the Chicago River. I've shut out any awareness of the office around me, completely focused on the events in Michigan. Plouffe makes repeated trips across the office to check on what's happening in Lansing. Each time, I tell him we're still fighting, and he walks away to wait nervously in his office for news of the outcome.

Finally, our allies disappear into the State Capitol for the final debate on the ballot legislation and put me on radio silence. My mind races through the implications of Barack losing Michigan on January 15th—even if no delegates are at stake.

Finally, I get a call from our Michigan legislative supporters. They have news for me. I listen and then hang up the phone.

Lost in a fog from the tension of the afternoon, I pivot away from my desk and pick up my head to see a large knot of our political and field staffers staring at me. They're waiting anxiously for the same news from Michigan.

"Jeff, what happened? Are we going to be all right?" someone asks.

"They couldn't get the votes," I respond. "The Michigan legislation is dead. Barack's name won't be on the ballot."

I've got to tell Plouffe. As I head off toward his office, word that the Michigan legislation has collapsed moves ahead of me. Still in my fog, I hear noise rising up around me, but don't immediately recognize why. As I make my way across the headquarters, I realize that the noise is moving all around me, literally following my path toward David's office. It's a spontaneous ovation from fellow staffers, applauding and cheering as I pass their desks, creating a wave of celebration across the headquarters.

When I reach David's office, I burst through the doorway to give him the good news. We both understand that we've dodged a bullet in Michigan. Our path from Iowa to South Carolina to Super Tuesday remains intact.

$$\star \quad \star \quad \star$$

On December 1st, 2007, the DNC's Rules Committee convenes by telephone to address the scheduling of Michigan's primary in January in violation of DNC rules. There is little debate about what must be done, as the Rules Committee already decided, in the case of Florida, to strip the delegates of any state violating the DNC's primary timing rule.

The Rules Committee votes unanimously, except for the abstaining member from Michigan and co-chairs, to strip the state of all its delegates to the Democratic National Convention.

With Michigan's delegates stripped, the DNC adjusts the list of National Convention delegates to show that Michigan will have none. This change reduces the national number of pledged delegates by 128 and unpledged delegates by 28. As a result, the National Convention now will have 3,253 pledged delegates and 798 superdelegates, for a total of 4,051 delegates to the National Convention.

The Magic Number drops from 2,103 to 2,026.

$$\star \quad \star \quad \star$$

In advance of the Michigan and Florida primaries, all the Democratic presidential candidates, including Hillary Clinton, reaffirm their pledge to boycott the two states. The candidates steer completely clear of Florida and Michigan. The states receive no presidential campaign visits, offices, staff, literature or advertising.

The press respects the decision of the DNC to revoke the Florida and Michigan delegates and include none in the national count of Democratic delegates. The two states are unable to disrupt the early New Hampshire primary or the DNC's nominating process.

6

Preparing in the States

AS SUMMER TURNS TO FALL IN 2007—and the DNC is still in the midst of its wrestling match with Florida and Michigan—we begin to pivot from planning to implementation for the early balloting that will run through Super Tuesday. The Campaign already has been hard at work laying the groundwork for the hugely important early states of Iowa, New Hampshire, Nevada and South Carolina. For us, Iowa is the first among early-state equals. Plouffe's handpicked lieutenant, Steve "Hilde" Hildebrand, is building the strongest early-state organizations these states have ever seen.

The Iowa organization already is massive. Plouffe spent a good part of his time during the Gephardt 2004 presidential effort in Iowa. While that effort failed, it was a great learning experience for David and he is schooled in all the key aspects of building a top-performing Iowa caucus operation. This means hiring capable staff, providing them with boatloads of money, and dedicating a good chunk of the candidate's campaign time to the state.

Now, Hilde is adopting David's laser-like focus to make sure our Iowa operation gets everything it needs to give Obama his best chance to win. Hilde has brought in his former consulting partner, veteran organizer Paul Tewes, to be State Director and Mitch Stewart to be Caucus Director. Behind them is an army of paid field organizers.

Our field team is blanketing the state to coordinate the thousands of volunteer Iowans who will be the backbone of our caucus operation. The goal is for Iowan Obama supporters to reach out to their families, friends and colleagues to expand our network of supporters beyond those who have participated in past Democratic presidential caucuses.

Beyond Iowa, we are constructing an elaborate organization in New Hampshire, in order to be ready to capitalize on our hoped-for success in Iowa. Running New Hampshire for Obama is New Hampshire Primary veteran Matt Rodriguez, who toiled there in the presidential run of Senator Bill Bradley in 2000 before serving as deputy political director—with Plouffe and me—in the 2004 Gephardt presidential campaign.

Our New Hampshire staff, to their consternation, won't see nearly as much of our candidate as they do in Iowa. Our Iowa-first priority makes sense, though, as our chance for success in New Hampshire will be determined, to a significant degree, by our Iowa performance. A strong win in Iowa can provide momentum for success in New Hampshire.

In Nevada, the next state to vote, we're developing a substantial caucus organization, though on a less elaborate scale than Iowa. This is the first year that Nevada will host a key early nominating contest, so it's difficult to estimate the level of turnout for the caucuses and how many supporters we'll need to win.

We're not putting all our eggs in the large basket of voters in the Las Vegas area, which is likely to be a stronghold for Hillary. We'll also focus on Washoe County, which includes Reno, and the smaller rural communities scattered around the state. In a close contest, the parts of the state that lie outside of Las Vegas could make the difference for us.

In the last of the approved early state contests, South Carolina, we'll almost certainly face a critical showdown with Hillary, if we're fortunate enough to be competitive with her at this point in the race. In order to win over the state's many African-American voters, we'll reach out to them in their local communities through a network we'll create of churches, barbershops, beauty salons and other centers of daily life. We'll also work to turn out young voters and as many white voters as we can, as success in this state requires a coalition of support.

*   *   *

While Hillary and the other presidential candidates are also organizing in 2007 for the contests in Iowa through South Carolina, the story is different for the Super Tuesday round of states. Thanks to our upwardly ramping fundraising success, we're able to allocate unexpected funds to those Super Tuesday states where early preparation might change the election outcome. I'm not talking about large primary states that are affected heavily by the momentum, press coverage and paid advertising that gels late in a campaign.

I'm talking about the caucus states we've targeted to win and where early organizing can make a big difference in the results. I break down the complexities of these voting systems and advise our field department on what it will take to win and maximize delegates.

Senior field advisor Jon Carson takes my analysis of the Super Tuesday caucus states and designs a campaign structure and operational plan for developing our staff and volunteer organization in each state. Jon is straight out of central casting for an Obama campaign leader. He's a self-effacing professional who uses every tool available to him (pus a few he invents) to implement those areas of our campaign plan that fall under his wing—and does it without drawing attention to himself. If this description sounds strikingly like one of David Plouffe, it's because Jon and David share a similar no-bull, honest approach to doing their work and working with others. Like many in our organization, they epitomize the approach that everyone calls "No-Drama Obama."

Jon constructs meticulous organizing plans for each targeted Super Tuesday state. He plans the budgeting, timing and logistics for standing up our Super Tuesday staff and grassroots organizations in one target state after another. One of his main focuses is determining how we will redeploy our staff from the four early states into our Super Tuesday state targets. They will need to interface with dedicated Obama supporters who aren't waiting for instructions from Chicago on how to prepare for the primaries and caucuses.

Even now, when Jon's first organizers arrive in their states, they often find themselves greeted by a well-oiled grassroots machine that can seem as impressive as the organized French Resistance that welcomed Allied troops liberating France after D-Day. I can only imagine the reception that will meet our redeployed staffers when they arrive in their new states in the days or weeks before Super Tuesday.

Jon and his headquarters team are developing unique organizing tools for field staffers to manage the work of grassroots supporters. One software application lets our paid field staff keep track of individual volunteer activity—such as voter contacts made—in real time through the Internet without having to rely on often unreliable self-reporting by volunteers. Now, our staff can know with precision how many voters our grassroots network is reaching every day and every week. This helps our supporters be more effective campaigners for Obama than activists ever have been for a presidential candidate before.

I help Jon train Obama supporters on the intricacies of the caucus process. Each state sets its own rules for caucusing, so I customize detailed guidelines for each caucus state. Since the vast majority of our caucus field staff and supporters don't know how their state's caucus system works, I boil this information down to understandable instructions.

In order to introduce our caucus staffers to their new state systems, we decide to do live training sessions in each of the Super Tuesday caucus states. This is in the late summer and early fall of 2007.

I go to as many caucus states as I can fit into my schedule to help lead the training sessions. Minnesota, Colorado and Kansas, here I come! In each state, huge crowds of Obama grassroots supporters come out to learn how to master their caucus system.

Minneapolis Mayor R.T. Rybak welcomes a boisterous group of Obama supporters who've come to learn about their caucus system in the Twin Cities. I'm stunned along with my colleagues from Chicago at the turnout for the training session. Obama supporters have packed the auditorium and are cheering like crazy for Obama at every opportunity. Senior Obama staffer Temo Figueroa—a good friend back at the Obama headquarters—extols the importance of organizing and energizes our supporters to focus on how they can win their caucus. I deliver the how-to part of the program, keeping things simple and walking everyone through a simulation of a caucus meeting. It's a lot of fun to interact with our grassroots supporters and a great opportunity to get a feel for the Obama support brewing in the states.

In Colorado, it's much the same. We rent a school auditorium in a struggling area of Denver and find it overrun with grassroots supporters. It's not just us from Chicago who are amazed at the attendance, so are the Coloradans who now see the support for Obama that already exists in their own communities. Many of our Colorado supporters are so excited about the prospect of caucusing for Obama that it seems they might not be able to wait until their caucuses on February 5th.

The scene in Kansas is no different. We hold a caucus training conference in a gleaming auditorium at the beautiful University of Kansas in Lawrence. I never thought Kansas looks like it does in Lawrence. The campus is hilly and landscaped in a way that seems like it could be anywhere but the Great Plains. I meet with Dan Watkins, a close advisor to Governor Kathleen Sebelius, at the training session and we marvel at the huge turnout and high spirits of our grassroots Obama supporters. Dan's been around the track a long time in state Democratic politics and can't remember seeing anything like this enthusiasm for Barack Obama— all we need to do is channel it and we can win these caucuses, Dan tells me.

After the Kansas training ends, I leave myself a few minutes to sneak over to the University's Allen Fieldhouse to take in the historic arena that has served as home to several great basketball stars. This was the college home of NBA Hall of Famer Wilt Chamberlain, and it's inspiring just to be here.

In subsequent weeks, these Super Tuesday caucus state training sessions are repeated over and over at ever more local levels to train a wider circle of Obama supporters within the caucus states.

At the same time, our state caucus organizations steadily expand their outreach, so that before long, we have designated leaders for each county and then down to even more local levels. After building this broad foundation for competing in the caucuses, I start to hear occasional reports that the Clinton campaign is showing the first glimmers of attention to organizing in these states. The reports aren't much, and certainly not something to cause us concern. By now, Obama has an organizational lead over Hillary in these states that she'll never be able to close.

* * *

While I'm helping Jon and his team organize for the Super Tuesday caucus contests, I have another important task that demands my attention. My son Joe is applying to college and he wants me to review his application essays. He's applying to 14 universities. Late at night, for several weeks, I take out my red pen and focus on Joe's drafts. He's a good writer, but he wants perfection. We go back and forth, discussing alternative approaches and wording, until finally he finishes the essays.

After we're done, I decide I need a day off from work and arrange with colleague Temo Figueroa to track down a small neighborhood bar, "Maeve," to watch the Washington Redskins on satellite TV. For 349 days per year, Maeve is a local wine bar, but for 16 days every fall, Maeve is the Sunday headquarters for Chicagoland Redskins fans. Temo and I pull directions to Maeve from the Internet, don our jerseys of Burgundy and Gold, and ride the subway to the closest stop to the bar. Then we hike from there.

When we arrive, we're in a Redskins wonderland, with team posters, banners and jerseys hanging on every inch of wall space. The place is packed with joyful Redskins fans, including one who has set up a grill outside to cook burgers and dogs for the crowd.

We all roar with approval at every Redskins first down and let loose the team fight song each time the 'Skins score. As a Redskins season ticket holder-in-exile, I'm in heaven!

When Temo and I get back to downtown after the game, I notice a noisy crowd milling about down the street. As we walk closer, I realize they're in front of the historic Chicago Theater and that Bob Dylan and Elvis Costello are about to perform inside. Without hesitation, we quickly scalp a couple tickets and within minutes we're inside enjoying vintage rock-and-roll. The concert is fantastic—you never know with Bob Dylan—making for a great end to our day off in Chicago.

★   ★   ★

When I return to the office, I throw myself into one of the most challenging parts of my job, which is to qualify Obama and his delegates for the primaries and caucuses. In many states, a candidate can't receive votes—and thus earn delegates—unless he or she earns a place on the election ballot.

Since my job is to assemble the delegate majority for Obama, I have to master the crazy quilt of state laws and party rules Obama must satisfy to compete in each of the primaries and caucuses. I recruit a battalion of 75 top lawyers in Washington, DC to join a volunteer committee whose sole purpose is to study the laws and party rules for ballot access in each state. At their typical hourly billing rate of $600, one of our hour-long meetings would cost me $45,000 if I had to pay everyone for their time!

★   ★   ★

I know from my work in Dick Gephardt's 1988 presidential campaign how awful it is to miss—or nearly miss—a primary ballot. At the time, all of the presidential campaigns were well into the ballot qualification process for their candidate. I was based in Gephardt's national headquarters in Washington, where I served as his deputy campaign manager for delegate operations. While his financial resources definitely were second-tier, Dick was a great candidate and had a lot of promise.

One day that started out not much differently than any other, I received a phone call from a campaign staffer for Governor

Michael Dukakis, one of our principal Democratic opponents. The staffer's voice was agitated.

"Jeff," he said. "We just got word that all the presidential campaigns may have blown a filing requirement today in Oklahoma. Apparently, the state elections office requires a new form to be filed and says any presidential candidate who doesn't file it today will not be on their primary ballot. The deadline is 5 pm!"

I was stunned: "What? Are you kidding?"

"I'm not kidding," he replied. "We're all screwed! We have to file today and nobody even knows what to file."

"Unbelievable! Thanks for the heads up," I said, my voice trailing off as I hung up the phone.

I sat at my desk, and for a moment pondered the nightmare I was about to face. Oklahoma was an important neighboring primary state for us and on our critical path to winning the nomination. Gephardt had good support in the state, including endorsements from statewide office holders and members of Congress.

Now, everything in the state was completely at risk.

The first thing I did was get on the phone with the lawyer who I had assigned the research on Oklahoma's legal requirements. She was as surprised as I was that this new filing requirement existed. This is not what you want to hear from your lawyer.

There was no point in assigning blame at this point. It was 10:30 am. I had six and a half hours before we would be off the ballot in Oklahoma. Our nomination chances would be measurably reduced, not to mention the hell there would be to pay as a result of this embarrassment.

I called the state elections office to find out what needed to be done and learned that all we needed to do was have our candidate sign a form, have a notary authenticate his signature, and file it in Oklahoma City. Ordinarily, this would be no big deal.

When I asked our scheduler, Jon Haber, where Gephardt was, so I could get the form to him by fax, I didn't like the answer.

"Dick is in New Hampshire, up north in the state," Jon said.

"Is he in Manchester?" I asked.

"No, that's not up north." Jon replied. "He's north of Concord."

"Are there any airports near there?" I asked. "I've got an emergency that involves getting an important legal paper from Dick, onto a plane, and in Oklahoma City by 5pm, or we're not going to be in the Oklahoma Primary. And I'm not kidding around!"

"You can't do anything fast from his location," Jon said. "Even if you drive the paper to the airport in Manchester, there are no non-stop flights from there to Oklahoma City. You'd need to get the paper to Boston in the next hour to get it on a plane from there that could get to Oklahoma City by 5pm. But you can't get to Boston that fast."

By this time, my stomach felt so upside down that I just wanted to puke. It turns out the other Democratic campaigns did not face as much of a problem as me, because their candidate was located closer to a major airport.

Jon recognized the urgency of the situation and immediately scrambled to check on other options, and then said, "There is one thing we can do. It turns out there is a Leer jet we could rent in Boston that we could fly to New Hampshire to get the form and then straight to Oklahoma City."

"What will it take to get this done?" I asked.

"Money," he replied. "It will cost $10,000. And there's no travel money in the budget to rent you a jet."

"I don't have any money to rent a jet, either," I grumbled back.

Then, with a smile emerging as he reached into his pocket, he said, "Since this is such a big deal, I'm willing to split it with you."

And with that said, he pulled his credit card out of his pocket and slammed it down on his desk in front of me.

I looked at him and thought for only an instant about our Campaign's lousy financial condition, and said, "Jon, that's a generous offer, but you're out of your mind. Neither one of us should be putting a jet rental on our credit card. We need to find another way to do this."

I put in a call to our outside counsel, Bob Bauer, to let him know we may have a legal problem in Oklahoma and get his advice. We talked back and forth about our options. We agreed to try to convince the Oklahoma elections office to let us have Dick sign the form in New Hampshire, get it notarized on the spot, and fax it into the elections office.

We then held a series of phone calls with elections officials and others in Oklahoma. But after an hour or so, it became clear they were going to be sticklers and demand an original signature on their new candidacy form.

By this time, it was too late to get a form with an original signature on the Leer jet from Boston, even if I wanted to pay for it myself.

So, we got back on the phone, and held more discussions with Oklahoma officials. By mid-afternoon, we reached an understanding that might get us through the day.

The Oklahoma elections office agreed to conditionally accept a filing signed by Dick and notarized in New Hampshire, if Dick and the notary certified it live over the phone and an agent for Dick signed a duplicate form at the Oklahoma elections office. This would give them an original signature. But the elections office said they wouldn't lift the condition on the filing unless the Oklahoma attorney general issued a legal opinion that the elections office could accept this kind of signature on the filing.

This was a relief, except for one thing. The Oklahoma attorney general might not provide the needed legal opinion. Unfortunately for Dick—and me—the attorney general already had endorsed our opponent for the presidential nomination, Al Gore.

I couldn't worry about that right away. First, I had to work with our advance staffers in New Hampshire to get the Oklahoma form to Dick and a notary on site to authenticate his signature on the document. With some difficulty, we finally got everyone and the paperwork in position in New Hampshire. With less than ten minutes before the state filing deadline of 5pm Oklahoma time, we convened our conference call with the Oklahoma elections office.

The state elections officer began the call: "Is Richard Gephardt on the line?"

"Yes, I'm here," Dick responded.

"Mr. Gephardt, are you a candidate for president of the United States?" he asked.

"Yes I am," Dick responded, while he probably wondered if this was sort of procedure from the Middle Ages.

"Mr. Gephardt, I need you to read the Oklahoma statement of candidacy and attest to the accuracy of each statement you are making on the form," the elections officer insisted.

And with that, Dick was forced to read aloud every line on the form. With very few minutes left until the 5pm filing deadline, this seemed like it took an eternity. When Dick was done reading, he signed the form in the presence of the notary, who audibly identified Dick as the signer of the document.

As soon as the notary stopped speaking, a nervous Oklahoma lieutenant governor, Dick's state campaign chairman, signed the same form in the state elections office and slid it across the counter to the elections officer.

At that point, I was ready to reach through the phone line and start strangling people, because the procedure was taking so long.

The elections officer took the form in his hand, turned toward the clock on the wall, and announced: "Mr. Gephardt, it is 4:59 pm, and you have filed the Oklahoma form for your presidential candidacy on time. However, I am accepting this filing only on the condition that its validity is affirmed by the Oklahoma attorney general. If he does not do so, I cannot place your name on the presidential primary ballot."

I couldn't celebrate for a moment. I needed to figure out how to get the state attorney general to agree that the filing could be considered legally valid. I got on the phone with our top political supporters in the state to let them know of the situation and get their ideas.

I asked the late Congressman Mike Synar, who was a great friend to Dick, if he could help. "Yes," he volunteered. "I'll call the state attorney general, and encourage him to work something out for Dick."

After they spoke, Mike called me with a report.

"The AG is going to work hard to find a legal justification for accepting Dick's candidacy," he told me. "I told him he needs to be fair to all the candidates. Plus, if he ever ran for office again he'd need votes from my district—and my help to get them. I was real frank about his chances for that happening if he was unfair to Dick now."

The next day, Oklahoma's attorney general called a press conference for noon under the State Capitol rotunda. The press corps assembled in front of the lectern set up in the historic hall and waited for the attorney general to begin.

"Ladies and gentlemen," he intoned, "the office of the attorney general has found a precedent from 1945 that guides my decision today. That year, at the end of World War II, the State Elections Board permitted the father of a soldier serving overseas to file a statement of candidacy for his son to enable him to run for public office upon his return. Based on that precedent, I am providing a legal opinion today that the State Elections Board may accept the statement of candidacy filed yesterday on behalf of Congressman Richard Gephardt as a valid filing for public office in Oklahoma. Mr. Gephardt will be on our presidential primary ballot."

With that action, my 24 hours of crisis had passed, and Dick was placed on the 1988 Oklahoma presidential primary ballot. Dick refused to let me apologize for this ordeal, but I have never felt as low as I did those two days.

*   *   *

Now, in 2008, I'm determined not to let anything like that 1988 near-disaster happen on my watch again. Our legal and field efforts in 2008 are first-rate. My Washington lawyers group produces extensive legal analyses for each state, and nobody misses a beat in helping me prepare for the blizzard of legal filings that are required for Obama around the country.

In a number of large primary states, the presidential campaigns have to conduct complex petition efforts, often during a limited period of time, to prove that the candidate has a threshold level of support in the state to earn a place on the election ballot.

These petition drives are fraught with risk for the presidential campaigns. Failure can deny a candidate the opportunity to win votes or obtain delegates from the state. In a close nomination race, this can cost the candidate the presidential nomination.

This is precisely what happened in 1984—the time of the last great delegate battle for the Democratic presidential nomination—when Senator Gary Hart lost the presidential nomination to former Vice President Walter Mondale.

Hart defeated Mondale in several large states, but he lost hundreds of delegate positions to Mondale because of a failure to meet state legal requirements for the primary elections. Hart's campaign was so underfunded and loosely managed that they could not do some of the basic "blocking and tackling" of presidential politics, leaving them vulnerable to all kinds of problems that prevented proper qualification for some important primary ballots.

In several states, Hart failed to meet petition requirements and was not allowed to have the names of his delegate candidates placed on the primary election ballot. In these cases, when Hart supporters showed up to vote, they could vote only for delegate candidates pledged to Mondale or another candidate, but not for Hart. This happened in state after state—with Mondale benefitting to the tune of up to 300 delegates—allowing him to slip by Hart to win the Democratic presidential nomination.

Hart would be treated better under today's Democratic nominating rules than was the case in 1984, but there are other ways to screw up. Now, the presidential campaigns have to ensure their candidate meets the current requirements to participate in all the primaries and caucuses. If 2008 turns out to be anything as close as the 1984 presidential nominating race, no candidate in the delegate hunt will be able to afford to lose delegates due to state petition and ballot qualification requirements.

It can mean the difference between winning and losing the presidential nomination.

*   *   *

In the Commonwealth of Virginia, qualifying for the ballot will be no walk in the park. State law requires us to collect 10,000 signatures statewide, including a minimum of 400 signatures in each of the state's 11 congressional districts.

The state is very diverse. Our effort will include Democrats from the African-American communities in the southeastern tidewater and Richmond areas, the deeply conservative Appalachian counties of southwestern Virginia and the liberal melting pot in Virginia's Washington, DC suburbs. Thankfully, we'll have the help of popular Governor Tim Kaine, who is deeply committed to Obama and serving as his national campaign co-chair.

As in other states, our grassroots supporters in Virginia will run this petitioning effort. Although Obama is well behind Hillary in the polls when we kick off the petitioning effort, this doesn't dent the enthusiasm of our citizens' militia. The problem they face is their unfamiliarity with the petition process.

Fortunately, though, we have our two Kevins—statewide petition director Kevin Wolf and Arlington County Obama leader Kevin Vincent. They'll guide the effort with no pay for themselves and no budget. They're both deeply committed to the effort. Kevin Wolf is a veteran of the Virginia ballot qualification process, having learned the ropes during Gephardt's 2004 presidential run. I coordinate with both Kevins to train our rank-and-file supporters in every detail of how to channel their enthusiasm for Obama into the very specific tasks that have to be accomplished.

After many weeks of work—in a triumph that hopefully is a prelude to success in the Virginia Primary next year—our petition team files their signatures nearly a month before the legal deadline.

The Clinton campaign is not on the same glide path toward success in Virginia. Reports from the Democratic frontlines indicate the Clinton petitioners are struggling. Hillary is backed by many local elected officials and party leaders, who should be able to get her petitioning done. But many of them are working only out of a sense of obligation and without the passion felt by many Obama supporters. Although it's unthinkable that Hillary Clinton would fail to qualify for the Virginia ballot, the petitioning isn't getting done and the danger for her is real.

In the final weeks before the filing deadline, the national Clinton leadership recognizes their state petition drive is not on course. They call in high-paid petition specialists to complete the effort. We hear through the Virginia Democratic rumor mill they are offering a cash bounty for each signature for anyone who walks in the door with signed Clinton petition papers. The last-minute scramble works, and Hillary submits more than 10,000 signatures just in time.

Waiting for Hillary's filing is a team of crackerjack Obama attorneys we've assembled to examine the validity of her petitions. While we have no information about her petitions' quality, I know that signatures paid for by the dollar sometimes are less likely to pass muster than those collected by volunteers, who are more dedicated to their work. The state Democratic Party—not the State Board of Elections—is responsible for validating each candidate's petitions, and the last thing the Party wants is a war over ballot qualification. I consider the pros and cons of opening a new front in the battle for the nomination and decide to have our lawyers stand down.

Hillary's petition filing goes unchallenged, and her name is placed on the primary election ballot.

*   *   *

In Pennsylvania, we have to complete a petition drive that also tests the mettle of every presidential campaign. State law requires petitions to be circulated statewide for the presidential candidate, plus a separate petition for every congressional district delegate and alternate. Since Pennsylvania elects 103 district delegates and 16 alternates, we'll have to circulate 119 petitions for our delegates and alternates plus a statewide petition for Obama. That's 120 separate petitions in just one state!

The whole process is made extra difficult by the fact that state law prohibits us from starting to circulate any of these petitions until 21 days before the petition filing deadline. The system is designed to test even the best-organized presidential campaign. And failure is not just a possibility but, for some campaigns, a likelihood.

When I begin laying the groundwork for our petition drive, we have zero paid staffers in the state. I have to build our statewide petition organization from scratch. I work with Greg Stewart, our indefatigable organizer from central Pennsylvania, to set up separate meetings in Philadelphia, Pittsburgh and Harrisburg to meet with grassroots Obama activists in each part of the state. Greg puts thousands of miles on his car as he drives from one end of the state to the other identifying Obama supporters who can lead the petitioning in the state's 19 far-flung congressional districts.

In Philadelphia, Obama supporters come together from all walks of life, representing the great and varied culture of the city. It's a boisterous group, shouting information and suggesting all kinds of approaches for tackling the task before us.

In Pittsburgh, the meeting is completely different. We gather in a glistening downtown office tower that reflects the evolution of this formerly downtrodden manufacturing city into a leading corporate, financial and educational center.

In Harrisburg, Obama supporters from the small towns that dot the vast, economically struggling center of the state gather on the second floor of a folksy restaurant. Since this spot is only two hours from my home, my family drives here to see me. It's not a resort destination, but an increasingly rare chance to get together.

In all these meetings, we devise detailed plans to collect the signatures required during the 21-day blitz mandated by law. The detailed procedures for handling the petitions can trip up even the most dedicated circulators, especially in the frigid weather and sometimes blizzard conditions of deep winter in Pennsylvania. We'll have to stay calm when the proverbial shit hits the fan—as it always does.

Our national headquarters will lend me two young staffers— one for the eastern part of the state and one for the west—to provide a means to physically gather the petitions. I borrow two of our petition experts from New York City, seasoned pro Jerry Koenig and young Andrei Greenawalt, to station them in the Pennsylvania state capital. Pittsburgh lawyer and election expert Cliff Levine will guide us on the petition intricacies unique to Pennsylvania.

As soon as completed petition pages make their way to our

makeshift Harrisburg headquarters, Jerry and Andrei are buried in piles of hand-scrawled petition pages. It's their job to ferret out any irregularity that could invalidate our signatures. They throw some petition pages in the trash and send others back out to the field for correction. Its onerous work, but we're determined that our petitions be complete and legally bulletproof.

For whatever reason, the Clinton campaign appears to struggle to get through Pennsylvania's petition process. Sometimes it seems nearly the entire state Democratic machinery is working for Hillary as a result of her endorsement by Governor Ed Rendell. Party leaders in every corner of the state should be supporting her petition effort, but the unglamorous work of petitioning appears to be dragging for Hillary. By the time her campaign realizes its Pennsylvania operation is better at collecting endorsements than completing petition pages, a portion of her delegates may be in danger of failing to qualify for the primary ballot.

As the filing deadline approaches, Governor Rendell issues an emergency proclamation declaring that snow conditions in the state necessitate an extension of the deadline. We have no problem submitting our petitions on time and file a 100% complete slate of delegates for Obama.

Hillary's campaign takes advantage of the Governor's extension to file late, but still fails to file petitions for a number of her delegates. With as much political support as she has, something must be wrong with her organization.

★　★　★

Rhode Island has a nasty system for qualifying for the primary ballot. It's complicated, requires multiple filings and petitions and has to be completed in just a few days from start to finish. The only way to master the system is to build a petition organization in advance and hit the ground running when the starting gun sounds.

Our effort will be led by state Obama co-chairs Joe Fernandez and Jeff Padwa. They're an enthusiastic leadership team, but they've never overseen a presidential petition operation in the state before. Joe, Jeff and I hold a series of conference calls to make painstaking plans for the petition drive. I make sure Joe and Jeff understand every nuance in the legal requirements and all the practical pitfalls they'll face once they begin petitioning. They put together special petition teams for each congressional district.

The petition forms are made available by the state Board of Elections on a Friday. Obama supporters from across the tiny state converge on Joe's home to pick up the forms and hit the streets. The atmosphere among the troops is upbeat, as everyone looks forward to carrying the banner for Barack. The petitioners work like a well-oiled machine, and by Monday they've finished the job, just as the other campaigns are getting ready to start.

Joe and Jeff contact the state press to let them know there will be a media event at the state Board of Elections that Monday afternoon. Rhode Island political reporters assume our guys have something up their sleeves, as no presidential campaign has ever filed petitions so quickly. To the astonishment of the Rhode Island press, the petitions are submitted to the Board of Elections and everyone realizes that this is no joke.

Our Rhode Island supporters are ecstatic. They have shocked the state political establishment, which cannot understand how our Rhode Island wizards pulled off their baffling petitioning feat. A few days later, I learn Governor Bill Richardson and Senator Joe Biden have failed to make the Rhode Island primary ballot.

★   ★   ★

During the grinding months in the fall of 2007, as I'm buried in the day-to-day work of qualifying Barack for the primary ballots in the states, other important things are happening for our campaign. Most importantly, our candidate turns the corner to being more competitive with Hillary both nationally and in Iowa.

For months in 2007, Obama has been trailing Hillary in opinion polls by a significant double-digit margin. Throughout this long "preseason" period, our candidate has been pacing himself. He's been developing his feel for the voting public, honing the delivery of his message and learning the general rhythms of the

2008 nominating race. While this time has been valuable for Obama, a lot of our supporters have become very antsy as time has gone on and he hasn't moved to more directly challenge Hillary.

Finally, that all changes on October 30th in a debate at Drexel University in Philadelphia. Obama signals in an article in the New York Times that he's going to put the pressure on Hillary during the debate. Aided by an even more aggressive Edwards, Obama takes his task to heart and bears down on Hillary throughout the debate.

Then, well into the debate, she cracks. In response to a question about the wisdom of granting driver's licenses to undocumented immigrants in her home state of New York, she seems to support the policy, only to then draw back and say she doesn't support it.

Her Democratic opponents pounce on her apparent stumble, and all of a sudden—after months of little change in her standing as the sole frontrunner in the race—there is a noticeable shift in the national nominating contest. I'm giddy that our guy has taken the offensive and—like Obama supporters around the country— am hopeful for good things to come.

Less than two weeks later, another pivotal moment takes place, this time in the critical opening state of Iowa. The Iowa Democratic Party is to hold its major fundraising event in Des Moines known as the Jefferson-Jackson Day Dinner. Our crack Iowa field organization has mobilized Obama supporters to turn out for this event. I'm ready for a break from my seven-day-per-week grind and make plans to drive from Chicago to the J-J Dinner to see my candidate on the stump.

Nothing can fully describe the pomp and circumstance of the Iowa J-J Dinner. The supporters of each of the candidates parade through the streets of the city and march straight into the Veterans Memorial Auditorium. Thousands of people throng the festooned arena to cheer for their candidates as though the Iowa Hawkeyes are taking on the Minnesota Golden Gophers.

When it's Obama's turn to take the stage, the Obama supporters mobbing the hall go crazy, chanting slogans and waving placards in anticipation of seeing and hearing their candidate.

Obama enters the center of the arena and climbs the stairs to the stage. He strides in like the strong competitor he's become in the wake of the Philadelphia debate. He gives a fantastic speech that gives me goose bumps as I watch the scene from the cheap seats up above.

The J-J Dinner is the last major chance for the Democratic campaigns to put their Iowa organization to the test, and our success here is obvious to media from throughout the state and country. We couldn't ask for a better night in Des Moines, and I'm comfortable that we're now on track as we close out the 2007 political exhibition season.

* * *

When I return to Chicago, I get straight back to the thankless, difficult work of satisfying the myriad, mind-numbing requirements for qualifying Barack for the 56 primaries and caucuses in the states and territories. As the end of 2007 closes in, all of the campaigns are being tested organizationally in a precursor to the massive get-out-the-vote efforts of the actual voting contests that are to come.

No matter how many lawyers I have cranking away, I know that, in the end, the buck stops with me in ensuring that Obama is qualified to win every possible delegate from every corner of the country.

While I'm focused on the competition between Obama and Clinton, the other candidates—John Edwards, Joe Biden, Chris Dodd, Bill Richardson, Dennis Kucinich and Mike Gravel—are struggling to survive the gauntlet of ballot qualification requirements. Some falter. Chris Dodd, the senator from Connecticut, for instance, fails to qualify for the primary ballot in the neighboring state of New York, which would have to be on his critical path toward the nomination. While no one state is essential to winning a presidential nomination, how can Dodd succeed without even being able to compete in such a major state neighboring his own?

It's not just the second-tier campaign organizations that struggle to qualify for the state nominating contests. The early ballot-qualifying season has revealed the organizational struggles that beset Hillary's campaign. While her ballot-qualifying difficulties are not transparent to the general public or even the press, I can see a harbinger of the organizational shortcomings that may affect her performance in the caucus states and even primaries that soon will start voting.

While I take some solace that the Clinton campaign might not be the steamrolling juggernaut that the political world expects, I am wary about any suggestion that she will be anything other than tough to beat once the voting begins.

*   *   *

After several days of non-stop work to qualify Barack for the primaries and caucuses, I'm at my wit's end. I'm feeling completely bogged down in this ballot qualification work which, for me, is the worst part of the presidential campaign.

Every state and territory establishes its own way-too-complicated filing requirements. This is treacherous territory that every presidential campaign must traverse. I'm a lawyer, Harvard-trained, but I'm nervous as a cat about meeting all the requirements. Now, I'm nearly through the worst of it, but by no means out of the woods.

On Tuesday of this week, I come back to my desk around 9 pm after getting dinner to find a note taken by a campaign receptionist. It's exactly the kind of note I never want to see. The note is so scratchy I can barely make out what it says. After giving it a quick glance, my stomach turns upside down as I realize the gist of the message. A call had come in from the Kentucky State Democratic Party to tell us that today was the presidential candidate filing deadline, but the State Elections Office hadn't received any submission from Barack Obama. Obama won't be allowed to compete in the Kentucky primary.

"Oh, crap!" I say to myself. I'm sure I had sent in the required documents. But now the State Party is telling me I didn't.

I have a system for keeping track of these requirements, but the requirements can change, sometimes being updated with no real notice to the public. I guess I might have made a mistake and blown the filing, but how could that have happened?

Since it's now 9pm—and way after the hour to find a state Democratic Party officer or government official in their office–I'm left to confirm the accuracy of the message on my own. Methodically, but nervously, I gather my files on Kentucky. As every minute goes by, I become increasingly anxious as I sort through the statutes, rules and filing materials.

I have memos from my Washington, DC group of high-powered lawyers on everything. I can't find anything wrong, but who am I to second-guess the Kentucky Democratic Party?

When there are no more places to look, no more rocks to turn over—around 1 o'clock in the morning—I reluctantly leave the office and trudge home to my apartment. I set the alarm for an early wake-up and then, exhausted, go to sleep.

When the alarm goes off in the morning, I sit up in bed and realize I'm still stuck in the nightmare I faced last night. Once again, my stomach begins churning, as I know I still haven't confirmed whether Obama will be on the ballot for the Kentucky primary.

After a quick shower, I scramble in to the campaign office so I can call the Kentucky elections office as soon as it opens. When I get the elections office on the phone, to my utter relief, they have no concern about our filing status. It was a damn false alarm!

Just to be sure, I call the Kentucky Democratic Party to learn why they called me in the first place. They acknowledge they in fact had put in the call to my office, but say it was only to say they hadn't seen the filing I made with the elections office, not to say that there was no such filing received. Despite this being a false alarm, I remain on edge for hours over what might have been a total disaster.

Wednesday passes relatively uneventfully, but on Thursday, it's hell all over again. This time, I receive another late night phone message, now involving Louisiana. Sitting on my computer keyboard when I return from dinner is a note saying I received a message from the Louisiana Secretary of State's office that Obama's election filing is not there and today was the deadline.

It would be one thing to screw up Kentucky, where I think we'll lose badly late in the primary season, but Louisiana is a must-win state for us early in the election calendar. Again, my stomach is churning, as I consider the possibility of Obama losing every delegate in the state.

As with Kentucky two days ago, it's way too late to return the call to Louisiana by the time I see the message.

"How can I receive a message from a secretary of state so late in the day?" I say to myself. "Damn it!"

I have to spend another night digging through the legal requirements and my filing records to figure out what has happened. Like with Kentucky, I feverishly look through my records and research materials to see how I could have had a problem with my Louisiana filing. I can't find anything to give me a clue. With no alternative, I leave the office for what, this time, will be a sleepless night.

In the morning, I scramble into the office early, tired to the bone, to call the Louisiana Secretary of State's office. Just as with Kentucky, the Louisiana election officials tell me they did make the call to me, but that there is no problem. They have my filing, and just wanted to let me know they had not reviewed it yet to see if there were any issues with it.

Now that they've looked at it, it's fine, they say. Nothing to worry about. While I'm relieved, I'm also seething at having had to lose sleep due to another screwed-up late-night phone message.

Now, it's Friday. I feel like I've had some kind of sinus headache through these last few days. It's been such a tough week that I want to get to a doctor to get some medicine before I feel even worse. With an appointment to meet Barack late in the afternoon to get his signature on a stack of election filing papers, I figure I can take a few minutes after lunch to slip out to the doctor's office.

Since I'm an out-of-towner, my doctor doesn't know me well. When I walk into his office, his nurse takes my vitals, and then disappears. A few minutes later, the doctor comes in and looks me straight in the eyes.

"Jeff," he says, "your blood pressure is through the roof. I'm concerned. I don't know you well enough to let you walk out of this office and go anywhere but straight to the hospital emergency room. You need to go there, now."

"I'm in the middle of the Democratic presidential campaign," I plead. "I can't just disappear into a hospital. I've got to meet Barack Obama in two hours to qualify him to compete in half a dozen presidential primaries."

The doctor screws his head around, disgusted, and lets it fly: "Go to the damn hospital. I'll let them know you're coming."

"Okay," I snort, "but first I've got to take care of some business."

When I get back to the campaign headquarters, I pick up the phone and call home to let them know what's going on. It's not an easy call to make, but I do it. Then I walk out of the building and grab a taxi to the Second City comedy club, where I'm supposed to meet up with Barack after a fundraiser there. Second City is the birthplace of Saturday Night Live's comedy concept, and it's beyond ironic that this is where I have to go in the minutes before checking into the hospital.

When I arrive at Second City, I head up to a small room behind the stage, where I meet with Theretha Reed, my notary for all the legal documents Barack must sign. We've been through this drill many times and we all have it down to a science. Today, I have a few more papers for Barack to sign than usual.

After a few minutes, Barack walks briskly in and says, "Let's go. What have we got today?"

When he sees all the pages I've laid out for him, he adopts a tone of slight annoyance. Of course, I didn't create all these ridiculous legal forms for presidential candidates, and being headed to the hospital, I'm a lot less happy to be messing with them than is he.

Silently, he signs paper after paper, as I lead him through the documents. Within minutes, we're done. After exchanging a few more words, he's on to his next stop and I'm headed back to the campaign headquarters.

It's now late on Friday night, and the campaign office is like a ghost town. Preying upon my mind more than anything is whether to call our campaign manager or political director to give them a heads up that their national delegate director is headed to the hospital just weeks before the start of the primaries and caucuses. I can't bring myself to do it. I don't know what's going to happen next and I don't want them to worry if I can avoid it.

Instead, I organize my desk, so that my papers would make some sense if somebody has to go through them without me. I pin a sheet on the wall with all my critical filing deadlines and information, to allow the staff to get through my responsibilities if I can't get back to work next week. On my way out the door to the hospital, I drop the filing papers signed by Barack into the overnight mail drop.

When I arrive at the hospital, I calmly step through the front door and into a medical twilight zone. Within minutes, I have every sort of tube hanging off me as doctors work to lower my blood pressure. Tests are run and medications injected into me as I lay on a bed staring at the ceiling in disbelief.

As the hours pass, the doctors and nurses seem to relax about my condition. Thanks to their intervention, all my tests and measurements are now normal.

In the morning, I'm cleared to leave. The first thing I do back at my apartment is get on the phone with my wife and kids to reassure them that I'm fine.

Then I decide to take the rest of the weekend off.

On Monday, I'm back in the office and determined to improve my work style, take care of myself, and prepare for the long campaign yet to come. Fortunately, we have some good news at headquarters. The latest batch of polling confirms that Barack is continuing to rise nationally and, even more importantly, in Iowa.

Any cockiness I might have felt about our prospects, though, is tempered by a new, deeper understanding that this truly will be a campaign not only to win, but also to survive.

★   ★   ★

By the time of the December holiday season, I've done most of the work needed to qualify Obama for the primaries. With just a few states still requiring filings in the new year, I now can say that he'll be on the primary election ballot everywhere. We'll also have qualified delegate slates to compete in every state and congressional district. This phase of the campaign has been a grueling crucible. I've leaned heavily on our grassroots network to do the required work in all the petition states. I've given them the direction and training needed to get the job done, and they've delivered—not for me—but for Barack.

Now this work is winding down and I can turn my attention toward the superdelegates and the upcoming start of the 2008 caucuses and primaries. Hallelujah!

7

Figuring Out
the Superdelegates

WHILE OUR CAMPAIGN HAS BEEN WORKING to prepare for the 2008 primaries and caucuses, we also have been focusing on the hundreds of superdelegates, who attend the National Convention without pledging to the presidential candidates.

From the day I arrived in Chicago, I've recognized the potential importance of this large group of delegates, who are free to support any presidential candidate they want. It's clear the superdelegates could well be decisive late in the race and can affect assessments of the national delegate race from the very beginning.

Who are these automatic unpledged delegates, and how did they get this special role in the Democratic presidential nominating process?

Superdelegates were created in 1984, when the Democratic presidential nominating rules were amended to authorize the automatic selection of "unpledged party leaders and elected official delegates." This group of superdelegates was to include all State Democratic Party chairs and vice chairs, 60% of the U.S. House Democratic Caucus and Senate Democratic Conference, and additional state and local party leaders and elected officials, with special preference given to governors and big city mayors. These automatic unpledged delegates would constitute approximately 14% of the total convention delegates for 1984.

The reason for giving these elected officials and party leaders automatic seats at the national convention was to make sure the presidential nomination decision was not made exclusively by "amateur" delegates selected through the primaries and caucuses. Members of Congress and other high ranking elected Democrats felt that they had lost their influence at the national conventions as a result of changes to the rules made prior to the McGovern presidential candidacy. These changes democratized the process and served to bring large numbers of activist party members into the convention hall.

Many Democratic elected officeholders also did not want to compete under the post-McGovern rules against their own constituents for the limited number of delegate positions apportioned to each state.

In advance of the 1988 Democratic National Convention, the Party created a special commission, known as the Fairness Commission, to review presidential nominating rules for possible improvements. As a result of their deliberations, the presidential nominating rules again were amended, this time to increase the number of superdelegates to include all members of the DNC, 80% of the U.S. House Democratic Caucus and Senate Democratic Conference, all Democratic governors, and all living former Democratic presidents, vice presidents, House of Representatives speakers and Senate majority leaders.

In 1992, the rules again were changed. In response to the perceived need to seat a few more senior Democrats from each state who were not already designated to serve as superdelegates and who also might not want to run for an ordinary pledged delegate position, new superdelegate positions were apportioned to each state in a new category known as "unpledged add-on" delegates.

Each state would be allocated one unpledged add-on delegate for every four of the state's DNC member delegate votes. The unpledged add-on positions wouldn't be designated to a specific person already in an elected office or party leadership position. Instead, the unpledged add-on delegate positions would be filled pursuant to a hodge-podge of procedures that vary by state and could be interpreted to allow nearly anybody to serve in these positions if they could get the support of a state convention or ruling political committee.

Finally, the last expansion of the superdelegates category occurred in advance of the 1996 national convention. As a result of consternation within the House Democratic Caucus and Senate Democratic Conference over having to choose who among them should get to fill the superdelegate slots reserved for only 80% of their members, the nominating rules were amended to simply include all of them. In addition, the Party decided to also include the Democratic President and Vice President as superdelegates, plus former Chairs of the DNC.

The aggregate result of this drip-drip-drip of decisions was to create a huge number of unpledged delegates. We now have just under 800 superdelegates (the original 849 minus the 53 stripped from Florida and Michigan). Superdelegates constitute nearly 20% of the national convention delegates, a percentage that strikes me as too high and possibly troubling in its impact on the nominating process. Besides being untethered to the primary and caucus results, the superdelegates don't reflect the makeup of Democratic voters—though this was never intended to be the case. The percentage of white males among the superdelegates is nearly double the percentage of white male voters in the Democratic electorate, and men constitute nearly two-thirds of the superdelegates even though a little over half of Democratic voters are women. This might not matter in most election years, but it could matter this year or sometime in the future.

* * *

Early in our 2008 nominating race, my concern about the number and makeup of the superdelegates is overshadowed with my worry about their possible early support for Hillary Clinton. Who could be tougher competition for the loyalty of these superdelegates than the wife of the former President of the United States?

I can only imagine the breadth of relationships that President Clinton has with Democrats across the country. With my candidate being only two years out of the Illinois state senate, I have no doubt that Hillary is going to grab a lead among the superdelegates from the get-go.

Matt Nugen, our political director, and I have a series of discussions on how to deal with the superdelegates. We decide to divide them into two groups and ask two of our staffers to oversee communications with their half of the superdelegate world. My deputy in the delegate operation, Myesha Ward, will handle all of the DNC members. Mike Robertson, who came to the Obama Campaign from Obama's U.S. Senate office, will be our liaison to the members of Congress.

Governors will be high profile targets for Matt's larger political operation. Any superdelegates not covered in these groups will be picked up by Myesha, who is helping on political outreach.

Throughout 2007, Myesha and Mike call through their list of superdelegates, taking their temperature on the nominating race, ranking them in terms of their presidential preference and, most importantly, trying to convince them to support Obama. At this early point in the campaign, the vast majority of the superdelegates are uncertain about who they'll support for president.

Each candidate does find a core of superdelegates who are willing to commit to a candidate. For Hillary, she'll find strong support among the healthy number of superdelegates who come from her home state of New York. This is a big state with a large delegation to the House of Representatives and to the Democratic National Committee. Beyond these superdelegates, Hillary also finds support from Arkansas, the former home state of her husband, where he served as governor for many years. Other pockets of superdelegate support for Hillary likely will come from several sources, including those in her home Northeast region, those who want to advance a strong woman candidate for the presidency, or those who have long ties to the Clinton family from their days in the White House.

Obama has a much smaller starting circle of support among the superdelegates. His home state of Illinois is mostly supportive, though it's not as large as New York and has fewer superdelegates. He also picks up support from some African-American members of the House of Representatives and the DNC. Initially, though, his support among these established black political communities is not overwhelming. They have longstanding ties to the Clintons and an inclination to wait and see if Obama can demonstrate the staying power of his candidacy.

The Obama and Clinton campaigns, the major national television networks, Associated Press and the New York Times and even some bloggers are all keeping separate counts of the superdelegates. These counts vary among the campaigns and media outlets, since each uses different methods for trying to reach the superdelegates and categorizing their responses. The fact is that no superdelegate count is completely reliable.

All of the counters face endless problems in talking to the superdelegates and getting a straight answer on whether they are committed to support a presidential candidate. With regard to the media, many superdelegates simply refuse to get on the telephone with the counters and will not return their phone calls. It might be a little bit easier for the campaigns to get a superdelegate on the phone, but the superdelegates can be tempted to give each presidential candidate's counters a more positive indication of the likelihood of support than may be the truth.

★   ★   ★

Periodically, I sit down with Myesha and Mike to get their read on what they're hearing from the uncommitted superdelegates and their reasons for not making a commitment to either presidential candidate. They report a lot of uncertainty among the superdelegates in how to proceed.

Some superdelegates say they can't make a commitment until they know which of the presidential candidates has received more support from voters in their state's primary or caucus. Others say they want to know which candidate would be more viable against the Republican nominee, or would make the better president, and that they need more time to make these determinations.

Also, some superdelegates have a loyalty to a presidential candidate other than Clinton or Obama, including longtime senators

Joe Biden and Chris Dodd, past vice presidential candidate John Edwards and Governor Bill Richardson.

There is more to the story, though, for how superdelegates are approaching their decision on whom to support for the presidential nomination. The large group of superdelegates who are members of Congress want to be particularly careful in deciding what to do about the presidential nominating race. They see a range of seriously qualified candidates, several of whom are longtime colleagues, especially in the Senate.

These superdelegates have to gauge how a presidential endorsement on their part will affect their politics back home. Clinton and Obama have unique images that can resonate with constituents and, putting aside the obvious benefits of an endorsement to the candidate receiving it, the endorser has to recognize that such a high profile move could affect his or her own public standing.

The even larger number of superdelegates who are members of the Democratic National Committee are a different kettle of fish. There is no one model for understanding these roughly 450 DNC member superdelegates. Fifty-six of them serve as chair of their state Democratic party organization and have significant representational responsibilities.

Some raise significant money for the Democratic Party, while others do not. Many are heavily involved in state politics on a day-to-day basis, with some being well-recognized in their community. Most work in the private sector, while some work in state or local government. Others may be retired or in school. Organized labor is represented on the DNC, though not as much as in the past.

For many members of the DNC, serving as a superdelegate has evolved into being one of the more important aspects of their DNC membership. Most members of the DNC are elected to the DNC by their state Democratic organization, either by a state convention vote or the vote of some other state Democratic body. They will attend two meetings per year to hear from national Democratic figures and approve various actions of the DNC chair and organization.

The decision of a DNC member to endorse a candidate for president thus reflects a different calculus than for a member of Congress or a governor, for that matter.

To a DNC member, their endorsement is a prized asset that only they are in a position to control. They will give it to a candidate they want to see as president, but also can seek a lead role in that candidate's state campaign—just like any political figure making an endorsement. Or the superdelegate can withhold a commitment, leaving the presidential candidates to seek it through a courting process, with the onus on the candidates to figure out the best way to seek the endorsement.

Usually, this comes in the form of repeated entreaties for support not just from the candidate, but also the candidate's staff and supporters within and outside the DNC member's state.

The most important information I'm picking up from Myesha and Mike, though, is that many of the superdelegates unwilling to declare a preference have little inclination to support Hillary. Whether right or wrong, some uncommitted superdelegates just don't think she'll do well in their part of the country and are afraid she'll reduce the electoral chances of other Democratic candidates on the election ballot in the superdelegate's state. It's nothing more complicated than the old political adage that "all politics are local."

Superdelegates who doubt Hillary's appeal in their state, however, need to be convinced that Obama actually could beat Hillary before they risk a public endorsement of him. For many Democrats, the idea that anybody could defeat the Clintons in an intramural Democratic contest is unthinkable.

With Bill Clinton, Hillary's campaign chair, Terry McAuliffe, and other top Clinton campaign supporters around the country making aggressive pitches to the superdelegates for their support, it's not surprising that many of them would be cautious about making a commitment to Obama too soon. For these superdelegates, it's better to keep their head down until Obama proves that "David" really can prevail over the Clinton "Goliath."

As messy as this superdelegate counting process may seem, as we near the end of 2007, we believe that Hillary is holding commitments from around 150 of them, while our number is somewhat north of 50, giving Hillary a lead of just under 100 superdelegates, with the vast majority—approximately 600—staying uncommitted. An independent superdelegate tally by CNN on the eve of the Iowa Caucuses shows roughly a 100-superdelegate lead for Hillary. Perhaps most importantly, we've seen no evidence that her superdelegate lead has been accelerating since earlier in 2007, or that this will change any time soon.

I'm comfortable with our read on the superdelegate race from Myesha and Mike. Given the Clintons' claim to Democratic loyalties, Hillary's lead over Obama is neither surprising nor intimidating at this point in the campaign. Until Obama shows tangible success against Hillary in the caucuses and primaries, Hillary will continue to lead in the superdelegate race and we won't make much headway beyond the early superdelegate commitments we've already received.

Mike and Myesha will keep nudging the superdelegates toward Barack while he and our campaign management focus their attention on preparing for the coming elections in Iowa and the other early states. Achieving electoral wins in these contests will be the best way to convince the uncommitted superdelegates that it's safe to support Obama. Then we can turn up the effort to catch up with, and overtake, Hillary among the superdelegates.

Until then, if some of the superdelegates want to enjoy the attention they're getting from the campaigns and media, so be it.

8

The Voting Begins

AS THE END OF 2007 NEARS, the calendar for the voting in the four DNC-approved early states—incredibly—is still in flux. Because Michigan has moved its contest up to January 15th in violation of DNC rules, New Hampshire and Iowa have been threatening to move their dates forward from the dates originally approved for them by the DNC. When will these two states hold their first-in-the-nation caucus and primary voting?

The uncertainty is driving Plouffe crazy, as it makes it very difficult to finalize plans for turnout operations and television advertising in the states. I'm sympathetic to what he's going through, but there's nothing we can do to get finality until these states set their dates.

Finally, New Hampshire's Secretary of State Bill Gardner sets his state's primary date for Tuesday, January 8th. This allows Iowa just enough time to hold its caucuses right after the Christmas and New Year holidays, on the night of Thursday, January 3rd.

Nevada agrees to stay on its DNC-approved caucus date of Saturday, January 19th, even though the DNC expressly authorized Nevada to precede the New Hampshire primary. South Carolina will close out the group of DNC-approved early voting states by holding its primary on Saturday, January 26th, three days prior to the Florida primary date that was rejected by the DNC.

With the early voting calendar now set, a sense of excitement and hopeful anticipation grips the Obama organization. Plouffe and our national campaign have thrown everything possible into building our Iowa caucus operation. David knows that with a win in Iowa, anything is possible for Obama, but with a loss, his hopes for the nomination almost certainly will be crushed.

Iowa played a critical role in each of the three presidential campaigns I have under my belt. In 1984, John Glenn's campaign tanked in Iowa, destroying his chances in New Hampshire, where he had been rising in the polls until the Iowa results were announced. In 1988, thanks to a brilliant television advertising campaign highlighting Gephardt's aggressive trade policy, Gephardt rallied to win Iowa—before faltering afterwards due to a lack of funding. My third presidential run in Iowa, in 2004, was the worst. That year, in Gephardt's second campaign for the presidency, he descended into a demolition derby with Howard Dean that destroyed both candidates' chances for the nomination.

The 2004 loss in Iowa was expected when it came, but still it hit me hard. It was the end of our 16-year wait for Dick's second chance at the White House and not the end we wanted. Within minutes after Dick learned the caucus results, he announced, without any hesitation or melodrama, that he was ending his presidential campaign and we were all going home.

So I understand the importance of Iowa in a way that many of my younger colleagues could not know. This year, I'm determined to be in Des Moines for this pivotal day, in order to pitch in however I can. With four kids who could learn more about how we do democracy in this country, I also want my family to be there with me. Hopefully, this will be a far happier night than I experienced in Des Moines four years ago.

The Iowa caucuses can do great things for the right candidate, running the right way, at the right time. And our Iowa campaign team has prepared for this night in a way that gives us all great hope for the boost we'll need to take on Hillary in the later states.

* * *

My family is meeting me in Chicago for the drive to Des Moines, the capital of Iowa and the nerve center of our state campaign operation. Unfortunately for us, at the same time we're driving to Des Moines in our minivan, a fierce snowstorm is moving in and generating blizzard conditions. Barely able to see, I drive for five nerve-wracking hours through mostly unplowed snow, sometimes with more cars on the shoulder or in the ditch than on the highway. Just passing a car means crashing through the wall of snow that has accumulated between the lanes. Finally, thankfully, we arrive.

When we get to the Obama state headquarters, it's a beehive of activity. Iowa state director Paul Tewes and caucus director Mitch Stewart have been working for months to build our Iowa campaign organization and the result is apparent. As I look around the headquarters, I see scores of staffers working furiously to manage the final days of our caucus campaign. They must tend to a massive field operation, which we created to empower grassroots supporters throughout Iowa to turn out their neighbors, coworkers and others to caucus for Obama.

When you come to Iowa from out of state to pitch in for the final sprint to the caucuses, you typically do one thing and one thing only: canvass door-to-door. While some out-of-staters bristle at the notion of knocking on the doors of strangers in the cold of January, I get a kick out of it.

Over ninety percent of the time in a presidential campaign, I'm cooped up in the headquarters talking only with other political people. The chance to spend time talking with ordinary voters gives me the chance to conduct my own roving focus group. I can learn what's on voters' minds and see the range of people affected by what we do in politics. This recharges my batteries and reminds me we're campaigning to represent real people with real concerns, and not for ourselves or our candidate.

I grab a campaign walking list for a gritty blue-collar neighborhood in Des Moines and my family and I hit the streets together. My wife and I go door to door on opposite sides of the street, talking to all manner of people about Obama. Our walking list gives us a list of addresses where people who support or lean toward Obama live. We'll ask each of them to turn out to their caucus and stand up for Obama.

Of course, in practice, going door-to-door is not always a glamorous experience. Before we're even halfway through our walking list, a certain four-legged warrior decides it's necessary to take back control of its neighborhood. From this point on, while my teenage son Joe drives, my girls Cassie, Annie and Molly take up watch duty to scan for any sign of our canine nemesis.

As we're making our way down the street—out of the blue—one of my girls screams, "Look out! He's come around the corner and going straight for you!"

Upon hearing that alarming warning, Trish and I politely end our canvassing encounters—"thank you very much, sir, make sure you caucus for Obama"—and high-tail it for our minivan as fast as we can run.

My girls are loving it, as we play cat-and-mouse with an enemy who knows the territory far better than us and isn't distracted by the hunt for Democrats who'll caucus for Obama.

As we near the end of our list, I realize that canvassing for Obama here is very different from my 2004 canvassing for Gephardt. Our 2004 Gephardt supporters were an extremely narrow slice of the electorate, including almost exclusively older voters, virtually no middle-aged Iowans and not one person under thirty. Obama backers, on the other hand, span all ages and backgrounds and have the kind of demographic balance that provides a sound foundation for competing in the state.

When we finally get through our walking sheets and return to the Obama Des Moines headquarters, we're exhausted, but exhilarated that we were able to complete our (unexpectedly dangerous) canvassing assignment.

As caucus night arrives, we're full of hope for a big night. The polls had been showing a close three-way contest among Barack, Hillary and Edwards, but now are trending toward Obama as we head into the caucuses. My family and I decide to return to the precinct where we canvassed to observe the actual caucus process. I wouldn't miss it and I want my kids to experience it, too, so they can see how ordinary Iowans come together to caucus for their choice for president and start the nation down the path to selecting our next president.

When we get to our caucus site and ask to enter the room, the caucus chair, a local elected official who has endorsed Hillary, questions me closely as to who we are and why we're here. Finally, he agrees to let us in, directing us to stand to the side of the room once the caucus begins.

It soon becomes clear that the Obama supporters in the room are total novices who lack any understanding of how the process works and how to win it for Obama. Though my work usually requires me to expound on the intricacies of the national nominating process, I realize I've got to do some local teaching before the caucus is called to order.

I gather the Obama supporters together and start, "Listen up, folks, tonight is all about maximizing the number of delegates you elect for Obama to the Polk County Convention. There will be two rounds of voting and only candidates initially supported by at least 15% of the people in the room will survive to the second round. It's just like the "Survivor" television show."

"I love that TV show," one of the Obama supporters interrupts to tell me.

"Great," I say, cutting her off before my time to speak before the caucus ends. "Look over there at the Richardson, Biden, Kucinich and Dodd supporter groups. Their candidate is not going to have enough support to get to the second round and those people are going to switch to another candidate or go home. We want them to come to Obama. Pick out the people you know—or at least don't scare you—and start talking to them now. Build bridges to them, so when the time comes, you can grow your Obama numbers and win more delegates to the County Convention. Get going!"

As the caucus is called to order, my family and I step back and lean on the rear wall of the room to watch the evening unfold. The voting goes about as I expected, as the minor candidates fail to make it to Round 2. Instead, their supporters join the Clinton, Edwards and Obama campaigns, with Clinton and Edwards gaining more ground than Obama. While disconcerting, this isn't surprising, because this precinct is in a hardscrabble, blue-collar area and isn't one of our stronger precincts.

When it's time for the caucus officials to calculate how many delegates are to be allocated to each of the surviving presidential candidates, my interest is piqued. I know the rules in Iowa as well as anyone, and I quickly realize the Clinton-supporting caucus chair is not doing the math right. He's using the wrong method to round the fractions, and it's shifting a delegate position from Obama to Clinton.

I can't stand to let this crime go undetected and saunter over to the leadership area to chime in that they're making a mistake with the math. The caucus chair gives me the evil eye and threatens to have me removed from the room. When I explain how the math should be done, he grunts at me and revises his calculation. Our purloined delegate is retrieved, and moves from Clinton to Obama.

It's a small victory for Obama, but satisfying nonetheless. The local Obama supporters are grateful and more than curious about how I changed the outcome. I give a short explanation, grab my family and then we're out the door. I want to get over to the Obama Iowa caucus night celebration before the caucus numbers are final.

As I drive to the party, my fingers race through the radio dial, trying to find a news station that might be reporting early results. Finally, the radio crackles with a local news broadcast. The announcer is discussing the statewide caucuses. After an instant, he gives us the news. Early reports indicate Obama is off to a statewide lead, with Hillary and Edwards in a tight race for second place.

"Yes!" I shout in the car. "Did you hear that? Obama's winning Iowa!"

When the results are tallied, the state Democratic Party reports that Obama has won over 37% of the delegates to the county conventions, a huge victory. Edwards has squeaked by Hillary 29.75% to 29.47%, pushing the now-former frontrunner down to third place. The results indicate that Iowa's national convention delegates are likely to be 16 for Obama, 15 for Hillary and 14 for Edwards. It's an oddity of the state's delegate system that Hillary would qualify for one more national convention delegate than

Edwards even though he won more delegates to the county conventions, but delegates are allocated regionally and sometimes the results can be quirky.

Our Iowa win is attributable to many causes. Barack's message of hope and change has fit perfectly with the desire of the state's progressive Democrats for a new beginning in Washington. Barack's grassroots supporters became motivated to take matters into their own hands and mobilized Democrats in their own communities to turn out to the precinct caucuses in record numbers. Caucus participation exploded from 124,000 voters in 2004 to 240,000 in 2008, with a lot of the growth coming from young people and first-time caucus-goers. Credit has to go to our Iowa field team and our messaging and media experts, all of whom worked diligently for a year to bring us to this great victory.

The Obama caucus night celebration in Des Moines is nothing short of magical. As more and more Obama campaign staff join the party, we're all hugging and high-fiving each other. My kids jump up on the bleachers behind the podium and enjoy Barack's celebration speech as the cameras whirl and click away. He gives a great speech, every bit as good as his boffo performance last fall at the Iowa JJ Dinner.

I'm feeling high as a kite. I know tonight's caucuses mean much more than winning one state or more delegates to the National Convention than Hillary. Tonight, Barack Obama proved he could beat Hillary Clinton. Now, the country knows that Hillary is not invincible, and that voters of all races will cast their ballot for Barack Obama.

Tonight, Iowa has put Barack Obama on what can be a winning path. Victory here has been our singular objective since we first formed our campaign battle plan. Now, we have achieved this goal and gained the kick-start we need to move on to New Hampshire and the primaries that lie ahead.

Below are the Iowa delegate results:

Date	State	Election	Pledged Delegates	Delegate Results Obama	Clinton	Edwards	Obama Lead
3 Jan	Iowa	Caucus	45	16	15	14	1

★   ★   ★

The next morning, we set off in our minivan for the five or six hour drive back to Chicago. In order to pass some time on the way, we flip a DVD of Pirates of the Caribbean into our car video system.

After only fifteen minutes, my cell phone rings. My wife answers and it's a campaign colleague wanting to talk about what happened yesterday and what will come next. We pause the movie so I don't have to speak over the sounds of marauding pirates. After an unfortunately long conversation, we re-start the film.

It isn't more than two minutes before my phone rings again. A loud groan rises up in the car.

"Dad!" they shout toward the driver's seat, realizing they have to hit the DVD pause button once again.

"Sorry," I plead, "but I'm in the middle of a presidential campaign, you know." The unyielding stares I receive tell me I may as well be talking out the car window, for as much sympathy as I'm receiving.

Finally, I finish up my call.

Immediately, they hit the play button on the DVD system and the movie is rolling forward again.

Then, within minutes, the phone rings again. My wife is in charge of the phone and it's only her intervention that prevents the kids from disabling it.

Needless to say, this sorry situation repeats itself over and over through the long ride back to Chicago. In the end, the kids, their patience stretched beyond any reasonable breaking point, consider it a miracle that they're able to finish the movie just as we pull into the Chicago area.

"We did it!" they shout. For them, this is a victory that rivals our caucus win in Iowa.

★   ★   ★

After saying goodbye to my family, who returns to our home in Washington, I put in a couple of long days at the Campaign headquarters. However, with New Hampshire coming next Tuesday, there is no way I can stay put at my desk. I'm going to go to New Hampshire to join in the final weekend of campaigning. This is my way to pitch in personally, and I pay for my own plane ticket and expenses as a volunteer for the cause.

Barack is now soaring in the polls due to his decisive Iowa win. He's up by ten percentage points, right in line with the polling bump we'd expect him to gain from Iowa. After all my prior failed presidential campaigns, I'm elated at the thought of achieving the one-two punch of Iowa and New Hampshire wins.

My good friend Matt Rodriguez is our New Hampshire state director. While he'll be busy as hell, but I'll be in the state to share the big win with him. He's been toiling away in Manchester, the state's political hub, for nearly a year, with his new wife, Renee, living back home in Los Angeles. Now, it looks like he'll get the crucial primary win that will allow him to feel his separation from Renee has not been in vain.

The final New Hampshire debate is relatively lackluster. At one point Barack is prompted to make an awkward comment about Hillary's personality. He says clearly that "she is nice enough,' but then continues in a much quieter, barely audible voice, "that's for sure." I don't think much of it, as these presidential candidate debates have become endless in their succession from one to another. Any way, Barack's performance in this debate is not that different overall from his last one.

On Monday afternoon, the day before the election, I'm doing my traditional final canvassing before election day, when an odd report appears in the news. Apparently, Hillary was crying today when, at a small gathering of supportive women, she became overwhelmed during her explanation of the difficulty of running for president as a woman. It would be only natural to be emotional on the eve of what may be the final blow to her presidential chances, so like with the recent debate, this doesn't mean much to me.

If anything, today's report reminds me of the famed New Hampshire presidential primary of 1972, when Ed Muskie was the Democratic candidate who was overcome by emotion—in that

case when confronting the publisher of the state's biggest newspaper over disparaging treatment of Muskie's wife. That didn't
work out well for Muskie, as it caused the public to question his
emotional fitness for the presidency. Now, I can't imagine anybody questioning Hillary's toughness, so I don't put much significance in the report of her emotionalism.

The morning of election day, I head out with a team of local
volunteers to do "visibility" along a major boulevard in Manchester, which means waving signs to remind commuters to go to the
polls to vote for Obama. Our work continues through the day, until the evening rush hour. Then, I make my way to the Obama
New Hampshire victory celebration at a Nashua restaurant.

The scene inside is tense. Throughout the day, the media has
been talking nonstop about Hillary crying yesterday. This chatter
strikes me as typical media overkill, but it may be having an affect
on the voting. The sympathetic narrative it has created for Hillary
seems to have interrupted the momentum we had been riding
since the Iowa caucuses. Now, unlike in Iowa, people are palpably
concerned about what the voting will bring.

In the rear of the room, an individual is pacing nervously back
and forth, looking like he's trying to ease his nerves. It's Larry
David, the creator and star of Curb Your Enthusiasm and co-
creator of Seinfeld. We're all here to celebrate a historic victory for
Obama on his road to the presidential nomination, but the wait
for results is not easy. I've laughed to every episode of Curb and
would love to discuss the series with Larry, but not until we get
the news for which we're all waiting.

Finally, the early returns start trickling in on the television
screens over the bar.

I'm stunned. Initial reports say Hillary is leading Obama.

"Holy shit!" somebody shouts, as I stare at the election map on
the TV. "We're losing!"

I'm mesmerized by the map on the TV screen, and can't believe what we're learning. New Hampshire is failing us—and
we're not getting our Hillary knockout punch.

"Wait a minute," I yell to nobody in particular. Thinking that
maybe these results are skewed toward Hillary's strong areas, I

ask out loud: "Have the votes from the southern counties or college towns come in yet?"

As the minutes unfold and the election coverage continues, it becomes clear that there is no cavalry coming to Obama's rescue. He's lost the New Hampshire primary.

The vote is close, with Hillary beating Barack by 39% to 37%. It's small consolation that we have tied her in delegates. The final tally is 9 pledged delegates for Clinton and Obama, with Edwards, still in the race, winning the other four.

Whatever momentum we had from the Iowa caucuses must have melted away over the final three days before the primary. Maybe it was Barack's comments about Hillary's likeability during the debate over the weekend or her tears yesterday, but something appears to have caused the voters to feel sympathy for her when it looked like she was falling out of the nomination race. The exit polls don't seem to explain the erosion of Obama's support in the final 48 hours, but the fact is that it doesn't matter.

We now know that Hillary is not going to fade away.

Instead, we're going to have a difficult fight on our hands. This is the situation that Plouffe feared, and for which he wanted me to join his staff. With no immediate knockout in Iowa and New Hampshire, we're facing a long struggle against a battle-tested opponent.

David quickly arranges a conference call with our entire campaign staff. After a recap of the primary voting, he lets everyone know it's time to buckle our seatbelts for a long, hard campaign ride. He closes the call with a confident, yet uncharacteristically off-color, call to action: "Let's go and win this fucking thing."

Below are the New Hampshire delegate results:

Date	State	Pledged Election Delegates	Delegate Results Obama	Clinton	Edwards	Obama Lead
	Prior Total	45	16	15	14	1
8 Jan	New Happshire Primary	22	9	9	4	0
	New Total	67	25	24	18	1

★ ★ ★

The next morning, I fly back to our Chicago headquarters and dive straight into my work. After the New Hampshire primary, the next primary to be held is in Michigan on Tuesday, January 15th—but this primary will not count for Democrats and there are no delegates at stake. Of course, this is because the primary was scheduled too early under national Democratic (and Republican) rules.

This is a frustrating situation for Michigan Democrats and a large number still want to vote any way. Voters supporting Hillary can vote for her since she allowed her name to remain on the ballot. Barack's supporters, though, cannot vote directly for him because he removed his name from the ballot. Some grassroots Obama backers refuse to let the primary pass without expressing their support for him. They organize among themselves and urge his supporters around the state to vote for "Uncommitted" to register their support for him. We in the national headquarters are careful not to get involved in this effort, as we're committed to not participating in the disapproved early primary.

When the Michigan votes are counted, I'm surprised to learn that a huge number of voters have turned out to vote for "Uncommitted." The final returns show that a whopping 40% of Democratic voters have cast ballots for "Uncommitted." Hillary has received 55% of the votes, giving her a win, though Michigan doesn't count. What's most interesting to me is that exit polls indicate African-American voters have supported Obama over Hillary by a lopsided 75%-25%. This 55 percentage point vote differential is huge news and bears out our long held view that African-American voters would vote overwhelmingly for Obama if he established his viability in Iowa. This can only presage a positive result in heavily African-American South Carolina.

★   ★   ★

The next state on the nominating calendar—and one that actually will elect delegates—is Nevada. The Silver State is holding an early Democratic presidential caucus for the first time ever. Nevada was chosen by the DNC to go early with Iowa and New Hampshire because of its Western regional location, substantial Hispanic population, organized labor presence, and less publicly but just as importantly, its strong backing by powerful Senate Majority Leader Harry Reid.

In the final days before Nevada's caucuses, things seem to be spinning just a little bit out of control. Obama wins the endorsement of the influential Culinary Workers Union, whose members include the many thousands of service workers in the hotels and casinos that line the world-famous Las Vegas Strip. This kicks off a harried effort by Culinary to let their members know Obama is the union's candidate. Since the endorsement has come in so late, Culinary has a mountain to climb to get this word out to its rank-and-file.

When caucus day arrives, Nevada Democrats are in a frenzy at the 520 voting sites around the state. Voter turnout explodes from the low level of 9,000 in 2004 to more than 120,000 today.

On the Las Vegas Strip, where the State Party has established caucus sites at nine major casino hotels to ease voting by the many thousands of hotel and casino employees, former President Bill Clinton is campaigning as though he himself is back on the ballot. He's hop-scotching from one Vegas Strip voting site to the next, rallying his wife's supporters to overcome any sense of obligation to follow the endorsement by the Culinary union for Obama.

Calls come into Obama headquarters alleging all kinds of voting irregularities at the caucus sites. One possibly apocryphal story has it that Clinton organizers instructed their supporters to arrive at caucus sites 30 minutes early, at which time their leaders locked the doors from the inside to prevent Obama supporters from entering to caucus for Obama. The Clinton campaign has its own complaints about caucus irregularities. At times, it seems that some version of chaos is ruling the day in Nevada.

As the returns begin to come in, I'm at my desk in Chicago, prepared to analyze the results. I'm in touch with our data advisor, Peter Appel, who is working from home in the Washington DC area. Peter is working with two more of our data team, Ken Strasma and Michael Simon, who are in Las Vegas obtaining caucus returns as they are made available by the Democratic state party.

The data that is coming in reflect the number of delegates to the county conventions won by each presidential candidate in the state's precincts. The press appears to be simply adding up the number of these delegates elected from the precincts to see who has won. The media concludes that because Hillary has a six-percentage point advantage among these delegates over Obama that Hillary is winning the state.

As the data develops, though, we start to see a pattern where Hillary is doing her best in the Las Vegas area, where there is an even amount of delegates to be elected to the National Convention, while Obama is excelling in the areas elsewhere around the state, from where an odd number of delegates is to be elected to the National Convention. This may sound technical, but the differences involved are significant.

It looks like we're doing well enough in the Las Vegas area to earn an even share of that area's National Convention delegates. In the rest of the state, though, we're earning not just a split of the National Convention delegates, but also an extra delegate in the district that has an odd number of delegates available. The bottom line is that we're able to project Barack will win a 13 to 12 victory over Hillary in delegates to the National Convention.

The *Associated Press*, which is a lead counter for media outlets throughout the country, announces that Clinton is winning more precinct delegates to the county conventions than is Obama and that Hillary thus is the winner of the Nevada Caucuses. As this news spreads in our headquarters in Chicago, I hustle over to Plouffe's office to let him know that *Associated Press* has oversimplified its analysis, and that, in fact, our candidate will take more delegates from Nevada to the National Convention.

David is surprised and asks, "Are you sure?"

"Pretty much," I say. "We have a little more data to go through to completely confirm it, but at this point, you can count on it."

"Let's get Burton in here," he calls out to his assistant, Katie Johnson, referring to Bill Burton, a deputy in our press department. Plouffe realizes we have an opportunity to try to change the national reporting that Hillary has won Nevada. If successful, we might be able to deny her the momentum she needs to overcome our likely strength in South Carolina.

I head back to my desk to see if the guys in Las Vegas have received the next round of data we need to conclusively declare we've won more national convention delegates from Nevada than Hillary. Finally, they've got what they need. Peter Appel confirms their math and I'm headed back to David's office.

Bill is there now and I explain to him what we've learned. He's excited to hear the news and says we need to get the word out as quickly as possible, before the Associated Press report that Hillary has won Nevada becomes gospel. David and he decide to do a conference call for the national political press for me to explain the results. The three of us squeeze into the small conference room next to David's office and Bill walks us through the call procedures.

When the call begins, it's impossible to know who is on the call. It seems hundreds of political reporters from every corner of the country have dialed in to join the call. Bill introduces David, who provides an overview on the day's voting and then introduces me.

I walk through our data analysis, trying to keep my explanation of the math as understandable as possible. When I finish, Bill announces that we'll take questions.

The first question is a simple one: "Are you saying that Barack Obama won Nevada, not Hillary?"

I look at David and he says, "It's up to the press to determine who is the winner."

"But you're saying you won more delegates to the National Convention, right?" the questioner persists.

"That's right," I respond. "Barack Obama will have more delegates from Nevada to the Democratic National Convention than Hillary Clinton."

A couple more reporters ask questions about the math calculation when a reporter from *Associated Press*, Steve Ohlemacher, speaks up. He wants to make a statement, not ask a question.

Ohlemacher then announces that he's issuing an alert that *Associated Press* is placing its projection that Hillary Clinton has won the Nevada Democratic Caucuses under review. He asks all news outlets to stand by for an update and possible revision.

Across the conference table, Burton quietly implodes with jubilation. I hear a jumble of noise from outside the conference room, but can't make out its source. I'm still focused intently on the conference call, aware that hundreds of political reporters remain on the phone line.

After a few more minutes of minor additional discussion, *Associated Press*'s Ohlemacher speaks up again. As I stare at the little telephone speaker box in disbelief at what is transpiring, Ohlemacher announces that *Associated Press* is revoking its projection that Hillary Clinton has won the Nevada Democratic Caucuses. Further analysis, he says, now shows that Barack Obama has won more national convention delegates than Hillary Clinton.

Ohlemacher provides an explanation that mirrors our mathematical analysis. While his statement is bland, its impact is electric. Obama has denied Hillary the Nevada win she needed to capitalize on her New Hampshire surprise.

With the *Associated Press* reversal now set for the history books, the conference call wraps up. David, Bill and I burst out of the conference room into the open campaign staff bullpen, and a huge roar rises up. Everyone jumps to his or her feet clapping and cheering. It's a standing ovation.

It turns out, unknown to the three of us on the conference call, that our staff broadcast the call throughout the campaign headquarters via the telephone system. Our entire staff heard *Associated Press*—in real time—reverse its call of Nevada for Hillary and announce that Barack had beaten her among the state's delegates to the National Convention.

When the celebrating dies down, we go into overdrive to convince the state Democratic Party, which operates the caucuses, to back up the delegate math that *Associated Press* has now adopted. The leadership of the Party is reluctant to weigh in on anything other than the tally of precinct delegates elected to the county conventions. They don't want to look down the road as to what the results will mean for the delegates to the National Convention. Those delegates will be chosen later in the caucus process—but based on the delegate representation that has begun in the precinct caucuses.

Nevada State Party Chair Jill Derby finally relents and issues a public statement that says:

> Just like in Iowa, what was awarded today were delegates to the County Convention, of which Senator Clinton won the majority. No national convention delegates were awarded. That said, if the delegate preferences remain unchanged between now and April 2008, the calculations of national convention delegates being circulated by the Associated Press are correct. We look forward to our county and state conventions where we will choose the delegates for the nominee that Nevadans support.

While throwing in a lot of verbiage to soothe the Clinton campaign, the State Chair has confirmed that our math is right and Obama has won more delegates than Hillary to the National Convention.

The reporting on Nevada begins to shift. *The New York Times* says:

> Mrs. Clinton scored a clear victory measured in the number of people attending the caucuses on her behalf. But Mr. Obama's campaign was successful by another measure—in the allocation of delegates to the national nominating convention, a result of a complex formula that gave more weight to votes in some parts of the state.

Even better, *USA Today* headlines their story on the Nevada Caucuses as "Clinton, Romney Win Nevada, Obama Claims Delegate Victory," with the opening text saying "Mitt Romney took Nevada's Republican caucuses Saturday, while Democrats debated whether their party had rendered a split decision. New York Sen. Hillary Rodham Clinton won the vote count among those at the caucuses, but Illinois Sen. Barack Obama claimed a slight advantage in national convention delegates on the strength of his showing in rural areas."

Thus, the delegate math has had a huge impact on the national understanding of Nevada's caucus vote. Yes, Hillary ends up with more precinct delegates to the county conventions, but Obama has earned more delegates to the National Convention. Coming off Obama's surprising loss of New Hampshire to Hillary, we needed to avoid an outcome in Nevada that would propel Hillary forward into South Carolina. Now, we've held her at bay, and perhaps even found our footing for the race ahead.

Below are the projected Nevada National Convention delegate results:

Date	State	Election	Pledged Delegates	Obama	Clinton	Edwards	Obama Lead
	Prior Total		67	25	24	18	1
19 Jan	Nevada	Caucus	25	13	12	0	1
	New Total		92	38	36	18	2

★   ★   ★

The next nomination contest is set for January 26th in South Carolina, the gateway to the South—and more importantly, Super Tuesday.

As we head into South Carolina, it's clear that Hillary has decided to contest the state fully, hoping to draw upon not only her husband's closeness to the black community but also his southern heritage as a son of Arkansas. But in the wake of Obama's strong victory in Iowa, African-American voters are choosing Obama over Hillary. Hillary's campaign could see this just as we did in the huge turnout for "Uncommitted" in the African-American areas of Detroit and elsewhere in Michigan. For whatever reason, though, Hillary sticks with her plan to campaign all out to win in South Carolina, putting the full prestige of her candidacy on the line.

During the final days before election day in South Carolina, it seems that the campaign circus we saw in Nevada has picked up and moved itself to the Palmetto state. Since South Carolina is a geographically compact state, both the Clintons and Obamas are able to move from town to town to bring their messages to the state.

It's not long before questions arise as to exactly what is the Clinton message to voters. Bill Clinton, who seems even more determined than his wife to visit every burg in South Carolina, makes a series of remarks that compare Obama's performance in the state to that of Jesse Jackson, whose presidential campaign won the South Carolina primary two decades ago. While Clinton campaign strategists deny any intent to brand Obama as "the black candidate," this is the effect that many in the media see and report.

As the voting approaches, it seems support in the state is shifting more and more to Obama. When the results come in, the popular vote is 55% Obama, 27% Clinton and 18% Edwards, producing an allocation of 25 delegates for Obama, 12 delegates for Hillary and 8 delegates for Edwards. Turnout, as in the three earlier contests, has exploded from previous levels, with 532,000 votes being cast in this year's Democratic primary compared to 280,000 votes cast in 2004.

The exit poll for South Carolina shows that 55% of all voters in the Democratic primary were African-American, with Obama pulling in a huge 78% share of this vote compared to only 19% for Hillary. Among white voters, Edwards actually has come in first with 40%—not entirely surprising given that he was born in South Carolina and won the state during his 2004 presidential campaign. Hillary follows with 36% of whites, while Obama attains a respectable 24% share. Obama has won an overwhelming 67% to 23% advantage against Hillary among South Carolina Democratic voters between 18 and 29 years old, which account for 14% of all such voters.

South Carolina thus delivers the sharp, unmistakable win around which we have based our strategy. This victory will allow Obama to move with strength into the upcoming Super Tuesday voting, when over 1,600 delegates will be allocated on a single day, dwarfing all the elections held so far.

Here are the South Carolina delegate results:

Date	State	Election	Pledged Delegates	Delegate Results Obama	Clinton	Edwards	Obama Lead
	Prior Total		92	38	36	18	2
26 Jan	S. Carolina	Primary	45	25	12	8	13
	New Total		137	63	48	26	15

⋆   ⋆   ⋆

Unlike the Obama campaign, the Clinton team doesn't seem to see the massive Super Tuesday voting as the immediate next step in the primary calendar. Instead, her campaign turns its attention toward Florida, which like Michigan, has violated national party rules by scheduling its primary earlier than allowed under the rules. Even though Hillary pledged publicly not to campaign in Florida due to this rule violation, she nonetheless heads to the Sunshine State. She is going to appear at fundraising events just before the Florida primary vote.

Her campaign asserts that her attendance at these fundraisers does not violate her pledge not to campaign in Florida's early primary, because she is soliciting money, not votes. In fact, the candidate pledge to boycott Florida might not cover these events, but their timing places her in the state just before the primary, potentially giving her a boost going into the voting.

When the Florida votes are tallied, Hillary wins the uncontested popular vote, with 50% for Clinton, 33% for Obama and 14% Edwards. Since the state has lost its delegates, none are awarded to the candidates.

Still, apparently seeing a chance to get some positive press from her Florida showing, Hillary holds a victory party in the state to celebrate the results. While the national press corps takes some note of the Florida vote, much of the reporting is laced with skepticism about the meaning of the results. On *MSNBC*, political commentator Chris Matthews states flatly:

> Just remember, for the people watching now, this doesn't count, what we're watching here. This is an unofficial, unratified, outlaw primary. It's banned and doesn't exist. We're watching what looks like a victory celebration in every other aspect. If you were tuning in, you'd think they just won something that matters. They did win something, but the question is does it matter in delegate terms? The Clintons are the ones that every second say all that matters are delegates. Yet, here they are celebrating the event of not winning any delegates tonight.

While Hillary may get some momentary publicity from Florida, the reality is that no delegates are awarded and the press dismisses the contest in its entirety. Instead, the focus shifts to the looming Super Tuesday mega-vote.

9

Super Tuesday
Train Wreck

COMING OUT OF SOUTH CAROLINA, we've had DNC-approved votes in four states—Iowa, New Hampshire, Nevada and South Carolina—which together have awarded 138 pledged delegates. The result so far is a delegate lead for Obama of just 15 delegates. But Obama's huge victory in South Carolina has put a big wind into his sails heading into the voting on Super Tuesday.

Of course, Hillary's campaign sees the voting so far as a virtual tie, since Obama won Iowa and South Carolina and she won New Hampshire and, in her view, Nevada (based on winning more of the precinct delegates). In fact, her campaign probably would say she's won more states than Obama—because of her victories in the disapproved contests in Michigan and Florida. Plus, they note whenever possible that she has a bigger lead among the superdelegates, than does Obama among the pledged delegates.

We're telling the press every day, though, that this race is about pledged delegates—the ones selected by the voters—and we've won more of them than Hillary. Superdelegates should do one thing in the nominating race, support the pledged delegates leader. They should intervene in the race only if the likely nominee is destined for defeat—which certainly doesn't apply for either Obama or Clinton. Thus, while media counts show Hillary supported by roughly 200 superdelegates and Obama by only around 100, we consistently urge the press to keep its focus on the primaries and caucuses that elect the pledged delegates.

★ ★ ★

And as we approach Super Tuesday, our early planning and organizing looks like it may pay off in the upcoming contests. By now, vigorous Obama campaign organizations have been working hand in glove with our grassroots networks for weeks and months to lay the groundwork for success in each of our targeted states. Senior field advisor Jon Carson has moved our top field organizers from Iowa, New Hampshire, Nevada and South Carolina to each of the new front lines that spread out across the country.

Small givers are showering Obama with financial contributions at levels never seen before. We now have more financial resources than expected, and Plouffe is using our newfound riches to double down on our Super Tuesday organizing strategy. He allocates additional sums of money to open field offices, hire staff, and engage in direct communications with voters in each of our targeted states and congressional districts.

The same treasure trove of financial resources is applied to buttress our Super Tuesday television and radio advertising campaign. Larry Grisolano, who coordinates our outside media consultants, invites me to join him in the consultants planning room at the campaign headquarters.

"Jeff, if I asked you to show me all the media markets where we might have a chance to win additional delegates, which markets would you choose?" he asks me.

I'm perplexed by the question.

"Are you asking me for a wish list that goes beyond anything we've already discussed?" I reply.

"That's right," he says. "We've got the money for anything you want."

"Even in Arkansas, where Hillary is certain to win?" I ask. "Is there money for me to chase down the one extra congressional district delegate in the state I think is within reach?"

"Yup. Let's go over the media markets together." Larry says.

After my 25 years of underfunded, losing presidential campaigns, I almost have to pinch myself to make sure I'm not dreaming.

"Alright, Larry. Let's do it," I respond.

And with that, I'm targeting small and medium size media markets that overlap the congressional districts where I believe Barack will be close to losing or winning a delegate in the 23 Super Tuesday election contests. For the first time in my delegate-hunting career, I have the funding to buy paid media in every congressional district where my analysis indicates we have a reasonable chance to win more delegates.

*   *   *

Besides targeting advertising to win extra delegates, I'm also working with Jon Carson and others to use the expanding early voting procedures around the country to maximize Obama's vote in the Super Tuesday primaries. My lawyers group and Carson's team have both been studying the thicket of state election laws that allow voters to vote before their scheduled election day without the hassles of long lines and other problems that may crop up at the polls.

Each of the states that permit early voting has its own procedures for doing so. In some states, the voters go to designated locations to vote on specific days in advance of the primary. In other states, voters may request a ballot to be mailed to them well before the election and mail it in without ever setting foot inside a voting booth. In either case, the voter need not offer any justification for voting early, such as being out of town on election day. It's just an option if they choose it.

Of course, voters might want to vote early for different reasons. Many want to avoid the inconvenience of having to go to their voting place and wait in line to cast their ballot on election day. Some don't want to be in the "straightjacket" of the polling hours of election day, which might impact their ability to get to work in the morning or home for dinner on time. Some simply prefer to vote by mail before the election, while others just want the freedom to vote whenever they please.

From our perspective, we want as many of our voters to vote early because we know that "a bird in the hand is worth two in the bush." Every vote that is cast early by our supporters is a vote in the bank for Obama. Who knows what distraction might emerge on election day that could keep a voter from making it to the polls? A child at home could become sick, or a car tire might go flat. In either case, an Obama vote is lost—and that is something we'll work hard to avoid. Also, if our strongest supporters vote early, we can focus our election day turn-out-the-vote operation on our less reliable supporters who need to be coaxed from their home to get to their polling place.

While we're doing our best to get our voters out early, we know this can be an uphill battle for us in some states. Since early voting may begin a month or more prior to election day, we're having to convince voters to vote early for Obama before he has established his candidacy in the days and weeks just prior to Super Tuesday. For many voters who might vote early for Super Tuesday, Hillary Clinton still is the inevitable Democratic nominee. We don't complain about this reality, but instead use it to motivate ourselves to get the most early votes we can.

★   ★   ★

In the immediate aftermath of South Carolina, Obama receives another great jolt of political momentum on the heels of his big South Carolina win. Senator Ted Kennedy—now a broadly-revered icon in the national Democratic Party—announces that he's endorsing Barack Obama over Hillary Clinton for president, along with other well-known members of the seemingly near-royal Kennedy family.

At a packed rally at American University in Washington DC, Kennedy robustly declares: "I feel change in the air," as he makes the case for Barack Obama to provide new leadership for the Democratic Party and the country.

His niece, Carolyn Kennedy, the daughter of the late President John F. Kennedy, takes to the microphone to say the Obama "offers the same sense of hope and inspiration" for the nation as did her father. Congressman Patrick Kennedy joins in the endorsement of Obama, and the crown of Camelot seems to pass from the Kennedy family to Obama, reinforcing to voters everywhere that Obama is worthy of their highest hopes for the future.

Nervous anticipation builds in our Chicago headquarters as we head into the final days before Super Tuesday. With data advisor Peter Appel at my side in Chicago, I'm running new election estimates and delegate projections daily as we obtain any new polling or other data that indicate a potential change in voter sentiment. Slowly but surely, as Obama's standing in the polls rises due to his win in South Carolina, his Kennedy endorsements and other developments, our delegate projections move from a slight net loss in total delegates to Hillary on Super Tuesday to a virtual tie in the delegates that will be elected.

David Plouffe is more than interested in our evolving delegate projections. He regularly makes the pilgrimage from his office to my desk to review the latest Super Tuesday numbers. Reflecting his respect for colleagues, he typically doesn't barge into my area, but instead hangs back behind me, sometimes lost in his own thoughts, as he waits for me to finish what I'm doing. Now, with Super Tuesday just around the corner, when I turn to him, he asks how I'm feeling about the pace of change going into election day.

"What do you think about the numbers today?" he asks.

"Barack's delegate projections are rising," I respond. "But I think Super Tuesday is going to be a head-on train wreck, with neither candidate coming out ahead."

★   ★   ★

I've been focusing so intensely on the upcoming vote on Super Tuesday, I've neglected to stay connected with my family back home. Consumed with planning and preparations all day long, I don't take a break to think about home or the day-to-day dramas that typically engage every family.

What is each child doing today, with whom are they going out tonight, and how are they getting to their destination and back?

The truth is I just don't know, and I'm not proud to say it.

Sometimes, though, late at night, around midnight, after everyone around me has left the campaign office, I emerge from my campaign cocoon and realize I've got a family back home. By this time at night, I can't call home on our family phone line. They've all gone to sleep by now. Except for Cassie, my high school sophomore, who's a night owl like me. So, on these late nights, I dial her up and—as I gaze out the floor-to-ceiling window at the frozen Chicago River below—I listen to her story of life at home. For a few minutes, I'm transported back to the reality I've left behind.

Now, with Super Tuesday approaching, I want to bring my family to Chicago to be here for what could be a potentially huge day for our campaign. Due to quirks in the school schedules of Cassie and Annie, my two older daughters, they can't leave Washington to come to Chicago. My wife Trish can't come until the Monday before Super Tuesday. On the other hand, Joe, my high school senior who worked as an intern with our information technology team last summer, can come a couple days early and bring my eight-year-old daughter Molly with him.

Joe wants to volunteer to work on what looks to be an historic primary election night, while Molly can spend her time at my desk until my wife arrives. Given Joe's familiarity with our computer and telecom equipment from his internship here, he could make a good addition to our election night boiler room, so I get the okay from our information technology team. It will be good to have him close at hand.

Our election night boiler room will include a dozen of our best data-crunchers and techies in a secure conference room in our Chicago headquarters. The team will scour state election and Democratic Party websites and online news outlets for the most current voting data, so we can interpret the election results, project delegate allocations and convey the information to Plouffe and our Communications Department as soon as possible. We'll be prepared if something unexpected occurs, as in Nevada, when the Associated Press called Hillary the winner based on a faulty analysis of precinct delegate data.

During the weekend prior to Super Tuesday, the data team lines up their data sources, prepares state-specific spreadsheets, and designates the computer and communications equipment they'll need to get their work done. Starting from scratch, the goal is to build the fastest and most accurate election night reporting operation possible.

Joe's job is to set up and test-drive the computer and communications equipment in the boiler room. He'll be responsible for keeping this equipment operating throughout election night on Super Tuesday. I'm amazed he can handle this responsibility, but our information technology team knows him and believes he's up to the task. Since, he's unflappable by nature, I'm not worried he'll crack under the election night pressure.

The data team in the boiler room has divided up the Super Tuesday states and each person will complete a spreadsheet to tally the votes for each of their states. Peter Appel has developed a master spreadsheet to combine the results from all the state spreadsheets into a single running tally for the night. But in the days leading up to Super Tuesday, he realizes that everybody will have to stop working on their state spreadsheets every time we want to combine the data into the master spreadsheet.

This could be a major pain in the neck at the worst possible time, so, in a big moment for my son, Peter asks him if he can create a software script that allows the state data to be combined into the master spreadsheet while the individual spreadsheets keep running.

"I think so," Joe responds, as he gets started on a short program that can keep the boiler room working without interruption.

It doesn't take him long until he shouts, "I've got it!"

The data team test drives Joe's software shortcut and see that it works like a charm. The boiler room will be able to hum along on election night without having to stop work every time they aggregate the date for the individual states. It's a small thing, but Joe has made a real contribution.

While Joe is working, my eight-year-old daughter Molly is sitting at my doublewide desk drawing and eating every type of candy that can be found in the office. My deputy, Myesha Ward, and a slew of other staffers are showering Molly with attention. Most of the staff is so young that they don't have children of their own. It's a rare treat for them to have a "little one" in the campaign office.

As Molly is living it up, I'm moving around the office preparing for Super Tuesday. I get a break from my preparation for election night when I take a batch of legal papers for the primaries to Barack for his signature. Since this will be a rare opportunity during the day to get my head out of my Super Tuesday work, I decide to take Molly with me.

My meeting with Barack is at a studio where he's filming a television ad. Molly and I head over to the studio and then wait for a break in the filming.

When Barack emerges from the studio to join us, in a nice gesture, he drops to his knees so he's looking at Molly eye-to-eye.

"Molly," he says, "I'm glad you're here so I can thank you for sharing your Dad with us in Chicago. He's doing a great job, and you should be real proud."

Molly blushes and doesn't know what to say. She understands, though, that this is a special moment for her—just as it is for me.

When my wife arrives in Chicago, she's ready for the excitement of Super Tuesday. There's a big election night party planned at the Hyatt Hotel next to our office, and she and Molly will head over there in the evening to celebrate the day's voting with our top donors and other campaign supporters.

Joe and I will be hunkered down in the boiler room, hoping for good news from the voters, but prepared for anything that comes our way.

* * *

As the Super Tuesday voting begins, I head into the office with my family, brimming with anticipation for the day ahead.

When I get settled in, I immediately engage our boiler room team to check on their final test drills for acquiring the voting data and populating their spreadsheets for each of the states and overall. I talk with our political staff, polling and media consultants and the crush of others in the office for this crucial election day. I let Plouffe know we're ready for business.

Throughout the day, we receive reports on turnout from different states and localities. Exit poll data start to circulate among our press and senior staff, much like it would on any other major election day. None of the early reports seems too far from what we've expected, but we're chomping at the bit for the real results to begin coming in.

We've prepared charts showing the flow of election reporting for the evening. The poll closings will begin in the East, and then roll west as the other regions finish their voting in earlier time zones. We'll be waiting for the last polls to close in the West and then hunker down as the final results dribble in through the night.

Once we hit the dinner hour in Chicago, the first states begin reporting results. Based on early glimpses into the voting, it appears our vote estimates are holding up. What a relief!

Today is pivotal to our chances for the nomination. We have to get through today to be poised to strike in the next phase of voting that starts this coming weekend. Tensions are running high in our campaign office as we await the initial election returns.

As results come in from an increasing number of states, it looks like we're winning more states than we're losing. The boiler room team now is cranking away. It doesn't take long before we can begin projecting initial delegate totals for each state. This requires calculating an allocation of the delegates for each congressional district, in addition to a separate calculation for the delegates allocated according to the statewide vote.

The major news outlets know from the earlier primaries and caucuses that it's our practice to produce timely and accurate projections, and are on the phone begging us for data and analysis. We're careful not to release information until we're comfortable it's accurate. Releasing faulty data or sketchy analysis would only come back to haunt us. We want our word to be like gold.

Of course, we're hoping our projections will show we've met our Super Tuesday goals to win more states than Hillary, to beat her in total delegates won for the day, and to win some of the day's marquis voting contests.

The Obama and Clinton vote totals in some states are so close that the networks, newspapers and *Associated Press* have trouble calling a winner. In Missouri, for example, *Associated Press* sees the early voting results from the largely white rural counties has given Hillary a lead as high as 9 percentage points statewide and finally calls the state as a win for Hillary. But the returns from more heavily African-American St. Louis and Kansas City are still far from complete. We see the mistake that *Associated Press* is making and call them to complain.

As more data from the cities come in, *Associated Press* has to revoke its call that Hillary wins Missouri, changing its assessment of the state to being too close to call. Ultimately, we gain enough votes to turn the tide completely, and *Associated Press* declares that in fact Obama has won the state. At some level it's hard to fault *Associated Press* for its mistaken call. After all, Hillary has swept vast expanses of the state, taking an astounding 109 of the state's 115 counties. But states are won on the basis of votes, not geography, and Barack has pulled out a narrow win in the state. His winning margin barely exceeds 11,000 votes out of over 800,000 cast, but it's a win nonetheless and we're more than happy to take it.

Exit polls for Missouri show strong support for Obama from younger voters, independents, African-Americans and affluent voters, while Hillary has prevailed with rural voters, seniors and working class voters. He's carried St. Louis and Kansas City, plus the college towns of Columbia and Maryville and the state capital of Jefferson City. While both candidates were helped by important endorsements in the state, I have to give a shout-out to Senator Claire McCaskill, who not only campaigned for Barack in Missouri, but around the country with other early Obama endorsers Governors Janet Napolitano of Arizona and Kathleen Sebelius of neighboring Kansas. The competition between the candidates is so close that each earn an identical share of the state's pledged delegates, with the final split being 36 delegates for Obama and 36 for Clinton.

New Mexico is another state that is very close. This state has an unusual primary election that is administered by the state Democratic Party instead of the state elections office, which is why some people call the election a caucus rather than a primary. Voting hours are unusual and run only from noon to 7pm, meaning there is no voting in the morning or on the way to work. Most of the ballots are thus cast late in the day, causing an intense evening rush hour that overloads some polling places. Making matters worse are difficulties at the polls that may stem from flaws in the data—supplied by an outside vendor—being used to verify voter identity by the state party.

Thousands of voters must cast their votes provisionally because their name is not on the voter list. These provisional votes—ultimately 17,000 of them—are counted separately, delaying the final statewide tally and making the country wait to know who has won what is turning out to be a very close race in the state.

Exit polls in New Mexico already show Hillary winning nearly 2 to 1 among the 35% of voters identified as Hispanic, while Obama is doing better among other voters in the state. Eventually, the final votes are tallied and Hillary has won the state by a razor-thin margin. She has taken 49.0% of the vote to Obama's 47.86% and gained a 14-12 delegate split over Obama.

The polls in much bigger—and more delegate-rich—California don't close until 8 pm local time, which is 10 pm in the Central time zone here in Chicago. It will be hours more before we have meaningful vote tallies. Votes must be tabulated in each locality and the results transferred to the state elections office in Sacramento. When considered with the contests in Missouri and New Mexico, California will make this a very long night in our election boiler room.

The first voting results from California are disappointing. They heavily favor Hillary. It seems these results include a lot of the votes that were cast days or weeks ago during the early voting period, when Hillary was running much stronger nationally than she is now after our big victory in South Carolina and the Kennedy endorsements. Based on what I'm seeing, I'd say that Hillary must have beaten us by around 20 percentage points in the opening days of the early voting period. Given that a reported 41% of Californians have chosen to vote early, it's clear we're going to have trouble in California.

But I'm interested not just in winning the state, but claiming as many delegates as possible. Somewhere around midnight, one of our research consultants, David Binder, comes over and asks how we're doing in the West. It's not long before we're hunkered down side-by-side outside the boiler room reviewing the California delegate numbers to see the potential for improving numbers as more results come in through the night and early morning.

Together, we watch an incredible phenomenon unfold. As the vote tallies are updated through the night and early morning hours, the percentage for Obama is rising. With 53 congressional districts in California, there are quite a few districts where Obama's rising vote percentage is moving us closer and closer to the threshold where he'll earn another delegate in the district. We know from our delegate math chart the breakpoint for gaining the next delegate in each district. Slowly, we pick up one delegate after another. David and I are enjoying the hell out of this, with each pick-up followed by a round of high-fives to celebrate Barack's good fortune.

★ ★ ★

Eventually, we're able to assess the Super Tuesday election results. Obama has won 13 states compared to 10 for Hillary. The two candidates have contested 16 primaries and 7 caucuses. Hillary has won 9 primaries to 7 for Obama. But Obama has won 6 of the 7 caucuses, losing only tiny, 3-delegate American Samoa.

The voting in all of the Super Tuesday states and territories allocates a whopping 1,681 pledged delegates, with Obama gaining 847 delegates to Hillary's 834. The net margin for Obama is only 13 delegates. The narrowness of his delegate victory is incredible given the number of delegates at stake, but it's a delegate victory nonetheless.

When we add this 13-delegate win to our 15-delegate lead from the four early voting states, we now have a lead of 28 pledged delegates nationally. While this seems like a measly lead in light of the 1,819 delegates that have been awarded to the presidential candidates so far, it is a lead nonetheless.

Here are the state-by-state Super Tuesday delegate results:

State	Election	Pledged Delegates	Delegate Results Obama	Clinton	Edwards	Obama Lead
Prior Total		137	63	48	26	15
Alabama	Primary	52	27	25	0	2
Alaska	Caucus	13	9	4	0	5
Amer Samoa	Caucus	3	1	2	0	-1
Arizona	Primary	56	25	31	0	-6
Arkansas	Primary	35	8	27	0	-19
California	Primary	370	166	204	0	-38
Colorado	Caucus	55	35	20	0	15
Connecticut	Primary	48	26	22	0	4
Delaware	Primary	15	9	6	0	3
Georgia	Primary	87	60	27	0	33
Idaho	Caucus	18	15	3	0	12
Illinois	Primary	153	104	49	0	55
Kansas	Caucus	32	23	9	0	14
Massachusetts	Primary	93	38	55	0	-17
Minnesota	Caucus	72	48	24	0	24
Missouri	Primary	72	36	36	0	0
New Jersey	Primary	107	48	59	0	-11
New Mexico	Primary	26	12	14	0	-2
New York	Primary	232	93	139	0	-46
North Dakota	Caucus	13	8	5	0	3
Oklahoma	Primary	38	14	24	0	-10
Tennessee	Primary	68	28	40	0	-12
Utah	Primary	23	14	9	0	5
New Total		1818	910	882	26	28

★   ★   ★

As I consider the day's results, I think back to my original view of what would be possible on Super Tuesday, if we implemented our plan for this crucial election day. I produce the following chart of which states I had projected as within Obama's Base, Competitive, and Clinton's Base, and the actual outcome for each of these states.

Projected Obama Base States	Winner
Alaska	Obama
Alabama	Obama
Colorado	Obama
Georgia	Obama
Idaho	Obama
Illinois	Obama
Kansas	Obama
Minnesota	Obama
Missouri	Obama
North Dakota	Obama

Projected Competitive States:	
American Samoa	Clinton
California	Clinton
Arizona	Clinton
New Mexico	Clinton
Oklahoma	Clinton
Tennessee	Clinton
Utah	Obama

Clinton Base States	
Arkansas	Clinton
Connecticut	Obama
Delaware	Obama
Massachusetts	Clinton
New Jersey	Clinton
New York	Clinton

This chart shows Obama has won every one of his Base States and Hillary has won 4 of her six Base States. Hillary also has won 6 of the 7 Competitive States, with Obama taking only Utah.

Next, I total up the Super Tuesday results in terms of the three key metrics I thought would be critical for winning the day's voting, most states won, most delegates won and marquis states won. I get the following results:

Most States Won
Total States Won by Obama: 13
Total States Won by Clinton: 10

Most Delegates Won
Total Delegates Won by Obama: 847
Total Delegates Won by Clinton: 834

Marquis States Won
Marquis States Won by Clinton: California,
    Massachusetts, New Jersey & New York
Marquis States Won by Obama: Georgia, Illinois

Obama has won two of the three key metrics that we targeted to achieve a winning Super Tuesday outcome. He's won the most states and the most delegates—even if barely. Hillary has won one metric, the most marquis contests, by prevailing in California and several states in her Northeast region. Two out of three isn't bad.

A primary reason for our Super Tuesday success is that Plouffe focused our resources from an early point in the campaign to win our Base States and maximize our delegate wins from all states to enable us to win the most states and delegates—two of the three key metrics. The third metric, most marquis state wins, would always be difficult to reach because most of the major Super Tuesday states have tilted to Hillary from the outset. David's discipline in pursuing our objectives has paid off, and is in sharp contrast not only with Hillary's campaign, but also that of all the Republican candidates, who seem to be scrambling from one week to the next without a focused strategic compass.

★   ★   ★

Some of the Super Tuesday results deserve a deeper dive to understand how we achieved our key delegate outcomes. In Obama's home state of Illinois, he has won the delegate count handily, taking twice as many of the state's 153 pledged delegates as Hillary. It's 104 for Barack and 49 for Hillary, giving him a net win of 55 delegates.

By comparison, in Hillary's home state of New York, where 232 pledged delegates were at stake, she has won 139 delegates versus 93 for Obama. This 46-delegate net win for Hillary pales in comparison to Obama's 55-delegate home state win—even though Hillary's New York has 79 more delegates than Barack's Illinois. This is exactly what I was hoping for when we laid our plans last summer.

Pretty much the same thing has happened in New Jersey, where Hillary has won 59 delegates to Obama's 48, giving her a modest net win of 11 delegates. Let's look at the math for the state's 20 delegate districts. In the ten three-delegate districts, Hillary has won a majority of the vote in seven, while Obama has won a majority in three (all northern Jersey districts with significant minority populations), producing a net win of just 4 delegates for Hillary in the three-delegate districts. In the ten districts with four delegates apiece, Hillary was able to win a 3-1 delegate split in only one district, netting her only 2 extra delegates in the state's four-delegate districts. Her net gain in the delegate districts thus is only 6 delegates. Add in the 5 more delegates Hillary won over Obama as a result of her 54% to 44% statewide vote victory, and you get to her 11 delegate win in New Jersey. This isn't much of a blow-out for Hillary when you realize it has to be combined with her 46 delegate gain in New York just to offset Obama's 55 delegate lead from Illinois.

Obama has met our projections for big victories in the two Deep South states of Alabama and Georgia, with their large African-American populations. He's won by more than 2 to 1 in Georgia, earning a net margin of 33 delegates. Exit polls show that blacks constituted 51% of the state's primary vote and favored Obama by 88% to 11% over Hillary. As discussed already, Obama was able to eke out a narrow win in traditional election bellwether

Missouri, relying on a strong vote in the large African-American communities in St. Louis and Kansas City.

★   ★   ★

Perhaps the largest credit for our Super Tuesday success, though, must go to Obama's performance in the caucus states. His enthusiastic grassroots supporters, led by our laser-focused field organization, have overwhelmed the Clinton campaign. Her leadership seems to have largely ignored the caucus contests, not having planned and prepared for them the way we did.

Our supporters swamped caucus sites everywhere. In some cases, so many supporters turned out that they couldn't fit in the building reserved for the caucus voting. Sometimes, voting had to take place outside in the parking lot, elsewhere down the street, or in sequential shifts within overcrowded buildings.

Obama's success in these states has produced significant delegate gains for him. Of the 206 pledged delegates available in the seven Super Tuesday caucus states, he has earned 139 delegates compared to 67 for Hillary. In percentage terms, this is a 67% to 33% delegate landslide for Obama. In fact, his net advantage of 72 delegates in these states is more than double the size of his entire lead of 28 pledged delegates coming out of Super Tuesday. Our wins in the caucus states have given Obama a huge boost in his tight race against Hillary Clinton.

★   ★   ★

I missed on a few of my projections for Super Tuesday. First of all, I was wrong regarding two states I considered to be in Hillary's base, Connecticut and Delaware. Regarding Connecticut, I had thought the fact that it neighbors New York and has a substantial white ethnic population would combine to deliver the state to her, but Obama pulled out a narrow 11,000 vote win. Exit polls show that Hillary did indeed win among white, less-educated, and Catholic voters, but Obama offset this strength by expanding turnout among his voters. He trounced Hillary among

independents by 62% to 32%, won African-Americans by 50 percentage points and, in a rarity so far, carried Hispanics in the
state—by 10 percentage points.

Concerning Obama's more comfortable, 53% to 41% win over
Hillary in Delaware, I also based my projection on the state's location in the Northeast and its substantial white ethnic population.
As Super Tuesday approached, however, our campaign saw
glimmers of opportunity and sent Michelle Obama to campaign in
the state twice. We then upped the ante and brought in Barack
himself just two days before the election, with his visit attracting
an estimated 20,000 people, a Delaware record for a political
event. While Hillary ended up winning white voters in the state
by 56% to 40%, according to exit polls, we increased African-
American participation from 16% of the vote in 2004 to a much
larger 28% in 2008. This made the difference, along with Obama's
sweep of the black vote by a whopping 86% to 9% enabling him to
win the state easily.

With regard to the Super Tuesday states I had hoped would be
competitive, Obama lost them all, except Utah. Of course, all these
losing states were far from slam dunks for him. California, Arizona and New Mexico have a high percentage of Hispanic voters,
who have consistently been part of Hillary's core support base. I
had hoped that other voters in these Western states would rally to
Obama's reform, anti-war candidacy to make these states winna-
ble for him, but it didn't happen in high enough numbers—other
than in Utah with its much smaller Hispanic population—to make
the difference.

Lastly, I had thought that Tennessee and Oklahoma might re-
ject the candidacy of a New York senator and prefer Obama, but
Hillary's geography does not appear to have played much role in
the outcome. Obama received low levels of support in these two
states among mostly conservative white voters. In Tennessee, for
instance, Hillary won the white vote, which constituted about
two-thirds of the primary electorate, by an insurmountable 50
percentage points. Obama could not offset this margin with African-American votes and took a drubbing at the polls.

⋆   ⋆   ⋆

How does the press corps interpret the Super Tuesday results? First, the press emphasizes Obama's win of more states than Hillary. The media coverage shows that while Hillary has won more primaries, Obama's caucus victories have enabled him to win the most state contests. As I'd hoped last summer, the Super Tuesday election map shows more states for Obama than Clinton, making clear the strength of his electoral performance.

The television networks also present charts of the day's delegate results. Of the 1681 delegates at stake, we're headed toward what appears to be the slightest of leads. Our final advantage for the day will be just 13 delegates once all the states report. It's the narrowest of victories, but we'll take it nonetheless.

Of course, Hillary has won California, the marquis contest on Super Tuesday, giving her important bragging rights. However, there is no shame for us here. Obama has won a huge number of delegates in California, and might have won the state outright if Hillary were not helped by the early votes cast before he fully emerged as the strong candidate he became following his decisive win in South Carolina.

Plouffe and our communications team gets right to the job of putting their best spin on the Super Tuesday results. David issues a statement that cuts straight to the chase: "By winning a majority of delegates and a majority of states, Barack Obama won an important Super Tuesday victory over Sen. Clinton in the closest thing we have to a national primary."

Senior Campaign Advisor David Axelrod says that "This was the night that Hillary Clinton announced she was going to close out our campaign and that's hardly happened. We're in a strong, strong position coming out of this night." Axe declares that "The momentum has shifted in this race," and that "in terms of the breadth of Senator Obama's appeal, winning in every region as he did, competing as strongly as he did and coming from as far behind as he has nationally, it's quite an achievement."

The national press seems to accept our interpretation of the results, though many news outlets recognize that the Super Tuesday voting produced no advantage for either candidate. *CBS News* reports that "Dems Fight to a Draw on Super Tuesday," while *Time Magazine* reports that "For the Dems, a Dead Heat Gets Hotter." *CBS* offers the same assessment in its online reporting:

> The Super Tuesday showdown between Democrats Hillary Clinton and Barack Obama gave both candidates plenty of delegates and plenty of things to brag about, but did little to bring the party closer to identifying a clear frontrunner. Obama won 13 of the 22 states holding Democratic primaries and caucuses, but Clinton won the night's two biggest prizes in New York, where her victory was widely expected, and in California, which polls had shown tightening up in the days leading up to the contest.

While this reporting reflects the "train wreck" scenario I'd foreseen leading up to the voting, it also represents a solid success for Obama, who faced major vulnerability on Super Tuesday if we hadn't offset Hillary's strength in the large primaries that day.

One important aspect of the media's interpretation of the delegate results concerns the caucus states. Given our success in their contests, it's important for us to have their results counted by the press. Unfortunately, some media outlets, particularly *The New York Times*, are reluctant to accept the results of the first round of caucusing — typically in local precincts — as indicating the final allocation of delegates to the National Convention. Plouffe makes eliminating this reluctance his special project. He gets on the phone with key political journalists and jawbones them on the need to include these states in their running national delegate tally. Ultimately, they all largely come around, and the delegates that will result from our caucus state victories are counted and help to put Obama in the pledged delegate lead.

The Clinton Campaign focuses its Super Tuesday push with the media on Hillary's success in leading in the popular vote tally for the day — thanks to her big state wins. *Time's* Swampland website reports that of all the votes cast in the Super Tuesday contests, Clinton has won slightly more votes than Obama, with the totals for the day being 7,347,971 votes, or 50.2%, for Clinton and 7,294,851 votes, or 49.8%, for Obama.

This is hardly much of a victory, and it's difficult to include the votes of the caucus states in any such calculation. The reporting of caucus results varies widely, with limited data available in some states. Exit poll results don't offer the kind of precise information that can establish specific levels of voter participation or candidate support.

For me, though, the bottom line is that I can't—and won't—waste any time on trying to analyze popular vote numbers. Democrats don't count popular votes at our National Convention to award the presidential nomination, we only count delegates. Our Press department can debate with Hillary's team the magnitude and meaning of Super Tuesday's photo-finish in the popular vote, but I'm staying focused on the delegate race, which actually matters.

For those who are interested in popular vote counts, I think it's more useful to consider what the voting so far might portend for the general election. A quick comparison of the popular vote totals to date for the major Democratic and Republican presidential candidates shows that voters across the country have voted nearly 2 to 1 for Democrats Clinton and Obama over Republicans McCain, Romney and Huckabee. Hopefully, this advantage for the Democratic candidates will translate into extra strength for the Democratic nominee in the fall.

★   ★   ★

Well into the night on Super Tuesday, when I'm still waiting on final vote tallies from California, I kill time with our data team talking about the Super Tuesday contests. When we've exhausted everything there is to say about the day's results, our conversation shifts to other topics. Instead of looking backwards at the Super Tuesday states, I suggest to Peter Appel and the group that we look forward to the remaining contests.

"Peter, can you create a new blank spreadsheet that includes all of the primaries and caucuses that are still to come, and I'll give you my estimate of the voting so we can crank out a projection of the road ahead?"

"Sure. Give me a few minutes to set up the spreadsheet," Peter responds.

Without much effort, Peter crafts a spiffy new spreadsheet and we get started. Peter announces each state in order. With the rest of the data team watching—and occasionally offering a cheer or boo—we march through all of the remaining contests, with me declaring the winner and likely vote percentage for Obama and Hillary.

For one or two states, Peter questions my call and I negotiate with him on a suitable adjustment. We're just shooting the breeze at this point, and I want everyone to enjoy the exercise. When we're done, we look at the final spreadsheet—which shows a tight race ahead—and agree that it actually appears to offer a realistic assessment of the remainder of the nominating race.

By 6 am, I've had it and want to go back to my apartment with my son to get a couple hours of sleep before dealing with press inquiries about Super Tuesday once the next business day begins. Most of the data team has dribbled out of the boiler room and only a couple of guys are left. I encourage them to also go home, as there isn't much more to be done at this point.

Joe and I ride down the elevator and emerge into the frigid Chicago winter night. I've heard we're experiencing the second coldest winter in Chicago history, and I have to say that the winter that was colder than this one had to be unbearable. It's cold outside! Still, I'm feeling good about the operation of our boiler room and the end result of all the Super Tuesday voting.

When we reach my apartment, Joe and I grab a bite and hit the sack. Finally, I'm able to get some badly-needed sleep.

"*Brrinnggg, brrinnggg.*" The telephone awakens me.

"Hello," I say, more asleep than awake.

"Jeff, it's Bill Burton," a voice shouts into the phone. "We've got a real problem and I need you back here. Now!"

"What are you talking about? I haven't been gone for an hour," I say, hoping desperately that there's some mistake I can clear up without getting out of bed.

"Bloomberg News just called and said they have our election forecasts for the remainder of the campaign and they're going to run a story with it. This is your stuff and you need to help figure out what's going on," he pleads.

"What the hell! I'm on my way," I respond, as I clear my head from sleeping.

I quickly say goodbye to my wife, Joe and Molly, and hustle back to the campaign office. They'll be heading out to the airport when they wake up later to catch their flight back to Washington.

When I arrive at the office, I go straight to the Press area to find Burton screaming into the telephone.

"Al, you have no right to that information! It was sent out by accident and you can't use it. Send it back!" he shouts into the phone.

"Bill, cover the phone," I say to Burton. "Who are you talking to, and exactly what does he have?"

"It's Al Hunt from Bloomberg News. He's got a spreadsheet of projections for all the remaining states. It has to be yours."

"Can you get it back?" I ask.

"He's not giving it up," Bill replies. "He's frustrated we haven't agreed to an interview request for Barack. Now we're paying for it."

"Well, who gave him the spreadsheet?" I ask. "I just left an hour ago."

Rather than wait for an answer, I walk over to our former boiler room to investigate. Although I'm not entirely clear on what occurred, it seems the spreadsheet was emailed out of the boiler room by accident after I left. The forward-looking spreadsheet looks a lot like our tally spreadsheet for Super Tuesday and the two spreadsheets inadvertently were sent together to our Press people for release. The Press Department didn't notice, and out went my projections to the entire national press corps.

Maybe if I hadn't left the boiler room to get some sleep I would have caught the error, but I did leave and now there's nothing I can do about the release of the projections.

It's not long before *Bloomberg* releases a detailed story "Obama Advisors Foresee a Delegate Draw with Clinton." Ben Smith, the journalist and blogger, posts the spreadsheet on *Politico.com*, and there it is, the "Bloomberg Spreadsheet" for all the world to see.

State	P/C	Pledged Del	Obama	Clinton	Obama	Clinton	Obama	Clinton
Louisiana	2/9	P	56	54%	44%	31	25	939	909
Nebraska	2/9	C	24	60%	40%	15	9	954	918
Virgin Isl.	2/9	C	3	60%	40%	2	1	956	919
Wash.	2/9	C	78	60%	40%	49	29	1005	948
Maine	2/10	C	24	49%	51%	10	14	1015	962
Dems Abroad	2/10	C	7	60%	40%	5	2	1020	964
DC	2/12	P	15	58%	42%	9	6	1029	970
Maryland	2/12	P	70	53%	46%	37	33	1066	1003
Virginia	2/12	P	83	50%	48%	43	40	1109	1043
Hawaii	2/19	C	20	52%	47%	11	9	1120	1052
Wisconsin	2/18	P	74	53%	46%	40	34	1160	1086
Ohio	¾	P	141	46%	53%	68	73	1228	1159
Rhode Isl.	¾	P	21	42%	57%	8	13	1236	1172
Texas	¾	P	193	47%	51%	92	101	1328	1273
Vermont	¾	P	15	55%	44%	9	6	1337	1279
Wyoming	3/8	C	12	60%	40%	7	5	1344	1284
Mississippi	3/11	P	33	62%	38%	20	13	1364	1297
Penn.	4/22	P	158	47%	52%	75	83	1439	1380
Guam	5/4	C	4	55%	44%	2	2	1441	1382
Indiana	5/6	P	72	53%	46%	39	33	1480	1415
N. Carolina	5/6	P	115	53%	45%	61	54	1541	1469
W. Virginia	5/13	P	28	43%	55%	13	15	1554	1484
Kentucky	5/20	P	51	42%	56%	23	28	1577	1512
Oregon	5/20	P	52	52%	47%	28	24	1605	1536
Montana	6/3	P	16	55%	44%	9	7	1614	1543
S. Dakota	6/3	P	15	57%	42%	8	7	1622	1550
Puerto Rico	6/7	P	55	45%	54%	25	30	1647	1580
Cumulative Pledged Delegates Through 2/5								908	884
Pledged 2/6 through 6/7								739	696
Superdelegates								159	209
Total (pledged as of 2/5 + Unpl)								1067	1093

Savvy journalists start speculating about the reason for our release of the Bloomberg Spreadsheet. They posit every imaginable reason for our giving it to *Bloomberg*. My favorite reportorial explanation for the Spreadsheet is that we released it in order to lower press expectations for Obama's performance in the coming states. Of course, it's true that I'm forecasting a fairly dismal series of losses in major states, but I didn't put my unfiltered statement of expectations into the public domain for this or any other purpose. The release was accidental.

There is nothing we can do about the Spreadsheet release and I don't waste any time worrying about it. We truly try to be "No Drama Obama." In fact, there is one positive effect from the Spreadsheet's release. The honesty and level of detail in the Spreadsheet seems to strengthen the view in the press that we know what we're doing in assessing the race. Earning this respect is not without value.

★   ★   ★

On Sunday mornings, I typically take my one break during the week. I sleep in just a little later and turn on the Sunday morning news shows. My favorites are *Meet the Press* with Tim Russert and *This Week* with George Stephanopoulos, though I like them all. I respect straight news reporters and analysts who cover the news without injecting their opinions. I know all news has an inherent bias from the perspective of the news organization doing the reporting, but the top journalists try to keep it to a minimum.

This Sunday, the first one following Super Tuesday, I'm interested to hear Tim Russert's commentary on *Meet the Press*. After his initial, high profile interview with Governor Mike Huckabee, one of the Republican presidential candidates, Russert immediately moves to a discussion of the Democratic presidential race.

To my amazement, Russert starts out by using the Bloomberg Spreadsheet to frame the race, taking it as gospel that we're headed to a virtual dead heat in the primary and caucus competition. Commentators Gwen Ifill, David Broder and David Brody proceed to pick apart all the possibilities of how the race might go, looking at the remaining primaries, the superdelegates, and the festering controversies in Florida and Michigan. None of them have a clear vision of how this is going to end.

The discussion on *Meet the Press* and at kitchen tables and office water coolers across the country would have been far different if

Hillary Clinton had delivered the decisive Super Tuesday blow to Barack Obama which she'd no doubt at one time expected. But Obama walked away from Super Tuesday's train wreck with his nomination path still intact. In fact, I'd say he's gained in strength from the Super Tuesday voting, as he's shown the country he can go toe-to-toe with Hillary Clinton in the broadest, most demanding electoral confrontation we'll see in this primary race. Now, he's in position to grab hold of the race in the days ahead.

10

Barack Breaks Through

HAVING SOLIDLY ACHIEVED OUR OBJECTIVES for Super Tuesday, the Obama campaign is poised to strike in the upcoming elections. In the next two weeks, eleven states will be holding primaries and caucuses that hold tremendous promise for Barack Obama. As identified last summer, these states include demographics and voting tendencies so favorable that Obama has the opportunity to win every one of them and take control of the race against Hillary—and just possibly knock her out of the race.

For David Plouffe, this is the opportunity of a lifetime, the chance to secure a presidential nomination for an extraordinarily talented, historic Democratic leader. In order to position our campaign to put in our maximum effort at this critical time, Plouffe has established a special, inviolable fund of several million dollars to finance our state operations in each of the states that will vote during the period that begins this Saturday, four days after Super Tuesday.

In order to prepare for the post-Super Tuesday states, Plouffe has directed our field organization to flesh out our state organizations in these states in the same manner undertaken for our targeted Super Tuesday caucuses and other states. First, put together skeletal staffs that could carve out a beachhead in each state. This is to pave the way for the redeployment of large numbers of organizers from earlier voting states to the new front lines. The goal is to stand up effective campaign organizations in little time in order to support the campaign effort in each state that follows Super Tuesday.

At the same time, Plouffe has been allocating funds to purchase advertising in the post-Super Tuesday states. The idea is to get Obama on the air in the states that follow Super Tuesday before the Super Tuesday voting has even begun. Thus, at a time when Hillary's campaign apparently is slipping into insolvency due to overspending on the early contests and Super Tuesday, Plouffe is tapping into a reserve fund to boost Obama in one post-Super Tuesday state after another. I can only imagine what Hillary's campaign managers are thinking as they learn of our purchase of this advertising while looking at their own depleted bank account.

★   ★   ★

The first contests after Super Tuesday are held on Saturday, February 9th. Three states and a U.S. territory in the Caribbean will vote, with a primary in Louisiana and caucuses in Washington State, Nebraska and the U.S. Virgin Islands. While these contests present the presidential campaigns with only a sliver of the amount of voting that took place on Super Tuesday, they'll extend the intra-party competition across not only the continental United States, but even into the Caribbean Sea.

As we look first toward Louisiana, I'm hearing a rumor in Chicago concerning Louisiana that could affect our adherence to our February 9th strategy. Apparently, there might be a concern that the exodus of African-Americans from Louisiana following the Hurricane Katrina disaster may have reduced the size of their vote so much that it could substantially affect the amount of support we could expect for Obama in Louisiana's primary.

I haven't studied the impact of Katrina upon African-Americans from Louisiana. I know it was severe, but did it really lead to the de-population of the black community in the state? My instinct is that while many people affected by the Hurricane have been displaced, that the numbers of people who've left the state would not alter the outcome of the presidential primary. My assumption is that many of those who've been displaced still remain in the state, if not in their former homes or cities.

Because Louisiana is the cornerstone of the February 9th voting, I decide to check in with one of our Obama supporters in the state, Louisiana House of Representatives leader Karen Carter Peterson. Karen assures me the primary will not be affected and puts me in touch with her political consultant, David Huynh, to obtain specific data on the state's African-American voting strength.

Dave and I hold a series of discussions on the affects of Katrina on Louisiana's voting population and he tells me emphatically "while a lot of African-Americans have been displaced since Katrina, most are still in Louisiana and the state is ripe for the taking by Barack." Huynh backs up his statement with detailed data showing that tens of thousands of African-Americans in Louisiana were displaced by Katrina, but roughly half of them have relocated within the state. In fact, according to Huynh's data, the state has lost only approximately 50,000 African-Americans to Texas and other states. I circulate the data in Chicago and never hear any concerns on this subject again.

When primary day arrives, I go into our campaign office early. I run through my routine for preparing for election day. Today, we've got one primary and three caucuses. I confirm our data team is ready to pull down the election results as they become available. I get a read on media expectations from our press staff.

It doesn't take long before we start receiving early reports on the voting from Louisiana. The news is good. Despite the difficulties many have trying to vote in Louisiana after Katrina, we learn that voters in the state, including African-Americans, are coming to the polls in great numbers and Obama is taking off like a rocket. When the polls close and the returns are in, we've won the Louisiana vote by a whopping 22 percentage points and earned 33 delegates to Hillary's 23. The exit polls say that African-Americans—who voted for Obama over Clinton by 86% to 13%—constituted 48 percent of Democratic primary voters. Huynh was dead on in assessing the impact of Katrina.

★   ★   ★

As the day rolls along, we're seeing the same kind of dividends from our early preparation for the February 9th caucus states as we saw on Super Tuesday. Our organization in Washington state is so well-organized that we are lapping the Clinton team in the level of preparation for caucus day. In fact, the Washington state caucuses are tailor-made for the Obama candidacy, with the Pacific Northwest's strong strain of anti-war activism and reform politics providing a sympathetic audience for Obama's opposition to the Iraq War and message of bringing change to the other Washington, Washington, D.C.

Although Hillary won the endorsement of both of Washington state's female U.S. senators, Patty Murray and Maria Cantwell, Obama is unstoppable in the state. In the final week before the first round of precinct caucuses, Obama receives the endorsement of Governor Christine Gregoire, but the real story for this caucus state is the great strength of Obama's support among grassroots activists. Our organizational efforts certainly help, but in Washington state, people know how to caucus without a lot of help from outside the state.

Washington state's caucuses begin at 1 pm local time, hours after the start of voting in Louisiana. Washington state Democrats run their caucuses like a finely tuned machine and there are fewer glitches in this state than we've seen almost anywhere. Turnout, like in other caucuses, is massive. As the results come in, our hopes for Obama are realized. Obama has won 68% of the precinct delegates elected in the caucuses, with Hillary earning only 31%. Obama has earned a 37 percentage point win in a state where African-Americans constitute less than 4% of the overall population.

The chances for Obama to do well in Nebraska, the other state holding a caucus on February 9th, may not seem obvious. Nebraska is a rural Great Plains state—with a small African-American population. When Nebraskans head to the caucuses, they swamp many of the caucus sites. Young voters, in particular, come out to support Obama, who campaigned in Omaha just before the caucuses. Obama's message of change is magnetic and he wins heavily in large Omaha and Lincoln, the home of the University of Nebraska, while Hillary does best in the rural west. The strong grassroots showing for Obama pushes him to another big caucus win, this time 68% to 32% over Hillary, producing a 16 to 8 delegate allocation in his favor.

A later uncontested, nonbinding primary in the Cornhusker State—won narrowly by Obama over Hillary 49% to 46%—shows how well Obama has performed, by comparison, in the state's caucus system.

The last contest on February 9th is the presidential caucus in the U.S. Virgin Islands, or "VI." The residents of the VI are American citizens, but without the right to vote for president or the members of Congress. As with other territories, the VI sends a non-voting representative to the U.S. House of Representatives and delegates to the Democratic National Convention. The VI gets to elect three delegates to the Democratic National Convention and I want them all to be for Obama.

The VI has a little over 100,000 residents concentrated in St. Thomas, St. John and St. Croix, the vast majority black, with only 6% classified as white. Virgin Islanders turn out in unprecedented numbers to back Obama. Governor John de Jongh has endorsed Obama and been in touch with me in advance of the caucuses. I'm looking for Obama to do well and want the caucuses to be implemented without incident, so the delegate results can be reported promptly along with the other February 9th contests.

It turns out that winning the delegates is simple, but getting the results reported is not. I'm on the phone with local Democratic officials on and off throughout the day to monitor the situation at the caucuses. I've heard that turnout is historically high and Obama is sweeping the delegates, but I need official results in order to claim the delegates for our national delegate count.

"Do you have the caucus results? I need the actual results!" I shout over the phone to local party officials.

"Not from all the islands yet. It could be a while," they reply.

"Why? The caucuses should have finished everywhere by now," I complain.

"You're not going to like the answer," they respond.

"Try me," I respond impatiently.

"Ok. The truth is that the caucus official from one of our major island caucuses is hand delivering the results to us here at Democratic headquarters and we haven't received any data by phone or electronically."

"Why don't you just call him and ask him for his final numbers. I can wait on hold while you make the inquiry."

"We can't reach him by phone," the official responds.

"For Pete's sake. How come?"

"Because he decided to travel here with the caucus results by boat, and the boat isn't due to arrive yet."

I thought I had seen it all in the presidential primary and caucus process, but now I know there's always more to experience. I've got the national press corps breathing down my neck for delegate totals for the day and the results for one of the contests are literally out to sea!

When the boat finally arrives and the results are reported, it's a three to zero delegate sweep for Obama, capping off the results for the first day of voting after Super Tuesday.

Overall, February 9th is a pivotal day in what has until now been a mostly deadlocked delegate race. On this day, in four small-to-medium contests, Obama has tripled his national pledged delegate lead from 28 after Super Tuesday to 75 at the end of today. While this addition of 47 delegates to our pledged lead might seem insignificant to the public, to me this is the first step in what I expect to be a series of victories that will change the dynamic of the nominating race and possibly even end it altogether.

Here are the delegate results for February 9th:

Date	State	Election	Pledged Delegates	Delegate Results Obama	Clinton	Edwards	Obama Lead
	Prior Total		1818	910	882	26	28
9 Feb	Louisiana	Primary	56	33	23	0	10
	Nebraska	Caucus	24	16	8	0	8
	Virgin Islds	Caucus	3	3	0	0	3
	Washington	Caicus	78	52	26	0	26
	New Total		1979	1014	939	26	75

★   ★   ★

On the morning of Sunday, February 10th, I'm still jazzed up about our four-contest sweep yesterday. This afternoon, we'll have a rare Sunday contest in Maine. The Maine contests, known as municipal caucuses, are held during the afternoon in 420 cities and towns across the state. It's citizens' democracy at its best. In the afternoon, reports from some of the caucus sites start flowing in to Chicago. Although I've thought that Maine might vote more like some of its Northeastern neighbors than the other caucus states that are all out west, all signals now are that our Obama activists will carry the day just as they have in nearly all the other caucus states. Obama wins the state solidly by 59% to 40%, with a projected delegate win over Hillary of 15 to 9.

Here are the Maine delegate results:

			Pledged	Delegate Results			Obama
Date	State		Election Delegates	Obama	Clinton	Edwards	Lead
	Prior Total		1979	1014	939	26	75
10 Feb	Maine	Caucus	24	15	9	0	6
	New Total		2003	1029	948	26	81

★   ★   ★

Hard on the heels of the voting this weekend are the Tuesday, February 12th Potomac Primaries of Virginia, Maryland and the District of Columbia, plus the close of the voting among Democratic expatriate Americans through their "Democrats Abroad" organization. The Commonwealth of Virginia is potentially the most challenging of these contests for our campaign, given its history as a southern conservative voting state, but this is no longer your father's Virginia. The state now is much more diverse, especially in northern Virginia, which has become a hotbed of reformist support for Obama.

In addition to northern Virginia, Obama has solid support in the large African-American communities in Richmond and the Tidewater area and the major university communities in Charlottesville, Richmond, Norfolk, Williamsburg, Blacksburg,

Harrisonburg, Fairfax, and elsewhere. With open eligibility for independents to participate in the Democratic primary, plus the backing of Governor Tim Kaine, our national campaign co-chair, Obama is in position to obtain a strong win here that could allow him to sweep the Potomac Primaries.

When Virginia's votes come in, we're ahead of Hillary by a stunning 64% to 35% popular vote margin. According to exit polls, African-Americans constitute 30% of the vote and Obama wins 90% of them. Independents comprise 22% of primary voters and Obama wins 66% of this group. Obama even pulls Republicans into the Democratic Primary, with the 8% of primary voters saying they're Republican and 72% of them voting for Obama. Obama wins every age category, though the younger the voter the better he does, with his support rising to 78% among those 24 years old and younger.

Obama's landslide win in Virginia earns him a whopping 54 delegates compared to 29 for Hillary, producing a net delegate margin from the state of 25 delegates. This delegate win is one of our largest so far and significantly increases our still-narrow national delegate lead.

The Maryland primary also sets up well for Obama. With its large African-American communities in Baltimore and the Washington, DC suburbs in Prince George and Montgomery Counties, plus the liberal white suburbs in Montgomery County, Maryland could be even stronger for Obama than Virginia. Our grassroots network in Maryland is so highly spirited and self-sufficient it sometimes seems they could operate the campaign on their own if we'd let them.

Obama beats Hillary in the Maryland popular vote by a thumping 61% to 36%. Exit polls show he's the leader among all categories of voters. In particular, Obama wins 84% of African-American voters, who constitute a substantial 37% of all primary voters. The delegate split is 42 for Obama to 28 for Hillary, a solid 14 delegate net gain for Obama.

The District of Columbia, where I live, should be in the bag for Obama. DC should provide us with just about the strongest vote of any primary in the country. Our population offers a mix of

African-American and liberal white voters that makes the only question: how big will our victory margin be?

When the votes are counted, Obama wins DC by a very big margin indeed. It's 75% for Obama to 24% for Hillary. We take 12 of the 15 pledged delegates, for a net gain of 9 delegates from DC. Obama's wins here and in neighboring Maryland give Obama a combined delegate gain that is more than double the size of Hillary's gain from her big Super Tuesday New Jersey win.

Finally, we have the tiny Democrats Abroad contest for Americans living abroad who identify as Democrats. That the Democratic Party would create such a voting entity shows the Party's desire to not leave anyone out of our presidential selection process. Each of the world's continents has its own Democrats Abroad organization. While some Democrats Abroad members are "establishment" employees of multinational corporations, others are reform-oriented liberals. Both Hillary and Barack have supporters in Democrats Abroad and I have no idea how this unusual delegate contest is going to turn out.

The Democrats Abroad members vote in an international contest during the period of February 5th to 12th. They can vote in person, by mail or online. They'll allocate 14 pledged delegate positions, each casting a one-half vote at the National Convention.

In advance of the vote, the Democrats Abroad organization arranges for a conference call for Hillary to address any members who want to join the call. When I hear about this, I'm livid. As amusing as this obscure voting process might seem, I'm not about to let Hillary get a leg up on us in it. I complain to the DNC, and Democrats Abroad, rather than descend into a brawl with me over the fairness of their process, immediately sets up a conference call for the Obama campaign to flog our candidacy to global Democrats.

The overseas voting attracts 23,000 Democrats. When the results are tallied Obama wins 9 delegate positions to Hillary's five. Since, under DNC rules, these delegates only have half-votes, we earn a total of 4 ½ delegate votes, while Hillary gains 2 ½. I happily put these nine "half-zies" in our delegates basket.

Here are the delegate results for the Potomac Primaries and Democrats Abroad:

Date	State	Election	Pledged Delegates	Obama	Clinton	Edwards	Obama Lead
	Prior Total		2003	1029	948	26	81
12 Feb	Dems Abroad	Caucus	7	4.5	2.5	0	2
	Wash DC	Primary	15	12	3	0	9
	Maryland	Primary	70	42	28	0	14
	Virginia	Primary	83	54	29	0	25
	New Total		2178	1141.5	1010.5	26	131

★ ★ ★

The post-Super Tuesday period winds up on Tuesday, February 19, when the traditionally important Wisconsin Primary and the Hawaii caucuses are to be held. Also scheduled for this day is the Washington state Primary, which will not be used to allocate delegates to our National Convention, but could offer some interesting insights into our national nominating race.

The Wisconsin Primary is one of the most established presidential contests in the country. At the turn of the twentieth century, Wisconsin, led by Fighting Bob LaFollette, the renowned prairie populist, introduced the concept of the primary election, whereby voters rather than party leaders choose each political party's nominees. Since that time, the Wisconsin Primary has served as an important barometer of public sentiment on the presidential race for both major political parties.

This year will likely be no different. Coming into Wisconsin, Hillary is desperate to halt Obama's string of primary wins. But Wisconsin is a bastion of progressivism. The state capital of Madison was the site of numerous demonstrations against the Vietnam War during the '60s and '70s. Scandinavian-American communities, with their dovish politics, dot the landscape just like in Iowa. When you add in the large African-American community in Milwaukee, we have every reason to believe we can win here.

Still, the Clinton team knows that Wisconsin's population is heavily white, older and working class—demographics that have tended to favor her candidacy. The campaign turns negative during the run-up to Wisconsin's primary. The Clinton campaign questions whether Obama has plagiarized material from the campaign of Governor Deval Patrick—an Obama supporter—and runs advertising that's critical of Obama.

When the votes are tallied, though, it's a big victory for Obama. He wins the popular vote by 58% to 41%. Exit polls show that whites constitute 87% of the primary voters, but this did not serve as a barrier to victory for Obama, as he handily won a majority of them. The delegate split is Obama 42 to Hillary 32, expanding our national delegate lead by ten.

The other contest on February 19th is in Hawaii, Obama's (real) birth state. We expect to do very well in the caucuses here. In somewhat of a surprise to me, a significant part of the Democratic Party establishment has declined to come to the aid of its favorite son and instead is falling back on old loyalties to the Clintons. Our grassroots supporters are not intimidated, and have been working steadily to organize for the caucuses. Their hard work shows, as our caucus-goers swamp Hillary's throughout the state. Obama wins 76% to 24%, producing a winning margin of over 50 percentage points! We gain a healthy 14 to 6 delegate split.

Our February 19th successes in Wisconsin and Hawaii serve as a powerful exclamation point to our string of victories following the standoff with Hillary on Super Tuesday. *Associated Press* sums up the importance of our wins in these two states by reporting:

> Barack Obama cruised past a fading Hillary Rodham Clinton in the Wisconsin primary and Hawaii caucuses Tuesday night, gaining the upper hand in a Democratic presidential race for the ages. The twin triumphs made 10 straight for Obama, and left the former first lady in desperate need of a comeback in a race she long commanded as front-runner.

The last event on February 19th is the Washington state primary, which is a "beauty contest" that does not send delegates to the National Convention, but still might say something about our race against Hillary. Although the state's delegates are chosen through separate caucuses, I'm interested in how the candidates will fare in the uncontested primary, as compared to the caucus process. It turns out that Obama obtains only a 51% to 47% win over Hillary in the primary in contrast to the 68% to 31% thumping he handed her in the caucuses. The huge 33-percentage point difference between these two showings offers unique evidence of the importance of Obama's grassroots network and field organizing team to his growing lead for the nomination. I imagine the Clinton team can see the same evidence, and must feel real remorse over their inattention to the caucus contests.

Here are the February 19th delegate results:

Date	State	Election	Pledged Delegates	Delegate Results Obama	Clinton	Edwards	Obama Lead
	Prior Total		2178	1141.5	1010.5	26	131
19 Feb	Hawaii	Caucus	20	14	6	0	8
	Wisconsin	Primary	74	42	32	0	10
	New Total		2272	1197.5	1048.5	26	149

⋆   ⋆   ⋆

With the February 19th contests now behind us, I have the opportunity to reflect upon the impact of the voting since Super Tuesday. During this period, we have competed in 11 primaries and caucuses and won every one of them, confirming my projections from last summer. In these 11 states we have competed for 424 pledged delegates and won 288 of them, increasing our national pledged delegate lead to 149 delegates. Given that we had earned only a paltry 28-delegate margin in the 27 nominating contests through Super Tuesday, the 121-delegate margin earned since Super Tuesday is extraordinary.

Our success during the post-Super Tuesday period is the result of our early planning and preparations and our discipline in sticking with our approach to the primary and caucus calendar. It would have been easy to get distracted by the urgency to win Iowa, New Hampshire, Nevada and South Carolina and to survive on massive Super Tuesday.

We didn't flinch, though. We kept our commitment—made many months ago—to target these post-Super Tuesday states for an Obama breakout against Hillary Clinton. Barack had some of his strongest grassroots support in these states, and it was incumbent upon us in Chicago to recognize this strength, enhance it and then capitalize on it. And that's what we've done.

Hillary's campaign must be rocked by the shellacking she's received since her earlier failure to pull ahead on Super Tuesday. Press reports circulate that her senior staff ranks are in turmoil, as they cast blame on one another for their inability to take charge of the nominating race.

A rare glimpse into their thinking comes in a small closed-door fundraiser during the period following Super Tuesday, when Hillary herself blames the Democratic "activist base" for some of her losses to Obama. According to an audio recording obtained by *The Huffington Post*, Hillary complains:

> We have been less successful in caucuses because it brings out the activist base of the Democratic Party. MoveOn didn't even want us to go into Afghanistan. I mean, that's what we're dealing with. And you know they turn out in great numbers. And they are very driven by their view of our positions, and it's primarily national security and foreign policy that drives them. I don't agree with them. They know I don't agree with them. So they flood into these caucuses and dominate them and really intimidate people who actually show up to support me.

Putting aside whether Moveon.org actually opposed taking out Al Qaeda sanctuaries in Afghanistan or whether Obama caucus-goers ever intimidated Clinton caucus attendees, the fact that Democratic base activists have been swamping the caucuses to advocate anti-war policies is like "dog bites man." That's what they do. Hillary's team could have mobilized their own supporters to contest the caucuses. A proactive Clinton caucus strategy might have diminished our winning margins and delegate gains, but we'll never know.

Having run the table on Hillary since Super Tuesday, we now have gained a 149-pledged delegate lead in the nominating race.

Our competition with Hillary, though, is not over by any means. While a lesser opponent than Hillary would have turned tail and quit the nominating race after suffering 11 straight losses, Hillary is undeterred and staying in the presidential contest. She knows major contests in Ohio and Texas lie ahead on March 4th, and expresses hope that they can return her to frontrunner status.

Some in the national press corps don't seem to understand the significance of our new 149-pledged delegate lead. On its face, it may not appear very impressive, especially with mega-states Texas and Ohio around the corner and huge Pennsylvania lurking just beyond. After all, these three states alone offer a total of 492 delegates, a number more than three times the size of our pledged delegate lead. But the leveling effects of the Democratic Party's use of proportional representation can't be ignored, and it will be nearly impossible for Hillary to now overcome Obama's lead.

The key, going forward, will be to deny Hillary the opportunity to use her potential wins in the remaining states to reduce our national pledged delegate lead to the point where it loses its significance. To me, that means our lead cannot fall under 100 delegates. A pledged delegate lead under 100 would enable Hillary to declare the race tied and best settled in an open competition at our National Convention in Denver. A 2008 convention floor fight of the type that took place in 1980 between Jimmy Carter and Ted Kennedy almost certainly would hinder Democratic unity for the fall election, and for the remainder of our nominating race we'll need to do everything we can to prevent this from happening.

11

Hillary Rebounds

HILLARY'S CAMPAIGN MUST BE STUNNED by her failure to dominate Super Tuesday or maintain any real competitiveness during the contests that followed. As if these losses alone were not enough to set Hillary's team on its heels, its heavy spending in the early contests and Super Tuesday apparently has caused the Clinton campaign to slip into financial insolvency. It's reported in the press that Hillary is placing a mortgage on her home to pump cash into her empty campaign coffers.

Less than a week after Super Tuesday, Clinton campaign manager Patti Solis Doyle resigns and is replaced by another longtime trusted aide to Hillary, Maggie Williams. Hillary's campaign is in danger of falling into a classic presidential race death spiral. Election losses, financial crises and abrupt management chances; the signs are all there.

Can Hillary find her footing in this disastrous political, financial, and organizational maelstrom?

Fortunately for Hillary, the answer is "Yes." Rather than crumble after her repeated electoral thrashings across the country, Hillary bucks up and announces she will fight on to the March 4th contests of Ohio, Texas, Vermont and Rhode Island.

Her campaign now seems to realize it has to be a lot smarter in how it operates. In order to compete financially, her leaders improve their use of the Obama model of grassroots Internet giving to fund Hillary's campaign. At the same time, Hillary sharpens her criticisms of Obama, targeting her messaging to those blue-collar voters who remain skeptical of Obama's novel candidacy.

The press corps sees a Clinton campaign that is regaining its footing and preparing for the next confrontation. That will be on March 4th when the candidates face off in Ohio and Texas.

★   ★   ★

In Ohio, we're facing a tough primary electorate. This state is a regional crossroads. In the northeastern part of the state, the Cleveland, Akron, Canton, Youngstown, and Warren areas have the feel of the mid-Atlantic region that is part of Hillary's base. These areas are peppered with the types of blue-collar communities that helped power Hillary through the primaries in New York, New Jersey, and Massachusetts. Columbus, Dayton, Cincinnati, and smaller communities in the central and western portions of the state reflect conservative Midwestern and German-American sensibilities. The southern region of Ohio, in particular the Hill Country that lies north of the Ohio River, is sharply conservative in outlook. Obama has strong support in the urban black communities, college campuses, and affluent suburbs ringing the state's large cities, but he's looking at an uphill battle against a resurging Hillary Clinton.

Notwithstanding the difficult demographic landscape in Ohio, Plouffe targets the state for victory. I don't blame him for one minute. Given our great run of wins in the weeks since Super Tuesday, wins now in Ohio and Texas offer what is probably our final chance to knock Hillary out of the race without having to contest every remaining primary. David dispatches a brigade of our top staffers to Ohio and dedicates a huge sum of money to compete on the television airwaves.

Our effort in Ohio is herculean, but we simply can't win the state. We lose the primary by 53% to 45%. Hillary's win, though, earns her only seven more delegates than Obama. The final delegate tally is 74 for Clinton and 67 for Obama.

An ominous harbinger of election difficulties still to come appears in the 6th congressional district, which sprawls across twelve counties along the Ohio River in hilly southeastern Ohio. This is Ohio's piece of Appalachia and I've expected we'd lose it handily. When the votes are totaled, Hillary has demolished Obama in the district 70% to 27%, producing a victory margin of 43 percentage points. When I bring it to Plouffe's attention, we're both sobered by this margin of defeat for our Democratic presidential frontrunner.

The other major contest on March 4th is Texas, which presents a very different, but equally difficult, electoral challenge for Obama. Here, we face not only a skeptical white conservative audience but also a large Hispanic community that typically leans strongly toward Hillary. While Obama will find strong support in the large African-American communities in Houston and Dallas, plus in the progressive state capital of Austin, this is going to be a tough state for him to win.

However, we have an ace up our sleeve in Texas. The state obtained special permission from the DNC to use a separate convention system—in addition to the primary—to allocate delegates to the National Convention. This dual Texas voting system, known as the Texas Two-Step, elects a total of 193 pledged delegates. There are 126 delegates elected from 31 state senatorial districts using the primary and 67 delegates chosen on a statewide basis using the convention system.

On election day, the voters will go to their primary voting location during normal daytime voting hours and then return in the evening to participate in precinct conventions that operate like caucuses in other states. The conventions typically are held at the same location as the primary voting, which means voters can hold over after voting and wait for their convention to begin. For the presidential campaigns, getting people to the polls to vote in the primary is hard enough, but getting them to come back in the evening to participate in the convention is a real challenge.

Ordinarily I might criticize the ungainly nature of this Two-Step voting system, but this year it looks like my candidate will benefit from it. By now, nobody should doubt the ability of the Obama campaign to outgun Clinton's team in a caucus or convention setting. With one-third of Texas's delegates to be elected through these evening conventions, we'll have the possibility of gaining a delegate boost in the state even if Hillary wins the primary.

There is another important quirk to the Texas presidential nominating system that is likely to help us. The apportionment of delegates to the state senatorial districts for the primary has the effect of accentuating the delegate strength of African-American areas. The 126 delegates elected through the primary are apportioned to each state senatorial district based on a formula that reflects Democratic turnout for president in 2004 and governor in 2006. State senatorial districts with strong Democratic turnout in the two elections—which tend to be African-American areas that vote near-exclusively for Democrats—will elect more delegates this year to the National Convention than other districts. This can only help Barack Obama. We had no role in the adoption of this delegate apportionment formula, but I can see how it might increase our delegate yield from Texas.

The potential impact of the structure of Texas's Democratic delegate system is noted just days before the Texas voting in the *New York Daily News* by political scientist Norman Ornstein:

> Under the Texas rules, it is entirely conceivable that Obama could lose the primary vote and still win more delegates. That may not be fair, but the rules were not set by Obama or crafted by his allies to work to his advantage. They were written long before he was a national figure, much less a presidential candidate.
>
> To Obama's credit, he studied his party's arcane delegate rules and adapted his campaign to maximize his delegate base—while the far more experienced Hillary Clinton missed the boat on the relationship between votes and delegates, and has suffered as a consequence.

The two Democratic presidential campaigns don't hesitate to throw every resource available into winning the two Texas contests. Millions of dollars are poured into television advertising and both campaigns import their top field staff to lead the organizing for the evening conventions.

The racial and ethnic tension between the Hispanic and African-American communities is palpable. Hispanic South Texas is aggressively pro-Hillary and Obama organizers struggle to break through in the region. African-American areas in Houston, Dallas and elsewhere are solidly for Obama.

Voter turnout for the presidential primary is the highest ever, and in the evening the convention locations are swamped with attendees. In many locations, so many people show up for the conventions that not everyone can fit inside the meeting room at one time. At some conventions, the discussions and voting drags on well into the night and early morning. While tensions between the Obama and Clinton supporters run high, partisans for both candidates feel the historic importance of their participation and revel in the political drama.

As in Ohio, though, Obama's best efforts in Texas are not enough to win the primary. Though pre-election polls showed the race tight as a drum, Hillary wins the vote by 51% to 47%, giving her 65 delegates to 61 for Obama.

Obama, though, wins a clear victory in the evening conventions, 56% to 44%. He takes a projected 38 delegates to the National Convention compared to 29 for Hillary. When the primary and convention delegates are aggregated, it is clear that our delegate strategy has worked. In Texas, it's 99 delegates for Obama and 94 for Clinton. Even though Hillary won the primary, she lost in the delegate race. Obama's lead grows by 5 delegates.

In the days following the Texas voting, the Clinton Campaign files a challenge with the Texas Democratic Party to dispute the outcome of the precinct conventions. The last thing the state party wants is an extended controversy that could cast a cloud over its delegation to the National Convention, and rejects the Clinton challenge. The Obama delegate win in Texas stands.

The other two primaries held on March 4th, in Rhode Island and Vermont, have a lesser impact on the nomination race. Both states are predictable wins, one for each of the candidates. In liberal, small town Vermont, Obama wins 69% to 39%, with the delegates split 9 for Obama to 6 for Clinton. In more blue-collar Rhode Island, Hillary wins 58% to 40%, yielding her 13 delegates to 8 for Obama. The two states give Hillary a net delegate gain of two delegates.

The March 4th drive of Hillary Clinton to reorient the nominating race has mesmerized the national press, but now it's over. The candidates competed for 370 delegates in four states. And how much ground has Hillary regained in the national pledged delegate race? She's reduced Barack Obama's lead by a total of four delegates.

Below are the delegate results for March 4th:

Date	State	Election	Pledged Delegates	Obama	Clinton	Edwards	Obama Lead
	Prior Total		2272	1197.5	1048.5	26	149
4 Mar	Ohio	Primary	141	67	74	0	-7
	Rhode Island	Primary	21	8	13	0	-5
	Texas	Primary	126	61	65	0	-4
	Texas	Caucus	67	38	29	0	9
	Vermont	Primary	15	9	6	0	3
	New Total		2642	1380.5	1235.5	26	145

★   ★   ★

Following the knockdown fight between Barack and Hillary in Ohio and Texas, the nomination race moves to a caucus contest in Wyoming on Saturday, March 9th. We prepare for Wyoming, an overwhelmingly Republican state, as seriously as we do for all the other caucus states. We open field offices and run TV and radio advertisements in advance of the vote. The Clinton campaign now is finally competing in the caucus states and sends Bill Clinton and daughter Chelsea to campaign on the Thursday before the caucus and Hillary herself on Friday, the day before the caucus.

Turnout in Wyoming is much higher than ever before. In Laramie County, which is home to state capital Cheyenne, turnout has increased from 160 in 2004 to over 1,500 in 2008, causing caucusgoers to wait in line for hours to enter the downtown auditorium to vote. Despite the greater effort put forward by the Clintons, Obama wins, though the pledged delegate split is a more even 7 to 5 than we've seen in other caucus states. Obama's win in Wyoming, however, puts him back on the winning track. After his losses in the major Ohio and Texas primaries, it's important to reorient the race back to a winning dynamic.

Here are the delegate results for Wyoming:

Date	State	Election	Pledged Delegates	Delegate Results Obama	Clinton	Edwards	Obama Lead
	Prior Total		2642	1380.5	1235.5	26	145
8 Mar	Wyoming	Caucus	12	7	5	0	2
	New Total		2654	1387.5	1240.5	26	147

★   ★   ★

Following Wyoming, there is an interesting contest on March 11th in Mississippi, where race still plays a significant role in elections. As I do before the voting in every state, I've been studying Mississippi's demographics and voting history to estimate the election outcome at the congressional district and statewide levels. I'm looking for a strong Obama win based on the state's large African-American population. In fact, African-Americans make up 38% of Mississippi's population—making it the highest percentage African-American state in the country—and should account for half or more of the statewide Democratic turnout.

Mississippi sends 33 pledged delegates to the National convention. I'm looking for Obama to win a majority of the vote and 3 delegates in each of the 3 five-delegate districts. I also see Obama winning 5 of the 7 delegates in the majority African-American 2nd district. Add in 7 of the 11 statewide delegates that I'm projecting for Obama and we should earn 21 pledged delegates.

When the votes are tallied, Obama beats Hillary 61% to 37% statewide, taking 7 of the 11 statewide delegates as I'd hoped. As expected, African-Americans constitute 50% of the turnout according to exit polls, with Obama winning them by a whopping 92% to 8%. White voters cast their ballots for Hillary by an also lopsided 70% to 26%.

At the congressional district level, my projections are off. Obama has garnered only 13 of the available district delegates, one less than the 14 I'd projected. It seems Obama is getting only two of the five delegates available in the 1st congressional district. What happened here? Where is this district?

The 1st district is in the north and includes the city of Tupelo. African-Americans constitute 26 percent of the population and I had estimated they might make up 40 percent or more of the Democratic primary vote. Assuming Obama pulls in his typical 90% or more of this vote, he'd need only 20% of the white vote to get to the 50.1% level needed to win three delegates in the district.

When the results come in, he's qualified for only two delegates. It turns out that he's scored only 48.5% of the vote in the 1st district. I don't know for sure, but my hunch is that he earned fewer than 20% of the white vote in this district, a low level consistent with our disappointing results in southeastern Ohio last week.

Unless something changes in Barack's showing among conservative white voters, he's going to struggle in the remaining primaries where that demographic dominates—apparently regardless of whether he's the frontrunner for the Democratic nomination.

Here are the delegate results for Mississippi:

Date	State	Election	Pledged Delegates	Delegate Results Obama	Clinton	Edwards	Obama Lead
	Prior Total		2654	1387.5	1240.5	26	147
11 Mar	Mississippi	Primary	33	20	13	0	7
	New Total		2687	1407.5	1253.5	26	154

★ ★ ★

After the Mississippi primary, the campaign schedule takes a six-week hiatus. There will be no voting anywhere in the country until the April 22nd primary in Pennsylvania. This is a state that traditionally has been associated with muscular industry, organized labor, and political party bosses. While much has changed over the years, vestiges of all these Pennsylvania traditions are intact today. Governor Ed Rendell, a fixture in both state and national Democratic politics, holds sway over the state Democratic structure.

We have no illusions that Pennsylvania will be anything but a tough state for Obama to win. Like Ohio, the state is a conglomeration of regions that, overall, favor Hillary Clinton. In the east, the Philadelphia metropolitan area is a politically moderate region, with a liberal inner core and sprawling moderate, generally more upscale suburbs wrapping around the city. In the west, smaller Pittsburgh and its suburbs offer a more working class voting constituency. In between the two big metropolitan areas lies the vast conservative center of the state, with its rural, small and medium-sized communities that form a "T" on the state map.

Obama can compete—and perhaps win—in the east by relying on African-American and liberal voters in Philadelphia and competing head-to-head with Hillary in the surrounding suburbs. Western Pennsylvania is likely to be more of a mixed bag for Obama, with pockets of strength in Pittsburgh, but weakness in the surrounding rural areas. In the central T, novel candidate Obama is going to take a drubbing.

Events during the run-up to the voting aren't doing us any favors. Obama is facing a boiling controversy over video footage and statements of Reverend Jeremiah Wright, Obama's pastor for a number of years at the Trinity United Church of Christ in Chicago. At the same time, Obama's association years ago with fellow Chicagoan Bill Ayers, who was a member of the '60s-era radical Weather Underground, is generating copious press attention.

Obama delivers a speech in Philadelphia that largely quells the concerns about Reverend Wright, but a new controversy erupts when Obama, at a San Francisco fundraiser, uses the following phrasing to explain his difficulty in winning over small-town Pennsylvania voters:

> ...it's not surprising then they get bitter, they cling to guns or religion or antipathy to people who aren't like them or anti-immigrant sentiment or anti-trade sentiment as a way to explain their frustrations.

Obama publicly explains that he meant no insult or condescension, but polling in advance of the voting consistently shows him not making up ground to have a chance to win the state.

When election day arrives, Hillary beats Obama 55% to 45%. The outcome is not close, as he's clobbered outside of Philadelphia and a handful of small counties, particularly in the economically depressed areas that spread throughout the state. The delegate tally is 85 for Hillary to 73 for Obama. Finally, she makes a dent in our lead, 12 delegates, but it's late in the primaries.

Here are the delegate results for Pennsylvania:

Date	State	Election	Pledged Delegates	Obama	Clinton	Edwards	Obama Lead
	Prior Total		2687	1407.5	1253.5	26	154
22 Apr	Pennsylvania Primary		158	73	85	0	-12
	New Total		2845.0	1480.5	1338.5	26	142

★   ★   ★

Hillary's easy win in Pennsylvania seems to give her supporters some hope that she still can challenge Obama for the nomination. The reality, though, as we saw dramatically on March 4th, is that the use of proportional representation to allocate pledged delegates to the presidential candidates limits her ability to change the course of the delegate race. Obama's lead may be narrow, but it is persistent and unless something changes, the remaining primaries will not change Obama's winning course.

But what could be that "something" that might save Hillary's chances?

12

Convention Chaos
in the Caucus States

To UNDERSTAND WHAT IS HAPPENING in the caucus states, we begin our story in the third week of February 2008, just after Obama's string of victories following Super Tuesday. While the primaries and caucuses have been contested in the glare of public attention, a parallel, largely hidden, front is about to open in the war between the two surviving presidential campaigns.

It's been clear in recent weeks that Obama's success in the caucus states has been underpinning his gains in the national pledged delegate count, winning big margins to more than offset Hillary's victories in the primary states. Our signature process of planning months in advance and putting key field pieces in place to capitalize on Obama's high-octane grassroots support has overwhelmed the Clinton campaign in one caucus state after another. Of course, we've also been helped by the Clinton campaign's relative neglect of all the caucus states to vote so far except early-voting Nevada.

Now, in late February, our national pledged delegate lead over Hillary is 149 pledged delegates. We have competed in 37 states and territories, including 22 primaries and 15 caucuses. In the 22 primary states, Obama has earned an aggregate pledged delegate advantage of 22 delegates. In the 15 caucus states, he has gained an advantage of 127 pledged delegates. This does not mean our caucus wins are any more important than our primary wins. All our state wins contribute to our national delegate total and generate political momentum for Barack.

But the fact is that almost our entire national pledged delegate lead is based on our strong performance in the caucus states, and the strength of this performance is not set in stone. I'm beginning to hear rumors that the Clinton leadership now recognizes its failure to aggressively contest the caucus states was a huge error. They want to reverse their disadvantage in these states to the extent possible by focusing on the upper rounds of caucusing that are yet to unfold. If they can change the delegate math in these states while winning upcoming primaries in Ohio, Texas and Pennsylvania, they might be able to reverse Obama's pledged delegate lead and even convince the superdelegates that Hillary is still the best bet to be the Democratic presidential nominee.

★   ★   ★

But how could the Clinton campaign undo Obama's success in turning out supporters at precinct caucuses around the country? Can the Clinton campaign use the strong loyalty of Democratic Party regulars to overturn or at least cut back Obama's early gains in the caucus states? What's going to happen next in all these states that our campaign needs to worry about?

Caucuses operate differently from primaries. In primary states, once the voters have gone to the voting booth, the delegate race in the state is over. Each presidential candidate is awarded delegates in proportion to his or her share of votes in the primary. The only business left is to decide who within the state should fill the delegate positions for each candidate and attend the National Convention to cast the delegate votes.

That's usually not the case in the caucus states. The typical caucus state has several rounds of caucusing, first by the public and then by the delegates, to determine how many delegates to the National Convention will be allocated to each presidential candidate.

Usually, the process begins with rank-and-file voters showing up at local precinct caucuses to support their presidential candidate and elect delegates to represent their candidate at county (or in some cases legislative district) conventions that will be held weeks later. These precinct caucuses have now been held in most of the caucus states and tens of thousands of delegates across the country have been elected to attend upcoming county conventions. These precinct caucuses are the events that have been reported in the press, and the basis for declaring who has won or lost in a caucus state.

The next step in the caucus states is for the county conventions to convene. At these conventions, delegates from all the precincts in the county gather to vote their presidential choice much like was done at the precinct caucuses. The county convention delegates then elect delegates representing the strength of the presidential candidates in the county to a congressional district convention and a statewide convention. The delegates to the congressional district and state conventions gather weeks later and hold another vote for president—this time to actually elect the congressional district or state's delegates to the National Convention.

At any round of convention voting, if a delegate does not show up to attend a convention, he or she can be replaced by an available alternate. In some states, the replacing alternate doesn't have to support the same presidential candidate. Delegates at any round of convention voting are free to change their presidential vote from whatever it may have been when they were elected as a delegate. Most convention delegates have no inclination to change their presidential preference—but the presidential campaigns can't practically vet the loyalty of their many thousands of county and state delegates—so there's always the possibility that one presidential campaign can entice some delegates to switch presidential loyalties.

Thus, while Obama's support at the precinct caucuses should translate through the county, congressional district and state conventions into a corresponding proportion of the state's delegates to the National Convention, this is not guaranteed. If the rumors are true that the Clinton campaign is going to try to reverse

Obama's delegate victories in the caucus states, our campaign is about to face a new confrontation potentially involving tens of thousands of delegates in thousands of state and local conventions extending across the nation. Overseeing our defense in this battle will be my job.

★   ★   ★

Nevada is the first state in the country to hold county conventions, on February 23rd, less than three weeks after the Super Tuesday voting. I'm not happy that we're beginning the county convention process first in Nevada, where Hillary achieved her greatest strength in a caucus state. The Obama and Clinton campaigns fought tooth and nail in the precinct caucuses here, with Hillary and her husband fully engaged against Barack. Supporters for both candidates retain bitter feelings from the precinct caucuses and have figuratively been sharpening their swords for the coming county conventions. Tensions between competing Obama African-American and Clinton Hispanic constituencies and opposing Obama Culinary Workers Union and Clinton Nevada Democratic Party leader and teachers union endorsements, plus the general "anything goes" reputation of Las Vegas add to my concern.

As I ponder how to approach the upcoming spate of conventions that will be held in all the caucus sates, I realize that we need to set up a new unit within our campaign that can provide the special forces we'll need to protect our initial caucus state successes. This new unit will require manpower, communications services and other support capabilities.

I go straight to Plouffe to lay out what we need to move forward on this front. David sees the need in protecting our caucus state gains and approves budget authority for a new unit under my direction. It's only due to the skill of our fundraising operation and the generosity of our donors, large and small, that we have the funding available to make this unit possible.

At the recommendation of our New Hampshire state director, Matt Rodriguez, my good friend from the 2004 Gephardt campaign, I bring in Brandon Hurlbut to be my deputy for management of the caucus states. Brandon is a rising star in the Obama universe who worked in Matt's New Hampshire political operation throughout 2007, before moving on to run our winning Super Tuesday operation in Delaware. To round out our small team, we add Mike French—an attorney like Brandon—to oversee the Western states and Mitch Wallace to run those in the Midwest. These staffers don't have specific experience in conventions or delegate operations, but they're canny operators and I'll get them up to speed on what needs to be done and how to do it.

The Nevada county conventions will be where our new convention unit first plants its flag. While Nevada is clearly in Mike French's wheelhouse, Brandon and I will both also give it significant attention to make sure we do our best in this first county convention clash. The first thing we do is arrange for our top Nevada precinct caucus managers to move onto our payroll to help lead our ground effort for the state's county conventions.

Because so much of Nevada's population lives in Clark County, roughly 75 percent, the Clark County Convention elects the lion's share of the delegates to the congressional district and state conventions where the state's delegates to the National Convention will be picked. To put the size of the Clark County Convention in perspective, it is expected to have as many delegates in attendance as will the National Convention this summer in Denver. The Clark County Convention will be located in the convention center facility located at Bally's Hotel on the Las Vegas Strip. As in the past, the County Convention will be administered largely by local Democratic volunteers.

Clark County covers the entire Las Vegas metropolitan area, and is a stronghold of support within Nevada for Hillary Clinton. Backing for Obama is stronger in Washoe County, where Reno, the second largest city in the state, is located and in the lightly populated rural counties that cover the rest of the state. While Obama can prevail in these outlying areas, he won't succeed statewide unless he competes effectively in Clark County.

Clark County has become something of an urban melting pot in the desert. Many voters here are relatively new arrivals with limited roots in their community. There are large Hispanic and African-American constituencies that diverged sharply during the precinct caucuses, with many Hispanics supporting Hillary and nearly all African-Americans backing Barack. Retirees have settled in Las Vegas in large numbers and tend to support Hillary, while waves of younger voters, drawn to the exploding construction and hospitality industries, are skewed toward Obama.

In the hours just after Hillary's big victory in New Hampshire, the important Culinary Workers Union, which represents a good part of the unskilled hotel and casino labor force in Las Vegas, came to Obama's rescue with a key endorsement—much to the dismay of the Clinton and Edwards campaigns. This Culinary jump to Obama led to a lawsuit—ultimately unsuccessful—by the competing teachers union to attack the precinct voting sites for Culinary members at Las Vegas Strip casinos as unfair and in violation of state law. The litigation between opposing units of organized labor heightened ill will among Democrats in the state, as did a tense struggle over the presidential loyalty of Culinary's many female Hispanic members.

Perhaps most significant at the moment, Hillary is backed by much of the leadership of the Clark County Democratic Party. The Democratic County Chair is John Hunt and he's appointed his close friend, Bill Stanley, to be the Chair of the Clark County Convention. Hunt and Stanley control the staff that is planning and overseeing the County Convention.

Our first order of business in preparing for the Clark County Convention is to figure out the rules for seating delegates at the Convention and to obtain a list of the Obama delegates to the Convention. We focus in particular on understanding the procedures for filling vacancies with alternates. Over and over, we press the county Democratic Party for detailed information on the delegates and procedural rules for the Convention, but the County Party is unresponsive. The State Party doesn't have the information we need and we're left in the dark on fundamental aspects of how the Convention will be constituted and run. Based on what we can figure out, any voter who is registered as a Democrat is eligible to be an alternate at the County Convention.

As the clock winds down toward the County Convention, we finally give up on getting the information we've been seeking for the county party. We can't go into the Convention less than fully armed for our first convention confrontation against the Clinton campaign. In particular, we can't show up without enough delegate and alternates only to see our delegate positions being filled by Clinton alternates. Accordingly, I direct our staff to mobilize Obama supporters in the county to come to Bally's convention center to register as Convention alternates. We'll fill all of our vacancies, and if there are Clinton ones available, then we'll have alternates available to fill those, too. The Clinton campaign gets wind of our push to turn out our alternates and reportedly responds in kind.

Expecting a major confrontation with Convention organizers and the Clinton campaign, I'm convinced Brandon and I need to be on site. Brandon and I will be able help direct operations at the Convention and gain valuable firsthand experience on what will and will not work in our national caucus state competition with the Clinton campaign.

When we head to the airport in Chicago, I can feel the excitement that always comes with a trip to Las Vegas. While we're not going to hit the blackjack tables or take in a dinner show, it still feels like we're headed somewhere special. We go straight to Bally's from McCarran Airport and do a quick walk-thru of the convention facilities. We meet with our in-state team to discuss plans for the Convention at a fabulous Bally's suite, which will serve as our headquarters until we deploy to the convention center. The floor-to-ceiling windows offer a shimmering view of the illuminated Strip below. I have to say this campaign office compares favorably with any other I've ever seen.

The next morning, we go to the convention hall early to check in with the Convention organizers and our grassroots leaders. County Party officials tell us everything is in order. As I survey the Convention set-up, the registration arrangements seem rather quaint to me for a convention of the large size we're expecting. Not to worry, say the Convention officials, they run the County Convention every four years and know what they're doing.

As the delegates and alternates stream into Bally's, the registration line for the Convention grows. The convention hall is located to the rear of the building, behind the main hotel and casino areas and the line begins to overflow into the front parts of the building. Convention officials struggle to figure out whom to credential as a delegate to the Convention. It appears they may be missing the names of a thousand or more delegates elected at the precinct caucuses.

How could this happen? Nobody has an answer, and after just an hour, the registration line extends all the way to the front hotel lobby. It's not much later until the line extends into the most inviolate of places in Bally's, the Casino.

Bally's security staff looks stunned. They watch as the registration line extends farther and farther into the Casino, snaking around slot machines and blackjack tables. Bells and buzzers sound and coins drop all around the Convention delegates. The security staff seems at a loss about what to do. I'm certain this has never happened before.

The Convention delegates who have been processed and allowed into the convention hall now number more than the convention hall can reasonably contain. Masses of delegates who can't fit into the hall start to back up into the adjoining central hallway. It becomes difficult to move through any part of the convention area. Rumors circulate that Convention officials chose a meeting space that couldn't accommodate a full county convention to save money—a Vegas gamble that now looks like a losing bet.

Democratic Party officials gather in a convention command center located off the main hallway near the convention hall. The command center is in a plush wood-paneled meeting room more appropriate for a corporate board meeting than a political party nerve center. The room is stocked with a luxurious luncheon spread. The heaping platters of food strike me as on par with some of the best Las Vegas resort buffets.

Inside the room, Clark County Democratic Party Chair Hunt, Convention Chair Stanley and senior county and state Democratic Party staff confer with Clinton and Obama campaign leaders.

Present for Hillary Clinton are Rory Reid, her Nevada campaign chair, who is Chair of the Clark County Commission and the son of U.S. Senate Majority Leader Harry Reid, and Karen Hicks, Hillary's senior advisor for field operations. Brandon and I are present for Obama, joined by Obama state political director Alison Schwartz and our state co-chairs Steven Horsford, the Democratic leader in the Nevada Senate, and Billy Vasilliades, a top Las Vegas political and business strategist, known by everyone as "Billy V." I also stay in touch by phone with senior DNC staff and counsel in Washington.

As the assembled honchos graze the buffet table, increasingly frequent reports make their way into the command center of registration delays and overcrowding in the building. At first, Hunt and Stanley do not appear fazed by the reports, but as their staff leave the room and return with firsthand reports, they seem to realize they have a burgeoning problem on their hands. They put on a brave face, as Convention staff struggle to handle the situation.

Through most of the morning, Stanley has held off filling delegate vacancies and finalizing the Convention delegate roll, in order to enable the thousands of delegates still in line to register their credentials and enter the convention hall. However, with the schedule for starting the convention slipping farther and farther behind—and order in the overstuffed convention hall beginning to unravel—he tells the two campaigns he's going to order all delegate vacancies be filled with alternates. Aware that thousands of delegates have yet to be credentialed, both campaigns express reservations about these delegates losing their positions.

Local Democrats are in charge, though, and the word goes out to begin seating alternates. As the filling of delegate positions with alternates begins, the news is not well-received by the thousands of delegates still in the registration line. Rumors run rampant. Many Obama supporters believe the County Party is replacing them with Clinton alternates—that Clinton allies in the Party are stealing the Convention for Hillary.

In the convention command center, Stanley is getting as agitated as the people outside. Obama leaders Horsford and Billy V suggest to Stanley that he consult with me on how to address the worsening problems. "Let Berman help," they plead. "He knows more about these delegate processes than anybody in the country."

Stanley growls, "This isn't my first rodeo. I don't need any help from someone out of Chicago." Then, in an instant, he shouts to the security staff in the room, "Get Chicago out of here. Throw him out."

As jaws drop, the security forces grab me and muscle me out of the room.

When I'm deposited into the hallway outside the command center, I can see for myself how far the situation has descended. It's bedlam in the convention center. In the main hallway, people are packed together like sardines in a can and screaming in every direction. Every now and then political chants rise up from the din: "Hillary! Hillary! Hillary!" or "Yes we can! Yes we can! Yes we can!"

As the chaos in the building escalates, the police arrive. They immediately set up barricades in the main hallway, hoping to stem the movement of the crowd toward the overloaded convention hall. Rumors begin to swirl among Obama delegates blocked by the barricades that the presidential voting has begun and the barricades are intended to keep them from voting. Determined to protect their candidate, the Obama delegates push forward to break through the barricades.

As a campaign official, I'm permitted to slip past the barricades to enter the convention hall. Once inside, I can see the scene inside is no more orderly than elsewhere in the building. Delegates are shouting and the aisles are jammed with delegates.

I can see that the Convention vote for president in fact has begun. I struggle to reach the front of the room, from where Convention officials are attempting to lead the balloting. One Obama delegate recognizes me and shouts to me that the ballot boxes are not secure.

I look around, and sure enough, I see a ballot box being carried above someone's head straight into the Men's Room. I wouldn't believe it, if I hadn't seen it.

Word of what is transpiring inside Bally's is starting to leak to the outside world. Television crews are arriving to capture what is growing into a major state and local news story.

Back in the convention command center, Horsford and Billy V continue to argue to Stanley that he cannot get things under control without cooperating with the national campaign organizations—and that he has no choice but to bring me back into the command center.

Apparently realizing he has no better alternative for restoring order, Stanley agrees to work with the campaigns. The door opens with the call to get "Chicago" back into the room.

Convention aides hunt me down and guide me through the mob back into the command center. While en route, someone pulls the fire alarm and sirens start blaring in the building. Fire trucks and—even worse for Stanley—fire marshals must be on their way.

Once back in the command center, I see a despondent-looking Stanley. Gesturing to the platters of food on the sumptuous buffet table, he says, "I'm finished. You may as well clear off a platter, because they're going to need it to serve up my head."

Rory Reid, the Clinton Nevada Chair, tells me he's worried about the unsafe conditions in the building and suggests that the County Convention be cancelled outright. Party officials can reconvene it later in the spring to elect delegates to the State Convention.

From a political perspective, I immediately recognize this wouldn't hurt us, since we expect to win a clear majority of the delegates being elected at the county conventions outside of Clark County. A non-result in Clark County, Hillary's state stronghold, would leave us with more delegates than Hillary elected to the Nevada State Convention. This would be an unexpected turnaround in the one caucus state in the country where she elected more precinct delegates than Obama.

I pull Rory aside and let him know that if the County Party decides to cancel the Convention, we'll join the Clinton campaign in supporting their decision. The fact is, I say, that none of us have much choice in the matter. Police and fire officials will make the decision for Convention officials, if they don't make it for themselves.

When Stanley hears the two campaigns are in accord, he's visibly relieved. He'll cancel the Convention if the campaigns publicly pledge their support for doing so and the delegates concur.

The first part is easy. Rory and I move to the front of the room and shake hands in agreement in full view of the assembled officials. We've delivered our joint consent.

With the campaigns behind him, Stanley and his entourage wheel out of the command center and head straight toward the Convention podium. A security escort leads us through the hostile crowd in the hallway and convention hall. It's slow progress even with our escort, since it's almost physically impossible to clear a path to our destination.

Inside the hall, the headline speaker is addressing the crowd. Of all the people that the County Party could have brought to Las Vegas to be its lead speaker, it's none other than famed Minnesota office-seeker and wisecracking comedian Al Franken. Franken is gamely making jokes about the chaos in the convention hall, disclaiming any personal responsibility for the grim situation. Despite his attempts at humor, nobody is laughing or even paying much attention to him.

When Stanley finally reaches the podium, the crowd is yelling every insult imaginable at him. They're angry about the mismanagement of the Convention and fearful that their delegate vote may be lost through the chaotic voting process that has been underway.

Ignoring the catcalls aimed in his direction, Stanley announces: "I'm going to ask for a privileged motion to recess due to a pressing situation affecting the privilege of assembly."

"No! No! No!" the mutinous delegates shout back.

"Therefore," Stanley says, "the Convention shall stand in recess for the purpose of voting, alignment, and the selection of delegates to the State Convention. This recess shall be until a date certain which shall not be less than 30 days..."

And then Stanley is shouted down by the delegates. They are enraged. They've endured long lines, inadequate facilities and more, all in order to cast their delegate vote for their presidential candidate. Going home to come back and start all over another time is the last thing they want to do.

Stanley tries to speak again, as delegates complain loudly that they don't want to recess without voting.

Stanley and others attempt to explain that too many delegates have been unable to register to vote and that even if they were registered, they cannot enter the convention hall, which is filled beyond capacity.

When the delegates finally vote on the Convention leadership's motion to recess, it fails.

Stanley looks speechless. The delegates have rebelled against him and refused to disband their Convention. He's lost control of the hall.

Watching this incredible scene is a group of very unhappy Bally's managers, police officials and fire marshals. They want the building cleared.

Unfortunately for everyone, Stanley can't make this happen.

Stanley and his group retreat back to the command center. He's stymied. The campaign leaders brainstorm together and decide the only way to convince the delegates to recess the Convention is to speak to them separately, with Rory to address the Clinton delegates and Billy V and Steven to speak to the Obama delegates. A defeated Stanley quickly agrees.

The state campaign leaders go to the Convention podium and obtain a temporary recess for the separate campaign caucuses. When the thousands of Obama attendees gather together, Billy V makes an impassioned appeal. He says too many of our Culinary Union delegates have had to leave to return to work. Many more have been blocked from registering. The size of our vote for Obama could be imperiled.

If there is one thing that unites all our delegates, it's their support for Obama. Billy V has found the formula for success. Our delegates will do anything to protect Obama and the strength of his representation from Nevada to the National Convention. The Clinton leaders talk to their own delegates and also convince them to allow a recess of the Convention.

All the delegates reconvene in the convention hall. Now, with the fire marshals insistent that the hall be emptied, Stanley again asks the Convention to approve the motion to recess. This time, the delegates grudgingly give their consent. They're not doing this for Stanley or the Clark County Democratic Party. They're doing it for Barack Obama and Hillary Clinton.

Finally, ten hours after the chaos began, the tired, hungry and disgusted delegates stream out of the building and into the parking lots.

The next morning, on the way to the airport, I pick up a cup of coffee and buy the Sunday morning newspaper. In large, bold letters, the banner headline yields the final public judgment, "Clark County Democratic Convention Ends in Chaos."

This is just the first of many county and state conventions to be held across the country. When I return to Chicago, I debrief my staff to determine lessons learned for future conventions. The first rule: expect Armageddon Day in every convention hall. The high levels of turnout and enthusiasm are likely to tax every convention, and we don't know what to expect from the Clinton campaign as we move forward. Given that we've knocked the barn doors off in every other caucus state we've competed in so far, we're going to have to do what we can to hold their conventions together and preserve our caucus states delegate lead.

★ ★ ★

The Clark County Convention reconvenes weeks later under much tighter operating rules. Unlike in advance of the aborted Convention, local Democratic officials collaborate with both campaigns to agree on who is qualified to attend as a delegate and on the procedures to be used. The resumed Convention runs smoothly and our preparation for it actually allows us to increase our delegate strength from the precinct level. When taken together with the county conventions that were completed on time, Obama's statewide delegate strength increases from the original 51% to 45% split favoring Hillary at the precinct level to a narrower 51% to 49% ratio in her favor after the county conventions.

When the State Convention convenes weeks later, the Obama delegates are full of enthusiasm. As at the county conventions, we prepare carefully before the State Convention to identify and fill delegate vacancies. Our strength on the State Convention floor grows from the level set at the county conventions, increasing to the level of 55% Obama to 45% Hillary. Obama now has the majority of delegates in the state.

By moving Obama over the 50% level at the State Convention, we gain two additional National Convention delegates. First, there is one more delegate earned from the group of 9 delegates to be allocated proportionally based on the presidential preferences of the State Convention delegates. Our majority on the convention floor earns Obama a 5 to 4 split of these delegates. If Hillary had held onto the state delegate majority, she'd have won this 5 to 4 statewide delegate split.

We also have the opportunity to obtain one more delegate for Obama due to our State Convention majority. This is Nevada's "unpledged add-on" delegate, a final delegate position from the state that can be awarded to anyone the Convention chooses. Brandon is on site at the State Convention and informs me by phone while I'm at the Colorado State Convention that there is a complication in our winning the add-on delegate. Rory Reid, Hillary's state chair, is imploring our state leadership to select a delegate who is not outwardly pro-Obama and our state leaders want to accommodate Rory to avoid any embarrassment for Clinton leaders in the state.

"Jeff, there's no way I can hold this add-on delegate," Brandon pleads with me. "Our state leaders want to let the Clinton people have it, and I don't think I can stop them."

"Brandon, I understand our guys have the best of motives," I reply, "but you need to find a solution that holds the position for Barack."

"But Jeff…" Brandon tries to start again.

"Talking to me isn't going to help," I cut him off. "Talk to our guys in Nevada. But don't come back without that damn delegate!"

And I end the call.

Within minutes, my cell phone is ringing.

"Alright, Jeff," Brandon says. "This is the best I can do and get out of the state alive. We're going to go with Rory's guy for the add-on position—but we have the guy's word that if the nomination is contested at the National Convention, he will vote for Obama."

"Do you trust this?" I question Brandon. "Is this an Obama delegate?"

"Yes," Brandon responds. "If push comes to shove, this is ours."

"Fine. Then that's how we'll score it," I respond. "Come on back to Chicago."

When Brandon returns to Chicago, we review our experience in Nevada. It's clear to us that the combination of Obama's grassroots strength and our convention leadership produced a multiplier effect that enabled us to grow our delegate strength in Nevada at the very time that the Clinton team was rumored to be looking to reduce it. As crazy as it was in Clark County, Nevada has proved we can more than hold our own against the Clinton campaign in the upper tiers of the caucus states.

* * *

My attention turns to North Dakota. Obama did very well in the Super Tuesday precinct caucuses and now we're approaching the legislative district conventions. The conventions are scheduled to occur over a month-long period from February 19th to March 14th. My caucus lieutenant, Mitch Wallace, is going to collect the precinct level results and develop a plan for us to maintain our strength at the district conventions.

When Mitch contacts the state Democratic Party headquarters for the precinct level data, party staffers tell him to contact the Democratic legislative district chairs directly, as they have the information for the delegates who are to attend their legislative district convention. This is a hassle for Mitch, but we need the data on who was elected at the precinct caucuses and I insist that he call through the district chairs to request the information.

After a week or two has gone by, Mitch comes to me to say, for some districts, he can't get any precinct results other than the vote for each presidential candidate. He's also hearing from some district chairs that they're getting little pre-registration by delegates for their district convention. The lack of information about our delegates and the uncertainty about convention delegate pre-registration concerns me as to what's happening in North Dakota.

While it's important to know how the presidential candidates fared in each of the precinct caucuses, I want to see the list of our delegates and alternates elected at those caucuses. Without this information, we can't contact them to make sure they attend their district conventions. I don't want any no-shows that could reduce our strength at these conventions.

Now, with the district conventions coming up on the calendar, we've run out of time to continue jerking around. Frustrated, I tell Mitch to get a knowledgeable person from North Dakota on the phone. I want to know how and when we're going to get our delegate names.

Mitch gets someone on the phone who says he knows what's going on with the convention process in the state. I join the call and immediately start boring in.

"Where are our delegate lists?" I ask. "Why aren't we getting more cooperation on this?"

Then I learn more about what's happening in the state. Incredible as it may seem, some precinct caucuses neglected to elect delegates to the district conventions. As explained to me, Democrats at each precinct caucus were to vote their presidential preference in a secret ballot and then elect delegates to attend the district convention. Sometimes, though, they cast their ballot for president and then went home. There are no delegates to the district conventions in these cases. This is why some district conventions have been seeing few or no delegates pre-registering, and why we can't get a list of our delegates.

This is not good news to me. Our hard-fought win in the precinct caucuses might be challenged at the National Convention if the district conventions can't be properly constituted, depending on how many district conventions are affected. Worse yet, if trouble in the North Dakota convention system fuels doubts—even if un-founded—about the caucus and convention process in other states, the legitimacy of our caucus state wins could be questioned. We have to figure out how we can make the best of North Dakota's situation.

Mitch asks me, "How can the district conventions function if they have no delegates from the precinct caucuses?"

"I've got an idea," I respond, "but first I need you to confirm the rules for delegate eligibility and the filling of vacancies with alternates."

After doing some research, Mitch returns and explains: "Under North Dakota delegate rules, any voter in a legislative district can serve as a delegate or alternate to their district convention. The delegates have to be elected at the precinct caucuses, but alternates don't have to be elected, they just have to be eligible to serve as a delegate."

"So here's what you should do," I tell Mitch. "Ask our North Dakota supporters to pre-register for their district convention as an alternate and then attend the convention. If the district is one where they're lacking delegates, then our folks can fill the vacancies."

Mitch immediately sends a message to our grassroots leaders in the state to ask their best Obama supporters to pre-register with their legislative district chair as a convention alternate. The word goes out to our supporters and greater numbers of alternates pre-register for the district conventions around the state.

When the district conventions meet, alternates fill vacant delegate positions as needed, and the conventions conduct their normal business. Obama's delegate strength doesn't necessarily increase, as he won overwhelmingly—nearly 2 to 1—in the precinct caucuses to begin with. Additionally, many districts attempt to follow the results of the precinct caucuses in the district when electing delegates to the State Convention.

What's important to me is that the district conventions have filled their delegate positions—in the manner expected—and not provided any basis for challenges to the state's delegation to the National Convention.

★   ★   ★

In Texas, the story is far different from North Dakota. The Texas precinct conventions, which were held on the night of the state's Two-Step primary, were conducted under the microscope of national media scrutiny. The state's convention system elects 67 delegates—one-third of the state's total—which is an amount equal to the number from a typical mid-size state. The next step in the delegate process is the March 29th county (or in some cases, state senatorial district) conventions. The results from these conventions will be closely watched by the media and both presidential campaigns.

The Clinton campaign fully contested the March 4th precinct conventions three weeks ago, much as they did the precinct caucuses in Nevada. In both cases, Hillary benefitted from strong support from Hispanic Democrats. Of course, Barack retained the solid support of African-American Democrats, plus the liberal reform wing of the Texas Democratic Party that is based in progressive Austin but spreads, to a lesser degree to other parts of the state.

Although the Clinton campaign put its best foot forward in the precinct conventions, Obama still won a victory that night. Now, our task is to maintain that success in the county and district conventions. What worries me is the large number of county and district conventions and the size of the largest gatherings. There are 254 counties in Texas, dozens of which will have conventions that rival our National Convention in terms of the number of delegates in attendance.

We move into our pre-convention drill. I check in with our state Obama leader, Ron Kirk, to get his advice on what we can expect. Ron is a good friend and revered figure in Texas Democratic circles. He gives me the skinny on the latest developments with the state Democratic Party and what to expect in the major county conventions.

Brandon gets in touch with the Texas Democratic Party to get lists of delegates for each of the conventions. It's not easy since there is so little time between the precinct conventions and the upcoming ones. We blast emails to as many of our delegates as possible to urge them to attend their convention. Brandon also puts together a plan for a state command center in Austin. In case there's trouble, I want us to be within shouting distance of the state party headquarters, which will be the coordinating point for the conventions.

For the major conventions, I'm convinced we need to do more than just staff an office in Austin that can relay reports of trouble to the state party. We need a capable representative on site at every major convention who will represent our campaign in any controversy that arises. The major conventions could be like that in Clark County, Nevada, where the Clinton campaign also fully engaged us and the proceedings spun out of control.

I put the word out through our Washington delegate lawyers group that we need help in Texas. Who is willing to go to the front lines and lead Obama delegates in a hotly contested convention hall? One by one, our best lawyers from the top law firms in Washington sign up. They'll be volunteers, travelling to Texas at their own expense, to be champions for Obama. They will be our eyes, ears and leaders in each of the top conventions in the state. In some cases, they might be the most calm and clear-thinking individual in the convention hall if events unwind.

The DNC also wants to set up shop in Austin, to look out for the national party's interest in having a well-run process when the national media descends upon the state to cover the convention results. DNC staff have been struggling for weeks to persuade the state party to increase its preparations for the conventions and the reporting of results. Now, the DNC wants to place its personnel in the state party's control room, where convention controversies will be resolved.

But this is Austin, Texas, not Washington, DC. The state party calls the shots here, and they push back against the DNC's request. There will be no national party staff in their convention control room. The DNC will have to locate its Texas operation elsewhere in Austin—where they'll be far from the action in the control room.

Brandon and I fly to Austin and join our in-state team at our downtown headquarters. This is a city of restaurants and music clubs that we mostly don't have time to enjoy. Still, when it's time to eat, we sneak out of the office and walk over to some of the best restaurants in the city. We've got to eat, and Texas barbeque is on our menu.

Our Washington legal team flies into every major city in Texas and takes up positions at each of the top conventions. Early field reports from the conventions and the state party headquarters indicates delegate turnout is high. We certainly worked our list of delegates to get our people out to the conventions, and I'm sure the Clinton Campaign has largely done the same. By this point in the campaign, they're pouring in resources to try and match our convention efforts, though it seems it's still mostly a game of catch-up for them.

It's now convention day. The convention system allows different conventions to start at different times throughout the day. We have a schedule for this on our headquarters wall and do our best to monitor developments around the state. As the morning rolls on and convention halls fill up, we're starting to get calls and see media reports that, at some conventions, things are not proceeding according to plan.

In San Antonio, a chaotic scene unfolds at one of the huge conventions in this major metropolitan area. In order to keep costs down, the county Democratic Party has rented a barren warehouse to serve as a "convention hall." The building recently was used to house the construction of large parade floats, some of which remain in the building, reinforcing a carnival atmosphere that greets arriving delegates.

Masses of delegates mob the property in advance of the scheduled convention start time of 8 am. Perhaps two thousand people show up, with many overflowing into the building's parking lot. The owner of the warehouse is on site and overseeing a set-up of barbeque grills, where he intends to roast chickens and cook burgers to make some more profits from the day's activities.

The delegates line up at the warehouse loading dock at the back of the building to receive their credentials to enter the convention. Convention leaders struggle to determine who is entitled to receive these credentials, as the delegate lists from many precincts are either missing or incomplete. Convention officials are unprepared for the delegate turnout.

Frustration grows and a group convenes in the front parking lot to establish a committee to hear complaints about missing credentials. Clinton and Obama partisans argue for two and a half hours over how to constitute the committee, as they know the granting of credentials could affect the relative strength of the two warring camps.

Despite Hillary's obviously greater strength in the heavily Hispanic county, the group agrees to split the credentials committee evenly between the campaigns and begins to address credentials complaints. It's slow going and it's not long before anxious Hillary and Obama supporters begin challenging one another's right to be in the building. The nervous building owner, seeing this chaotic situation unfold, panics and orders everyone out of his warehouse. Fistfights among the delegates break out in the parking lot, and the police are called to restore order.

The police can calm the delegates down, but can do nothing to help convention leaders conduct their business. It's now well into the afternoon and convention leaders still cannot determine who should be recognized to receive credentials to the convention.

The phone rings at our state Obama headquarters, and one of our staff tells me I need to take the call. It's northern Virginia lawyer Kevin Wolf, one of the lawyers I called into volunteer service. Kevin and local Obama leaders are struggling to deal with the situation.

"Jeff," he says, "its utter chaos here at my convention in San Antonio and it's headed towards a collapse. I don't know whether to let it go—since this area is Hillary country—or try to save it. What should I do?"

The Clinton campaign has been complaining about the Texas convention system since the precinct voting weeks ago. I assume they'd like nothing more than to see the state's county conventions break down to strengthen their case against the legitimacy of our strong precinct-level win. If the conventions can't elect delegates to the State Convention, the Clinton team might be able to challenge the seating of delegates to the Democratic National Convention that were elected through the state's convention system. These are mostly our delegates, so I have a simple answer for Kevin.

"You've got to get the situation under control," I instruct him. "That's why you flew to San Antonio. You can't let the convention collapse. It could affect all our convention delegates from the state."

We end the call and Kevin turns around to view the swirling mass of hostile Democrats in the warehouse parking lot. Realizing that the only path forward is to start the convention system over, he jumps up on a picnic table in the parking lot and screams as loud as he can to capture people's attention. With no authority whatsoever, he begins shouting commands to whoever is within earshot to meet in different areas of the parking lot for each precinct. Everyone attending from that precinct will simply vote again for president and allocate the delegate votes in accordance with the vote in the parking lot.

Appreciating that someone finally is bringing order to the day-long chaos, the crowd slowly organizes itself as Kevin has instructed. Delegates meet in precinct units and select delegates to today's convention. Kevin's system is working.

By early evening, the building owner is convinced that delegates will not destroy his warehouse and lets them re-enter the building so the convention can convene. At 7 pm, the convention is called to order and the convention organizers prepare to call for the Pledge of Allegiance. It's now that they realize nobody has brought an American flag. The delegates need an American flag.

Someone shouts above the noise in the hall: "Who has an American flag? We need a flag."

"I do," a voice screams back.

And then, rising into the air above the heads of the crowd, is a baseball cap. It's covered with the Stars and Stripes.

Making do, the 2,000 delegates—proud to be participating in today's voting despite the nearly unending difficulties they've endured—face the raised cap and together recite the Pledge.

The convention moves to the business of electing delegates and by 9 pm elects its delegation to the State Convention. Thanks to the resourcefulness of Kevin and his local team, we've helped save a major Texas convention from collapse. The challenge for us at many conventions today came not from Hillary's campaign, but from simple inadequate preparation.

In South Texas, though, the situation is nothing like that in San Antonio. Here, the Clinton forces, which are aligned with the dominant local Democratic Hispanic organizations, are in full control. Several days before the county conventions, the state Democratic Party proposed sending parliamentary experts to numerous major conventions, including some within South Texas, to assure a fair vote. In what may be an apocryphal tale, I hear a rumor that the state party was told by some local Democrats not to bother, that the parliamentarians aren't needed and perhaps their safety couldn't be guaranteed.

When the county conventions are held, Obama delegates in several major conventions struggle to obtain a presidential preference vote according to the rules. In the worst cases, convention officials are conducting the presidential balloting in ways that reduce the number of Obama delegates to the State convention.

Unable to make any headway within the convention hall in these situations, Obama delegates call our state command center in Austin to ask for help. But in most cases there is little we immediately can do for them. We instruct our delegate leaders to take notes of any rules violations so we can challenge the results later. We promise our delegates we'll not let them down and will fight to ensure their full representation at the State Convention.

In Harris County, which includes Houston, the situation is different yet again. Here, the Obama delegates have clear control of the delegate process, bolstered by our strength in the city's large African-American community. But our delegates are turning out in numbers so much higher than expected that they're having trouble getting to the convention hall to vote.

Starting early in the morning of convention day, delegates, alternates and others hoping to attend the convention jam access roads to the convention hall. The traffic back-ups are so bad that delegates, fearing they'll arrive too late to vote at the convention, abandon their vehicles and walk for a mile or more to get to the hall. The abandoned vehicles make matters even worse for other delegates and police who are called in to remedy the situation.

When the delegates finally reach the convention hall, they find registration lines that go outside the building and snake around the structure. Convention leaders see no alternative but to hold up the voting to allow people to register and get inside. The delays cascade one on top of the other, pushing the convention vote by the delegates until well after midnight.

Days later, after all these conventions have finished, we keep faith with our delegates at conventions where they believe they suffered in the presidential voting from rules violations. We lodge numerous challenges with the state Democratic Party and, where appropriate, ask for a change in the delegate allocation to seat more delegates for Obama at the State Convention. There are so many challenges around the state—from both campaigns—that the state party puts together an informal traveling court to go from one county to another to hear challenges and change for Obama and Clinton delegate allocations when justified.

All in all, we survive the Texas county and state senatorial district conventions but, for many attendees, it has been an experience of political battle and chaos they'll never forget.

★   ★   ★

In Colorado, the delegates from the congressional districts to the National Convention are selected in separate conventions, some of which meet on the same day in the same hall and some of which meet on different days. As these conventions approach, our delegate hunter for Colorado, Mike French, identifies specific districts where we might possibly snag one more National Convention delegate at the congressional district convention.

As it happens, one congressional district convention where we have a chance to pick up another delegate will be meeting on the same day immediately after another convention in the same ballroom. The first convention is scheduled to run from late afternoon to dinner time, and the second convention, the one where we're close to winning one more National Convention delegate, is to run from the dinner hour into the evening. This kind of stacking of conventions—one right after the other in the same hall—is fraught with risk that the first convention will run over and force a delay for the second one. Foreseeing this possible problem, we'll take steps to prepare our delegates to settle in for a long night.

Mike and I will attend these two conventions to see if we can't win the extra delegate we've identified as within reach. We ask for the rules for the congressional district conventions to be clarified to permit each of our delegate candidates to give a nominating speech for themselves. It's only fair for candidates to be able to say a few words on their behalf, and this will allow us to control the pacing of the conventions by adjusting the number of our delegate candidates who'll speak. Knowing that delays are likely, I have Mike arrange for a holding area where our delegates to the second convention can wait if the first convention runs over.

When convention day arrives, the scene at the convention center is like so many we have seen this year. Delegate records are incomplete, leading to confusion and long delays in registering delegates. It isn't long before some grumble about going home. Mike works patiently with convention officials and Clinton representatives to review the lists of delegates from the counties to produce a final roll of the convention delegates. We do what we can to reduce the number of our delegate candidate speakers to move the proceedings along.

Still, the first convention drags on. We're able to hold our delegates for the second convention, however, because of our planning and the arrangements we've made to provide a suitable waiting area for our delegates. We activate an informal organizational structure to stay in touch with our waiting delegates to make sure they don't leave before the voting begins.

As time goes on, it becomes clear that we need to pump our delegates up to keep them from dropping out of the convention. We move all our delegates down the central hallway into an empty lounge room for a pep rally. The room turns out to have little ventilation, and as our forces gather, the temperature rises from all their body heat. Realizing we have to capture the moment before the situation literally melts down, I squeeze up through the crowd and jump onto a table to address the hundreds of Obama delegates.

"On behalf of the Obama campaign," I shout at the top of my lungs. "I want to thank each of you for coming to your convention to elect Barack as our next President of the United States. Thank you! We have a special guest with us today, Federico Peña, your former mayor of Denver and also a member of President Bill Clinton's Cabinet. Now, in 2008, Federico is one of the hardest working, most important supporters—anywhere in the nation—of Barack Obama."

And with that, I reach my hand down into the throbbing mob to find Federico's hand. I pull as hard as I can and raise him up onto the table next to me. When Federico appears above the crowd, the delegates cheer wildly. Federico gives a fabulous impromptu address that thrills the delegates. When he finishes, the room is thundering with chants of "Yes we can! Yes we can! Yes we can!"

When it's finally time for the second convention to convene, our delegates make their way proudly into the convention hall. It's late, damn late in the evening, but they're fired up and ready to go. When the convention votes on the presidential candidates, we grow our delegate strength by the one delegate we've targeted as being within reach.

★   ★   ★

In Iowa's March 15th county conventions, we have an unusual opportunity to improve our delegate standing. The state soon will be electing two-thirds of its National Convention delegates at congressional district conventions. Iowa's earlier precinct caucuses, of course, delivered the rocket boost of momentum for Obama that started him down his nomination path. At the precinct caucuses, Obama won 4,707 delegates to the county conventions, or 37.5% of the total, while Edwards won 4,207 delegates, or 29.75%, and Hillary came in a close third with 4,103 delegates, or 29.47%.

Since then, John Edwards has dropped out of the presidential race and now the 4,207 Edwards delegates to the county conventions are up for grabs.

I'm all over this opportunity for Obama and gather my caucus lieutenants to prepare for a blitz to win as many of these Edwards delegates as possible. The key will be to focus on the Edwards delegates in counties where we can increase the number of delegates for Obama.

"Let's do the math," I say. "We need to target the counties in congressional districts where we have a good chance to win more delegates. Also, look closely at our statewide percentage of county delegates and figure out how many Edwards delegates we'll need to increase our number of statewide delegates to the National Convention."

In the next few days, our team calculates that we can win significant additional delegates to Denver at the county conventions if we can win over the Edwards delegates. I'm going to Iowa with Mitch Wallace to work with our well-organized grassroots network in the state to reach out to as many of the Edwards delegates as possible. We ask the remnants of the former Edwards high command for help, but they can't deliver much assistance at this point in time.

At the county conventions, Obama leaders and supporters reach out to as many Edwards delegates as possible. In one targeted county convention after another, our supporters convince Edwards delegates to switch to Obama. In many cases, the Edwards people already are headed in Obama's direction, but certainly not always.

When the voting is done, the convention results are sent in to the state party headquarters, where they're to be tallied and reported to the press. At the headquarters, I can see there is confusion over how to calculate the effect of the movement of the Edwards delegates to Obama and Clinton on the projected number of national convention delegates for each remaining candidate. I know from our internal calculations that we've done better than anybody expected. After making suggestions on how to do the math, I finally just sit down with the party staff and show them how to make the calculations. A state news reporter covering the conventions looks over my shoulder and jots down my results.

Thanks to the movement of Edwards delegates to Obama, our share of the statewide delegates has grown from 37.5% to 52.33%. Hillary's statewide delegate share has hardly budged, moving only from 29.47% to 31.68%. The now-suspended Edwards candidacy continues to maintain some diehard strength, dropping from 29.75% to 15.64%.

When these results are extrapolated to national convention delegates, we have increased Obama's overall Iowa delegate strength from 16 at the time of the precinct caucuses to 25 now. Hillary's statewide delegate total actually drops by one from 15 to 14, while former candidate Edwards holds on to six delegates from the 14 he earned at the precinct caucuses.

The net result of these changes is that we've increased Obama's advantage over Hillary among Iowa's national convention delegates by 10. We've negated Hillary's seven-delegate win of eleven days earlier in the Ohio Primary. Given that we've spent virtually no money to prepare for the county conventions, this is a good bang for our buck. I can't imagine what the Clinton campaign will think when they get the news.

★ ★ ★

The bottom line with all of the caucus states is that our study of the math is helping us preserve and, in some cases, improve our delegate standing in the caucus states. We pursue every opportunity to ensure that the Clinton campaign cannot reverse Obama's important lead among caucus state delegates.

We're empowered in our efforts by the enthusiastic and disciplined involvement of our locally-elected delegates throughout the country. The teamwork of these delegates and our national delegate staff creates a powerful advantage that the Clinton campaign can't match. In addition, when necessary, we've developed special strategies to overcome unexpected challenges in the sometimes chaotic real-world settings of the caucus state convention systems.

Our original purpose in building our caucus state convention operation was to prevent the Clinton campaign from rolling back our success at the precinct level in any of the caucus states. As I review the results of our efforts, I cannot find one instance where the Clinton team in fact has reduced our number of national convention delegates from what was expected after the precinct caucuses.

To the contrary, while we've held on to all of our initial caucus state delegate strength, in some states—such as Iowa and Nevada—we've actually increased Obama's number of national convention delegates from what was earlier projected. This accomplishment was not expected, but strengthens Obama's position in his running competition with Hillary.

13

Mining for Delegate Gold

HILLARY'S HOPE TO BECOME THE NEW Comeback Kid in the Clinton family is going to run into a dead end if her campaign doesn't find a way to more strongly challenge our position in the delegate race. Winning even the largest primaries, like Ohio and Pennsylvania, isn't going to enable her to make up ground that she's already lost in the national delegate competition. Proportional representation in the allocation of delegates limits how many more delegates she can win than Obama in any state. Her campaign will have to figure out another way to catch up in the delegate race if she's to mount a comeback.

One avenue open to Hillary to make up ground is with the unpledged add-on superdelegate positions allowed under national party rules. The unpledged add-on delegate positions are extra slots granted to each state party to send one or more additional delegates as part of its state delegation. The idea is to accommodate people not otherwise chosen to go to the National Convention, such as a senior Democrat in the state who wants to attend the Convention but isn't an automatic superdelegate. There are 76 of these delegates nationally, after eliminating the three assigned to Florida and two assigned to Michigan.

Not every state is allowed to elect the same number of un-pledged add-on delegates. A small state might be authorized to select just one unpledged add-on delegate, while a mid-size state might get two and a larger state might be entitled to three, four or even five, as in the case of California.

The add-on delegates from each state are to be chosen by the vote of a state convention or high-ranking state party committee, without being allocated in accordance with results from the state's primary or caucus. Rather, the unpledged add-on delegates are picked at the complete discretion of the body making the selection. Many state party chairs, in fact, consider these unpledged add-on positions theirs to assign however they believe is best for the state party.

In this unique presidential season, though, with Obama's delegate lead over Hillary being as narrow as it is, these unpledged add-on positions could serve as a vehicle for Hillary to reduce her delegate disadvantage and find her way to contest the presidential nomination at the National Convention.

While many state party leaders see these positions as theirs to assign, I see them as up for grabs by the two presidential campaigns. To me, they're delegate gold. And we'll do everything possible—within the rules—to win these unpledged add-on positions for Obama. I'm determined to protect his delegate lead for the presidential nomination.

Many of the party conventions or other meetings that select the unpledged add-on delegates are operating in chaotic circumstances in this hyperactive nominating cycle. The lack of predictability at these events elevates the importance of planning early and making preparations to capture as many of these delegate positions as possible. Whenever it makes sense either myself or one of my staff will attend the decision-making event to coordinate on the ground with our in-state Obama supporters. Working as a team will give us our best chance for success.

*　*　*

At the spring North Dakota State Convention at the Alerus Center in Grand Forks, there is one unpledged add-on delegate to be elected by a vote of all the Convention delegates. Before the Convention delegates are scheduled to conduct any business, they'll be treated to a special show, as both Hillary and Barack will be coming to address them and the public in the large Alerus arena.

I make plans at the last minute to fly to the State Convention with delegate staffer Mitch Wallace to oversee our pursuit of the unpledged add-on. We soon learn that every hotel room in the city is booked, except for a few at a nearby motel. With no alternative, we book the room and I soon find myself shaving in a bathroom with no working light. Another colleague from Chicago forced to stay in the same motel reports to me that her toilet fell over when she sat on it. The campaign trail is not always a thing of glamour.

With Obama and Hillary as the marquis attractions, 17,000 North Dakotans show up and join the Convention delegates for what turns out to be the largest political event in North Dakota history. I enjoy the show myself, until its time to get down to business. When the delegates convene to begin the State Convention, I lay out the situation to our state Obama leaders.

"Anybody can be selected to be North Dakota's unpledged add-on delegate," I say. "We need to use our strength among the State Convention delegates to elect an Obama loyalist for the add-on position. We have to nominate one Obama supporter for the position and put all our votes behind that person."

After some energetic discussion among our leadership, they agree that our Obama state chair, former state Democratic Party chair Dan Hannaher, will have the best chance to win the most votes and should be nominated for the add-on slot. Without any communications gear, we use word of mouth down each row of delegate seating to instruct our Convention delegates to vote for Dan and not be distracted by any other candidate running for the position.

The selection of the unpledged add-on will be the last item of business for the State Convention. As the Convention proceedings unfold, delays begin to pile up and the delegates get restless. It's getting late and I notice a significant number of them have started drifting out of the convention hall. I'm concerned that we're losing our delegate strength.

Why would any State Convention delegate leave before the most important vote of the Convention? There's no good reason, but a lot of bad ones. For instance, some delegates get hungry and want to go to a restaurant. Others live a long drive away from the convention hall and want to get a head start for the long drive home. Some get tired and just can't stay awake any longer, while more than a few decide their most important priority is hitting the local bar.

When I can no longer bear to watch our delegate numbers continue to shrink, I take matters into my own hands.

"You, you and you, get up!" I shout to Obama delegates who I've never met before. "Guard those exit doors. Identify every person who wants to leave. If they're for Obama, they have to stay. No Obama delegate is allowed out!"

Most of our delegates, when questioned, agree to stay, some, though, try to bust through our makeshift blockade, leading to vigorous discussions about loyalty to our cause. Overall, we seem to be winning the struggle to keep our delegates in the convention hall.

Hillary's delegates, on the other hand, continue to saunter right out the doors. Our door minders don't stop them. It's not their job. So, quite a number of Hillary's delegates head out— whether to the bars, restaurants, hotels, or maybe to head for home.

Finally, the time for the selection of the unpledged add-on delegate arrives. By this time, it's not clear what proportion of Obama and Clinton supporters are remaining in the convention hall. After the nominating speeches, we know that Hillary's forces are putting one main candidate up against Dan, producing a test of strength for the two sides. I'm hopeful we're still in control, but nervous about the outcome.

When the votes are tallied, it becomes clear our State Convention delegates have hung on and claimed the state's last delegate position for Obama. I'm relieved we've won, but determined to leave less to chance when other states make their add-on selections.

★   ★   ★

Later in the spring, we have a tense situation developing for New Mexico's selection of its one unpledged add-on delegate. The New Mexico State Democratic Central Committee will be meeting to elect the add-on delegate. Under the state Democratic Party's delegate selection plan, the State Chair alone is empowered to nominate two candidates for the position, though the full State Democratic Central Committee approves the selection.

The State Chair is a loyalist for Governor Bill Richardson, who endorsed Obama after dropping out of the presidential race. In this case, I have only one strategy, which is to see who the State chair might pick to fill the two nomination slots for the position. I want those picks to be Democrats who we can reasonably hope to vote for Obama at the National Convention.

In a phone conversation with the State Chair, my tracker for the state, Toni Morales, learns that the Chair is still deciding whom to pick for his two candidates for the add-on slot. The is hoping to nominate people who can help fill the affirmative action goals for the state. His search is focusing on two Native American women, neither of whom has endorsed a presidential candidate.

Toni's gives me a report on both possible candidates and I can see either one would make a fine delegate to the National Convention. Neither is for Hillary, and that's what I care about. Either one would help the State Chair meet his goal for the state's delegation to reflect the ethnic make-up of its Democratic voting constituency. State party leaders are supposed to ensure their delegation meets this goal and is equally divided between men and women. The presidential campaigns are supposed to help the states get this done, and we help whenever we can or are asked to do so.

When the weekend of the State Committee meeting arrives, I've got other work to do and send Toni to Albuquerque to look out for our interests. When she gets to the State Party headquarters the day before the State Committee meeting, she finds a very nervous State Chair. He's talked with some of his Executive Committee members and he's wary about how to proceed. Toni gives me a call to let me know what's going on.

"Jeff, we could have a problem here," she warns me. "The State Chair says he's being barraged with questions from Clinton backers in New Mexico about plans for the unpledged add-on nominations. The Clinton people want to split the nominations and have him put up an endorsed candidate for Hillary as a choice for the add-on slot."

"The State Chair has no obligation to give a nomination to any presidential candidate," I reply. "He just has to put up two people for the position. That's it."

"I know, but..." Toni starts to interject, before I cut her off.

"Toni, I know this isn't easy, but you have to help get the process finished and the delegation finalized." With that, we end the call and she's back on her own.

Not long after the scheduled start of the State Committee meeting, my phone rings. It's Toni calling again, this time from the meeting room. I can barely hear her over the loud cacophony of voices in the background.

"Jeff, all hell is breaking loose at the Central Committee meeting," she yells into the phone. "The Clinton forces are shouting objections to the selection process for the add-on. They're demanding the State Chair give one of his nominations to a declared Clinton supporter and are threatening to challenge the credentials of the state delegation if he doesn't do it."

"Don't worry," I yell back into the phone, so she can hear me. "They don't have grounds for a credentials challenge. The rules let the State Chair make these nominations. If they don't like it, they can re-write the rules for 2012."

"I know, but the State Chair is under a lot of pressure," Toni pleads. "People are screaming at him and disrupting the meeting. Some people are so upset they're crying!"

"He's the State Chair. It's his job. He just needs to make his nominations and call the vote—before the room spins out of control."

Toni hangs up, and within minutes, the process unfolds in the meeting room. The State Democratic Chair, over the angry shouts of the Clinton supporters, announces his nominations. They're the two Democrats he's wanted from the beginning.

The Clinton supporters in the room seek to add their own add-on candidate to the State Chair's nominees, but the State Chair knows the rules and calls for a vote on his two nominees.

Within minutes, Toni is back on the phone. She's calling me with a report on the meeting. Her voice trembles with emotion as she says: "They elected one of the State Chair's nominees. He did it according to the rules, but I've never seen such turmoil."

New Mexico Democrats have chosen their add-on and now have a full delegation.

★ ★ ★

Our work to build our unpledged add-on delegate numbers lasts for three months, running from February 23rd to June 21st. Throughout this period, we never take our eye off the ball to let the Clinton campaign find any traction among these delegates. At times, when we pluck an add-on—seemingly unopposed—in some state committee vote, I wonder if the Clinton campaign even is paying attention to this part of the delegate competition.

By the end of the primaries, I take stock to see how much of an advantage we've built up in this category of delegates.

When I look at the add-on selections in all the states, I see that we've shut Hillary out in 32 states compared to her 8 shutouts of Obama. 8 states split their add-ons and 2 states elect truly neutral Democrats for the positions. I feel no shame in losing the 8 shut-outs to Hillary, as she won the primary in every one of those states, usually with strong insider support.

My attention goes to the 12 caucus states with add-on delegates, where my special caucus state unit has watched over each state like a hawk. In these 12 states, 10 were to pick one add-on delegate, while 2 were to select two add-ons. When I look at the final record, my team has pitched a perfect game. All 12 states selected delegates loyal to Obama. Not one caucus state chose a delegate for Hillary. In terms of delegates, it's a shutout of 14-0 among these delegates—giving us a winning margin greater than our 13-delegate Super Tuesday win when 1681 delegates were at stake.

Plouffe is very interested in this aspect of the national delegate strategy, and I keep him closely apprised of our progress. When all is said and done, I count roughly two-thirds of the unpledged add-on delegates for Obama, meeting my goal for this category of 81 delegates.

Rather than take any chance that the Clinton campaign might gain ground among these unusual, non-automatic superdelegates — we've strengthened Obama's position in the national delegate race.

14

Hillary Hopes for a Superdelegate Rescue

THERE IS ONE AVENUE for the Clinton campaign to overcome Obama's delegate strength that is constantly discussed by the national political press, the automatic superdelegates. Obama delegate trackers Myesha Ward and Mike Robertson have been communicating with these superdelegates diligently through the many months of 2007 and early 2008.

Now that Super Tuesday is behind us and we're deep into the primaries and caucuses, it's time for us to step up our activity in pursuit of the superdelegates. After Super Tuesday, Hillary still has a lead, numbering just over 50, among superdelegates, with almost half of the superdelegates yet to commit to either presidential candidate.

Matt Nugen, our political director, sets up a special unit to increase our pursuit of the still uncommitted superdelegates. While I'm focusing on the pledged delegates and combat in the primaries, caucuses and conventions, Matt will lead the wooing of the superdelegates.

A number of the young delegate trackers who had been coordinating with our pledged delegates are providing the backbone of Matt's efforts to expand our outreach to the superdelegates. The work of these trackers is being augmented by calls from senior campaign staffers and advisors, as well as high-level supporters around the country—anyone who potentially could persuade a superdelegate to commit to Obama.

Many of those making the phone calls to court the superdelegates—and I suspect this applies to those calling on behalf of Hillary as well—don't particularly relish having to chase down these commitments.

Some superdelegates in states that haven't voted yet say they want more time to learn whom their state will support. Other uncommitted superdelegates may be putting off their decision on supporting a presidential candidate to make sure they know they'll be backing the nomination winner. Of course, some want to make the best decision they can and simply aren't certain which of the two candidates to choose.

But why should presidential candidates have to spend so much time and effort to win the endorsement of automatic delegates to the National Convention? While presidential candidates certainly will want to seek the backing of important Democrats around the country, it doesn't make sense for the national Party to create a need for the candidates to chase after every superdelegate, including those who are not major figures in their home community. Candidates already spend so much time pursuing well-heeled donors that it seems everyone would be better off if they spent the rest of their time reaching out to the tens of millions of voters who are the bedrock of our democracy rather than the automatic superdelegates.

I know there was a perceived need after the tumultuous '60s and '70s to reinforce the role of party and elected leaders in our presidential nominating process by guaranteeing them delegate positions. But the number of these reserved positions has grown well beyond what originally was envisioned to a level that now might overwhelm the democratic aspect of our primary process.

Ironically, the Republican Party provides each state and territory with only three superdelegates—for a national total of 168—compared to Democrats' 849 superdelegates (before the reductions in Florida and Michigan). I hate to say it, but maybe we Democrats could learn from the Republicans how not to overload the nominating system with unpledged delegates.

As the Democrats' delegate race proceeds toward the finish line, public debate develops as to whether there is a danger that the superdelegates could cast their votes in a manner that over-rules the choice of the voters. If Hillary were able to command the loyalties of established party and elected leaders to the degree that's been widely assumed in the press, she'd be able to use the superdelegates to win the nomination despite Obama's lead among the pledged delegates. It's not hard to imagine such a sce-nario unfolding and it might only be the apparent reluctance of many superdelegates to embrace Hillary's candidacy that's pre-vented this from occurring right now. This system certainly could benefit from some fresh thinking in the future.

★   ★   ★

Whatever ambivalence our campaign may have about the need to court superdelegates, our team—as well as Hillary's—has no choice but to do everything we can to woo the superdelegates for their endorsements. The calls get made and the pleading for superdelegate support continues.

Our team tells the superdelegates they can make an important difference in determining the outcome of the 2008 presidential race, that they can change the country. We tell those who might be willing to endorse Obama and campaign on his behalf that they could earn a significant role on our campaign for their state. We make clear that superdelegate support for Obama won't be forgot-ten. We just want the superdelegates to make a decision, and hope it's to support Obama.

Of course, the superdelegates are hearing not just from us, but also from the Clinton campaign. The Clintons, their staff and sup-porters are throwing the same arguments we're using at the su-perdelegates, plus a bunch of others that won't work for us. We hear reports that some Clinton callers are raising questions about Obama's readiness for office or that he might not be the strongest Democratic candidate to prevail against the eventual Republican nominee in the general election. These themes echo what we're seeing in some of Hillary's paid advertising, which stress a supposed difference in the level of candidate preparation to handle an unexpected crisis.

By Super Tuesday, the two campaigns have kicked the chase of the superdelegates into the highest gear. The Democratic presidential race now is virtually deadlocked and likely to continue as a drawn-out race for delegates. *Time Magazine* reports on February 6th:

> Neither campaign will publicly divulge its precise tally of superdelegates. However, one Clinton strategist said she had 257 commitments from superdelegates, with another 11 "in the wings," going into the Super Tuesday balloting, having picked up an additional 14 in the previous five days. The Clinton campaign estimated Obama's total at 159, leaving around 370 superdelegates still up for grabs. However, Obama campaign manager Plouffe insisted in an election-night conference call with reporters that the disparity between the two campaigns' superdelegate tallies was far smaller, having narrowed to around 55. "We've made a lot of progress," Plouffe added.

During the next couple months, the two Democratic campaigns trade shots privately and in the press over the role of the superdelegates and how the competition among these delegates is proceeding. Plouffe never misses an opportunity to reinforce our basic message that the superdelegates should vote in line with the preferences of the voters, as reflected in the pledged delegate total. Under no circumstances, he adds, should the superdelegates substitute their own judgment for that of the voters in this historic nominating campaign. In private conversations, he warns about the impact on the Democratic Party if superdelegates were to deny Obama the nomination even if he ends up the pledged delegate winner. What would young and African-American voters think after investing so much in Obama's presidential candidacy?

Of course, the Clinton campaign has a rather different message of its own for the superdelegates. It focuses on the strength of Hillary's national popular vote and on the need to pick the most electable candidate for the fall race against the Republican nominee. Once Hillary reverses the string of losses she suffered during the post-Super Tuesday period with wins in the Ohio, Texas and Pennsylvania primaries, she has more fuel for her argument that she'd be the stronger Democratic nominee for the general election.

Plouffe is no more impressed than I am with the Clinton contention that her success in winning popular votes is relevant to the presidential nominating race. David articulates our argument best when he writes in a letter to the superdelegates that:

> Just as the Presidential election in November will be decided by the electoral college, not popular vote, the Democratic nomination is decided by delegates. If we believed the popular vote was somehow the key measurement, we would have campaigned much more intensively in our home state of Illinois and in all the other populous states, in the pursuit of larger raw vote totals. But it is not the key measurement. We played by the rules, set by you, the DNC members, and campaigned as hard as we could, in as many places as we could, to acquire delegates. Essentially, the popular vote is not much better as a metric than basing the nominee on which candidate raised more money, has more volunteers, contacted more voters, or is taller.

As the campaign winds toward the conclusion of the primaries and caucuses, the Obama and Clinton teams go round and round about what the remaining uncommitted superdelegates should do or not do. While this rhetoric flies, our superdelegate tracking crew keeps plugging away, picking up a superdelegate endorsement here and another there. Matt complains to me constantly about the miserable nature of the work and how hard it is to get the superdelegates to make a commitment.

But the underlying dynamic among the uncommitted superdelegates has not changed. They are resistant to supporting Hillary, as they have been since we began monitoring them last year. Now, Matt and his team are making slow, but steady, progress toward reversing Hillary's early superdelegate lead.

The superdelegates, if nothing else, can read the writing on the wall, namely that despite her primary wins in Ohio, Texas and Pennsylvania, Hillary is not making up the ground she needs in the delegate race and is highly unlikely to be the presidential nominee. For a campaign arguing the importance of candidate electability, this is the kiss of death.

Still, Plouffe remains as frustrated as ever in having to deal with the superdelegate holdouts who refuse to commit to one presidential candidate or the other. To David, these superdelegates are holding the Democratic presidential nomination hostage to their refusal to announce an endorsement for a presidential candidate.

Finally, he sets out, in the most succinct terms possible, our view that the remaining uncommitted superdelegates need to end the long-running melodrama and support Obama, who by the late stages of the primaries, is all but certain to win the pledged delegate count:

> As we head into the final days of the campaign, we just wanted to be clear with you as a party leader, who will be instrumental in making the final decision of who our nominee will be, how we view the race at this point.

> Senator Obama, our campaign and our supporters believe pledged delegates is the most legitimate metric for determining how this race has unfolded.

As results of the superdelegate competition trickle in day after day, it becomes clear that Hillary's effort in this area has stalled, just like the rest of her campaign. Obama's superdelegate commitments surpass Hillary's by the second week in May, after which he slowly begins to open up a lead of his own. Matt's team has done a fantastic job. Drip by drip, Hillary's hope of a superdelegate rescue runs down the drain, and her team is forced to look elsewhere for a last-ditch effort to save her campaign.

15

Florida and
Michigan Déjà Vu

WITH HILLARY CLINTON FALLING BEHIND Barack Obama in the pledged delegate count, the Clinton campaign needs to get their candidate back into the pledged delegate game. Proportional representation will make it difficult for Hillary to cut into Obama's national lead in pledged delegates without some change to the primary or caucus landscape.

While Hillary's campaign team is publicly placing its faith in obtaining more commitments from the superdelegates to blunt our pledged delegate lead, her political operation has to know they're not gaining on us among the superdelegates. If anything, her lead among them is slipping. The Clinton camp will have to find a different way to make up ground against Obama if their candidate is to stop his movement toward a national delegate majority.

At the same time, Democrats in Florida and Michigan remain frustrated by their inability to participate in the historic 2008 presidential nominating race. Florida's leaders gambled that they could outmaneuver the Democratic National Committee to achieve an early date to boost their state's national influence. Michigan officials decided to use their primary contest as a battering ram to knock down New Hampshire's first-in-the-nation primary. Now both states have had their entire delegations to the

National Convention stripped and have a lot of irate rank-and-file Democratic voters.

We at the Obama Campaign support Michigan and Florida being represented at the National Convention. But we believe their delegates should be split 50-50 between Obama and Clinton since the states' primaries were invalid and neither candidate—in compliance with DNC rules and the pledge to the DNC-approved early states—campaigned in the state.

Now, well into spring and months after Michigan and Florida had their delegates stripped and primaries nullified, a new idea is developing in these two states. Why not just re-do the two states' primaries, since the campaign has now moved into the approved DNC timeframe for holding these contests?

When I first get wind of the budding discussion of redoing the Michigan and Florida primaries, all I can think of is, "Are you kidding me?" There are no do-overs in electoral politics. Once an election is held, its history. I can't think of another instance where an election was re-run, certainly not in a presidential race.

I talk with Plouffe about the possibility of Michigan and Florida re-doing their elections, and he can only shake his head. Redoing a government-run election is unheard of, and it's hard to imagine how this could be done. David and I are sympathetic to Democrats in these two states who've lost a meaningful role in this year's presidential nominating race, but we find it hard to see a feasible remedy that goes beyond sending an evenly split delegation to the Democratic National Convention.

DNC Chair Howard Dean, in response to a press inquiry on the subject, says that a do-over of the Florida and Michigan primaries could be accepted by the DNC – but only if the state parties and presidential candidates agree on a re-do plan. Dean makes it clear, though, that the DNC will not foot the bill for a second primary for either state. The DNC's Rules Committee, whose leaders and staff have begun discussing the topic with both presidential campaigns, issues a letter stating that delegates elected in a re-do primary or caucus within the DNC's permitted timeframe could be seated at the National Convention as far as the Rules Committee is concerned.

For weeks, Democratic Party leaders in Michigan and Florida had clung to the mantra that their January primaries were valid elections and had to be used to allocate and seat national convention delegates from their states. Now, the possibility of re-do elections has the two states considering a pivot to dump the earlier primaries and re-do them with new ones.

The possible re-do of Florida's and Michigan's primaries also gains the attention of the Clinton campaign, which would want nothing more than the chance to win these states all over again and seat their delegates at the National Convention. Winning new primaries in these states could generate important new momentum for Hillary and the resulting delegates could cut into Obama's pledged delegate lead.

In addition, as Pennsylvania Governor and Clinton campaign booster Ed Rendell lays out to *CNN*, Hillary could use new wins in Florida and Michigan to win new commitments from the superdelegates:

> Let's assume for the moment Hillary Clinton wins Ohio and Texas, she wins Pennsylvania, Florida and Michigan have primaries in June, she wins both of those. Then, the superdelegates can look at that and say, "Gosh, she's won the last five big primaries in a row. She's won almost every big primary since we began."

I have to assume that Hillary's campaign will leave no stone unturned in the effort to implement this re-do strategy, so that new contests in Florida and Michigan can deliver her the boost she needs to blunt or even reverse Obama's lead in the pledged delegate race.

★   ★   ★

While Florida and Michigan Democrats both pursue primary re-do plans, different circumstances in the two states lead them to take different approaches. Florida's Democratic leaders are in the weakest position to legislate a re-do primary. Republicans control the state legislature and governor's office, and they have no appetite for funding a second primary for Democrats at taxpayer expense. The Republican National Committee is allowing state Republicans to use the January primary to allocate their national convention delegates, though the number of delegates was cut in half as a penalty for the early timing of the primary. The Florida primary was fiercely contested by the Republican candidates, and Florida Republicans show no interest in holding a second primary in their state. There will be no government-run re-do primary in Florida.

This doesn't stop Florida Democratic leaders from considering an alternative caucus system for the state, though. Remember, they discussed the adoption of a state party-run caucus system with the DNC during the summer of 2007 before the DNC stripped the state's delegates. While it seems they never were really interested in pursuing a caucus alternative to their January primary, the circumstances are different now and they float the concept of holding a mail-in primary or caucus as a trial balloon.

As we discovered when the idea of a Florida caucus system was first kicked around last summer, there are substantial challenges to pulling off such a process. The state party doesn't have a dime to spare and only a bare bones office operation that almost certainly couldn't manage a complex statewide caucus system. They also have no caucus system experience, so it's completely unrealistic for them to contemplate planning, financing and implementing caucuses, especially in a state as big and populous as Florida. To top it all off, there are only a few weeks left before the end of the window for primaries and caucuses. So, it's seemingly impossible under even the best of circumstances for Florida Democrats to pull off a party-run contest at this point.

Not surprisingly, it doesn't take long for the Florida Democratic re-do trial balloon to fall straight back to earth. Soon after the proposal for the state party to run a statewide caucus system hits the street, Florida's Democratic delegation to Congress convenes in Washington, DC to discuss the prospects for this plan. Congressman Robert Wexler, our top endorser in the state, will join in the discussion.

There is little stomach among the congressional Democrats for any notion that the state party can or should run their own election. Everyone remembers the 2000 presidential election fiasco that threw Florida's electoral votes and the presidency to George W. Bush, and nobody wants to risk another "hanging chad" election debacle in the Sunshine State.

Even Hillary's supporters in the delegation, including Congresswoman Debbie Wasserman Schultz, understand the dangers in such a course of action and, to their credit, they join with Wexler and the uncommitted members of the state's congressional delegation to promptly issue a joint statement to the press and public:

> After reviewing the party's proposal and individually discussing this idea with state and local leaders and elections experts, we do not believe that this is a realistic option at this time and remain opposed to a mail-in ballot election or any new primary election in Florida of any kind.

Faced with the united opposition of their Democratic congressional delegation, the Florida Democratic Party has no choice but to announce they will no longer be pursuing a re-do of the Florida primary.

★ ★ ★

The story is not so simple in Michigan. Senator Levin and Michigan DNC Member Debbie Dingell have been locked in an effort for many years to end New Hampshire's hold on the first primary slot. I have never doubted the sincerity of their effort to achieve what they believe to be a fairer system for all the states. But with New Hampshire still in possession of the first-in-the-nation date and Michigan having lost all its delegates, Levin and Dingell could use a new approach for Michigan in the Democratic nominating race. The same is doubly true for Clinton forces in the state. The possibility of a re-do of the primary could be just what these Michiganders need.

Levin and Dingell ally themselves with Governor Granholm, the senior Michigan Democrat supporting Hillary Clinton's campaign, in backing a primary re-do. Governor Granholm creates a four-person committee to develop a plan for re-doing the primary and solicit support for it from the presidential candidates. The committee is to include Senator Levin and Debbie Dingell, plus United Auto Workers President Ron Gettelfinger and Congresswoman Carolyn Cheeks Kilpatrick.

All four appointed by the governor say they are uncommitted in the Democratic presidential race. Of course, the Governor is all-in for Hillary. The Obama Campaign is not consulted on the creation of this group, and we're wary of being dragged back into the state for a brand new primary controversy after all that has happened there during the past few months.

The Gang of Four, as the group is named by the press and on the Internet, promptly contacts our Chicago headquarters and asks for a conference call with our leadership. Plouffe, political director Matt Nugen and I get on the phone with the group. They make clear to us that it's their mission to re-do Michigan's January primary. They want to know what it will take for us to sign on to the concept, and who at our campaign will serve as our lead negotiator.

We haven't conferred within the campaign about who should handle these discussions, but when the question is asked, David immediately speaks up.

"Berman," he says. "He's our guy for Michigan."

"Thanks a lot," I mutter to myself, after which I jump right in.

"Look," I say, "we're open to discussing anything, but we're concerned that any new primary be feasible and fair to both candidates. If you send us an outline of your plan, we'll evaluate it and respond."

In the days following the conference call, rumors float in the press about various scenarios for a Michigan re-do. Soon enough, the Michigan group presents us with a plan for a re-do primary to be held on June 3rd, the last available date under DNC rules for a primary. Several aspects of their plan immediately give us cause for concern.

First, the plan calls for the Michigan state government to run a new, full-fledged primary, but without paying for it. The state already paid for the January primary, and there's no government funding available to pay for a second primary. The re-do proponents say this problem can be overcome by having the state Democratic Party raise the funds and place them in a trust account to fund the state's re-do expenses.

This strikes me as an odd approach, as I can't think of one example where private interests have paid for a government election. Who, in their right mind, would give millions of their dollars to pay for a public primary?

It's not long before I have my answer. Rumors begin to swirl in the national press that a handful of top Clinton donors are being recruited to write millions of dollars in checks to pay for the Michigan re-do. *Slate* reports that there's an:

> 11th-hour proposal being championed by Governors (and Clinton supporters) Jon Corzine of New Jersey and Ed Rendell of Pennsylvania [in which] a handful of rich Clinton donors, including baseball team owner Peter Angelos, investment banker Roger Altman, supermarket magnate John Castimatides, attorney Calvin Fayard, Jr., and philanthropist Brooke Neidich are willing to put up $12 million to cover the cost of a new state primary.

I hear one third-hand story of a high-end restaurant diner in New York who walked by a table at which billionaire Democratic activist George Soros was seated and looked down to see notes in front of Soros that detailed how he could help fund a second Michigan primary. I find this tale to be so preposterous that I can't believe it, at least not until I read in *USA Today* that Soros spokesman Michael Vachon has confirmed that Governor Rendell in fact asked Soros to help pay for the re-do primary. According to the account in *USA Today*, Soros turned Rendell down.

I can't understand how anyone could think it would be a good idea for the Michigan state government to hold a primary election funded by the richest supporters of one of the competing candidates. This would inject an appearance that the election process is owned not by the public, but one of the candidates. This could strain the legitimacy of the process for voters and potentially undermine the ability of Democrats to unify for the general election. It looks like a generally bad idea.

Another big concern for me is the voter eligibility rule in the proposed Michigan re-do plan. Michigan has traditionally held an open primary where voters are free to take either party ballot—whether they consider themselves to be a Democrat, Republican or Independent. In fact, voters in Michigan don't even register their party affiliation. Now, the re-do group says that any voter who cast a Republican ballot in the first primary will be unable to vote in the re-do primary.

This new limit on voter eligibility would be unfair to Obama supporters who, when the original primary was held, voted in the Republican primary because they had been told that the Democratic primary wouldn't count. Their presidential choice wasn't even on the Democratic ballot. For them, voting in the Republican primary might not have been an act of disloyalty to Democrats, but an effort to help the Democratic nominee by voting for the worst possible Republican candidate. This isn't a problem for Hillary's voters, because her name was on the ballot and they were more likely to vote on it to support her.

Perhaps the most important problem with the re-do plan, though, is that there simply isn't enough time to start down this path of a primary re-do. It takes time to plan, legislate, finance and implement a statewide primary, and with only weeks before the proposed primary day, there isn't adequate time for this plan.

For the re-do plan to become a reality, both houses of the Legislature and the Governor would need to change the election law, with many details to be worked out. The DNC, which would have to approve the plan in order to restore the state's delegation to the National Convention, also must review any final details and obtain the approval of both the candidates to prevent complaints of unfairness.

Notwithstanding the discussions about Hillary's supporters paying for the re-do primary, the Michigan Democratic Party still would need to assure the state that it would not end up with the estimated $10 million tab for the primary before anything could be done to prepare for the primary. The state party and Clinton funding efforts would be scrutinized closely and have to meet a basic test of transparency and credibility with the press and supporters of both candidates.

State election officials would be hard pressed to print the ballots and send them out to absentee voters with enough time to be returned before election day. County election clerks, who would have to administer the process, are up in arms about having this rushed election dumped in their laps. Concerns also are being expressed as to whether Michigan members of the armed services serving overseas would have enough time to receive and return their ballots, as required by federal law. Litigation would be almost certain to cloud the election results.

We convene another call with the re-do proponents joined this time by our campaign counsel, Bob Bauer. Bob and I have collaborated in two previous presidential campaigns, both in support of Dick Gephardt, and we know how to work together when the politics of the delegate process meets the legal requirements of the election system. Bob has studied each of our concerns with the re-do plan and prepared a detailed memorandum that makes clear the seriousness of the issues involved. We present the memorandum to the Michigan group for discussion on the call.

The group listens carefully to Bob's points and responds that while they hope our issues can be resolved, they must move forward now if they are to enact their re-do legislation. They're not waiting to resolve our issues.

From our perspective, they are laying down the gauntlet. There is no way we can support legislation that would mandate a primary re-do while our concerns are put to the side. It's now clear that we're headed to another nerve-wracking showdown in the Lansing state capitol. This time, though, the political calculus will be different.

Last fall, when we were dragged into the Michigan Legislature to prevent Barack from being forced back onto the primary ballot, we had not yet won the Iowa Caucuses and were the equivalent of political beggars in Michigan. We had little credibility of our own among legislators and had to rely on the political kindness of strangers. Now, Obama is the frontrunner for the presidential nomination race. He also has gained the endorsement of former Detroit Mayor Dennis Archer and other leading Democrats around the country.

On the other hand, with UAW President Ron Gettelfinger now serving in the primary re-do group, we're without an important organized labor ally for the legislative battle. We also can't turn for help to the campaign of John Edwards, who has since suspended his presidential campaign. Edwards was our key to gaining the support of Congressman David Bonior's Michigan network last fall.

I get on the phone and start talking to our supporters in the Michigan House and Senate. What are the prospects for the legislation? Who will be the key decision-makers on whether it passes or fails? Is there a deadline for legislative action?

It's important to understand every facet of the legislative battlefield, but as a Michigan outsider, I've got my work cut out for me. I quickly learn that the Michigan House and Senate have to approve the legislation before the end of the week, when they'll be departing for their two-week spring recess. There is such little time before the proposed June 3rd primary date that even a two-week delay over the recess would make it impossible to implement the re-do plan. Of course, it's our opinion that there isn't enough time to implement this plan even if it were adopted before the recess.

For now, the bottom line is whether or not there'll be a final vote on the legislation before the start of the recess. In the Michigan Senate—where Republicans are in control and happy to help Democrats spend millions in private funds for another intra-party shoot-out—the timing and outcome of the vote is not in doubt.

The real action will be in the Michigan House, where the Democrats are in charge and need to hang together to pass the legislation. Some among them are skeptical about the wisdom of embarking on a new, adventurous plan for a primary re-do after the first plan to violate DNC rules with a January primary led to the total loss of the state's Democratic delegates. To some Michigan House Democrats, this looks like they'd be doubling down on a losing bet in a Las Vegas casino, which is rarely a wise strategy.

Obama supporters in the House begin to coordinate with neutral House members who believe that the re-do plan is too problematic to be good legislation. Our supporters call me to let me know the latest developments.

Given the clout of the re-do proponents, some House members understandably want to maintain their distance from the Obama Campaign. I don't communicate directly with any House leadership members or staff, but instead communicate via an Obama loyalist from northern Michigan, Representative Matt Gillard.

Gillard tells me that the Governor and re-do group want to address an urgent meeting of the House Democratic Caucus to press for their plan. But rather than attend in person, the re-do advocates participate via telephone. This turns out to be a mistake, as it prevents them from being able to read the crowd in the room.

The re-do proponents lay out their plan and why they think it needs to be adopted. They emphasize the need to move quickly, as the legislation must be adopted immediately so the plan can become law before the impending spring recess. What happens next is unprecedented.

Normally, members of the House Democratic Caucus would accord substantial weight to the words of Governor Granholm and Senator Levin, not to mention the President of the United Auto Workers. In Michigan, state legislators are subject to strict term limits and many legislators enter office in their late twenties or early thirties and retire from office while still young. Legislators thus lack the seniority of other top Democrats in the state and can find themselves having less impact in important policy debates, such as the current one on the primary re-do.

But this in no ordinary policy debate, as the re-do plan can affect Barack Obama's path to the presidency. As soon as the re-do proponents finish addressing the House Democratic Caucus, a torrent of questions and opposition fly from the legislators. Those supporting Obama feel they're being pressed to enact a primary re-do that will be funded by wealthy out-of-state Clinton donors and possibly be an embarrassment that rivals Florida in 2000.

One legislator, outraged at being asked to approve re-do legislation by those that pushed the January primary plan that led to the state's loss of delegates, demands to know whether the Governor would support a re-do of other elections, such as the one that elevated her to office. Other legislators also voice opposition to ramming the re-do proposal through the Legislature. It becomes clear to everyone that there's no consensus to adopt the legislation and it can't be enacted before the spring recess.

Back in Chicago, I'm waiting for the House Democratic Caucus meeting to wrap up, when my phone rings. Knowing the stakes of the legislative debate in Michigan, I pick up the handset with a sense of trepidation for what I'm about to hear.

It's Gillard and he can barely contain himself. He reports how his fellow House Democratic Caucus members have stood up against the re-do plan. The legislators have refused to approve the primary re-do and are adjourning for the spring recess. The re-do plan is dead.

I hustle over to Plouffe's office to give him the news. We both recognize that although the public is generally unaware of this defense of Obama's candidacy in the Michigan House, it's an important moment on his path to the presidential nomination.

16

Hillary Cannot Defeat the Dynamic

WHILE WE'RE SKIRMISHING OVER CAUCUS STATE CONVENTIONS, primary re-do legislation, superdelegate commitments and unpledged add-on selections, Hillary is preparing to extend her primary wins in Ohio, Texas and Pennsylvania into the next rounds of voting in May. Her campaign is hoping to use her recent primary wins and aggressive campaign messaging to instill doubts among voters in the upcoming primary states (and the superdelegates) as to whether Obama would make the strongest presidential nominee. With Barack having lost several major contests during the prior two months, this is not an idle threat.

The use of proportional representation to allocate delegates still denies Hillary the ability to cut very much into Obama's national delegate lead. During the recent run of March and April primaries, Hillary has done the following: won 7 delegates in Ohio, lost 4 in the Texas Two-Step, lost 7 in Mississippi and won 12 in Pennsylvania. Although this period is her best during 2008, it produces a net gain of only 8 delegates, which isn't much progress for her given that we're entering the final weeks of the primaries.

★   ★   ★

To add insult to injury for Hillary, we are succeeding beyond expectations in converting the 18 pledged delegates that have been won by Edwards, including eight in South Carolina, four in New Hampshire and six in Iowa. Since Edwards left the race, we have engaged in an ongoing campaign to convince as many of his delegates as we can to switch their allegiance to Obama. Senator Edwards is of no help to us in winning over these delegates, as he hasn't made a quick endorsement of Barack's candidacy since dropping out of the presidential race. Much of the work is being led by Ed Turlington, who chaired the Edwards presidential campaign, along with the Obama leadership in all three states with Edwards delegates.

For the Edwards delegates in South Carolina, we arrange a conference call directly with Obama. While I envision this to be a perfunctory exercise to grease the transfer of their presidential loyalty, the Edwards delegates use it to pepper Obama with questions and display their reluctance to commit to him. I'm unhappy about this treatment, but hold my tongue to let Ed and our South Carolina leaders do their work to win over the Edwards group. Hillary is competing hard in the race, so we can't be too presumptuous.

Eventually Edwards endorses Obama for president, but the burden for winning over his delegates remains with Turlington and the Obama leadership in the states with Edwards delegates. After much cajoling, our shepherds for the Edwards delegates convince every Edwards delegate in South Carolina, Iowa and New Hampshire to switch their pledge to Obama. It's a clean sweep of 18 delegates for Obama that can't be good news for Hillary.

*   *   *

So, now in May, where does the campaign go after the late April contest in Pennsylvania? Guam. Yes, the faraway Pacific island sits all alone next on the nominating calendar. Of course, hardly anybody in either campaign is thinking of the May 3rd caucus on this U.S. territory, but I don't want Hillary to gain even the smallest opportunity to chip away at our lead—whether with Guam's four delegates or otherwise. When I speak with our local organizers in Guam on caucus day, they tell me turnout at the village caucuses has been heavy and we've gained a 2 to 2 split of the pledged delegates. No gain for Hillary here.

Here are the delegate results for Guam:

Date	State	Election	Pledged Delegates	Delegate Results Obama	Clinton	Edwards	Obama Lead
	Prior Total		2845	1480.5	1338.5	26	142
3 May	Guam	Caucus	4	2	2	0	0
	New Total		2849	1482.5	1340.5	26	142

*Some Edwards delegates changed their loyalties earlier at the Iowa county conventions, but the chart identifies them as originally pledged.

★   ★   ★

Following Guam, the campaign moves on to the real main events that will follow Hillary's big win in Pennsylvania, the May 6th primaries in North Carolina and Indiana. The national press corps is focused intensely on the importance of these two contests. While we're determined to use these elections to cut off any momentum Hillary might have gained from her recent big state wins, at what seems like the worst possible time, the Reverend Wright flap re-emerges.

This controversy, which bedeviled us so greatly prior to the Pennsylvania primary, was quelled when Obama delivered his convincing speech in Philadelphia on race in America. Now, Reverend Wright—without any consultation with our Campaign—is rolling out a series of public events to try to explain anew his controversial views on race and other matters.

Reverend Wright appears oblivious to his impact upon Obama and engages in one media appearance after another. First, it's a TV interview with Bill Moyers, then it's a well-publicized speech to the NAACP, and finally he gives a full-blown address to the National Press Club in Washington, DC. Serving as a one-man wrecking crew for Obama's presidential campaign, Reverend

Wright leaves Obama no choice but to denounce Wright's controversial statements. Obama then resigns from the church Wright once headed.

Once again able to focus on the voters and their needs, Obama sets out to campaign across North Carolina for its May 6th primary. Once a conservative southern state, North Carolina is increasingly integrated into the national economy and less dependent on regional industries. The state has developed a sophisticated university research complex and national banking center. Its western mountains and eastern coastline have become home to large numbers of Midwestern and Northeastern transplants. All these economic and demographic changes—combined with the state's large African-American population—have opened the door to a strong Obama performance.

The North Carolina polls are relatively tight coming into election day, though Barack consistently has been ahead. When the votes come in, it becomes clear this will be a runaway win for Obama. He carries the state by 56% to 42%. According to exit polls, Obama has won 91% of black voters, who make up about one-third of the electorate, and a solid 36% of the white vote. Obama's big win provides him a 67 to 48 delegate blow-out.

Hillary's last hope to maintain even a scintilla of political momentum after Pennsylvania now depends on her winning Indiana, also voting on May 6th. Hillary campaigns aggressively in the state, even though it's in Obama's backyard. She banks on the conservative rural communities and large number of blue-collar workers in the state for support, proposing a summertime federal gas tax holiday to offset rising gasoline prices that are affecting middle class households. Obama criticizes the proposal as nothing more than "phony ideas, calculated to win elections instead of actually solving problems," and Hillary gains little traction from it.

Obama expects a big vote from the large African-American communities in Indianapolis and the state's industrial northwestern corner, in addition to a share of the vote elsewhere around the state.

The opinion polls are close heading into the Indiana primary.

Both campaigns work to get out their vote. With our election night operation in place, I'm able to leave our office early in the day for the short drive to Gary to pitch in and canvass—like I did in Iowa at the very start of the 2008 voting. When I walk the streets, voters of all backgrounds seem aware of the primary and the feeling at the door fronts is electric. After hours of nonstop walking and talking, I head back to campaign headquarters to settle in for the nighttime reporting of voting results.

After the Indiana polls close, the votes trickle into the state elections office. It's not long before it's apparent that the race is extraordinarily close and might not be called until late into the night. Because Obama's win in North Carolina was announced quickly, Hillary needs an early projection of victory in Indiana.

This early projection of victory never comes. Instead, in Lake County in northwestern Indiana, the reporting of the primary results drags on and on. Lake County is the home of Gary, the largely African-American city that is expected to vote heavily for Obama. Voters had poured into the city's polls all day long, casting far more votes than usual. Also, voters cast a large number of absentee ballots, delaying the vote count and preventing the projection of a statewide winner. Lake County election officials are too overwhelmed to release even minimal results by 11 pm.

Finally, well beyond midnight, after the press has focused all night on Obama's win in North Carolina, enough Lake County votes are reported to show that Hillary will carry the state. Clinton partisans view the reporting delays with suspicion, but there are no specific allegations of wrongdoing for these delays.

The final vote tally shows Hillary has narrowly beaten Obama by 50.5% to 49.5%, taking 38 delegates to 34 for Obama. This margin of victory is so narrow and so late-reported that Hillary gains no political momentum from it. Exit polls show that African-American voters have given Obama over 90% of their votes. He does relatively well among white voters, taking 39%, exceeding is concurrent 36% share in North Carolina.

One disconcerting finding in the Indiana and North Carolina exit polls is that substantial numbers of Clinton voters are saying they'd choose McCain over Obama in the general election. In the

Indiana exit polls, almost 40% of Clinton voters say they would vote for McCain. In the North Carolina exit polls, less than half of Hillary's voters are willing to say they'll definitely vote for Obama in the general election. These deep divisions among Democrats hopefully will fade over time.

Tim Russert, the host of *Meet the Press* and America's foremost political oracle, appears on *MSNBC*'s election coverage to review the North Carolina and Indiana results. He believes they reflect a key moment in the race. With all the authority that might come with a papal pronouncement, he declares: "We now know who the Democratic nominee is going to be."

Without his name even being uttered, Barack Obama is anointed by Russert as the certain 2008 Democratic presidential nominee.

Here are the delegate results for North Carolina and Indiana:

Date	State	Election	Pledged Delegates	Delegate Results Obama	Clinton	Edwards	Obama Lead
	Prior Total		2849	1482.5	1340.5	26	142
6 May	Indiana	Primary	72	34	38	0	-4
	N. Carolina		115	67	48	0	19
	New Total		3036	1583.5	1426.5	26	157

★   ★   ★

After her blowout loss in North Carolina and whisker-thin victory in Indiana, Hillary gamely fights on to the May 13th primary in West Virginia. All the polling data indicates Hillary will obtain one of her strongest primary wins of the year here. She continues punching away with her proposal for a federal gas tax holiday, knowing that rural, lower-income West Virginia voters are feeling the pinch of higher gas prices. Obama moves his campaign focus away from West Virginia and the remaining primaries to the battleground states for the general election.

With her sizable advantage in West Virginia never in doubt, Hillary beats Obama by 67% to 26% in the vote. That's a 41 percentage point victory for Hillary! Even long-withdrawn candidate John Edwards pulls 7% of the primary vote away from Obama. To me, the 26,000 voters who cast their ballot for Edwards are saying they'd vote for nobody before they'd vote for Obama or Clinton — not a very inspiring message from those voters.

The exit polls indicate Hillary's huge margin can largely be explained by West Virginia demographics. Ninety-five percent of voters are white and, of these, approximately three-quarters don't have a college degree, more than half have a family income of less than $50,000 per year and almost a quarter are age 60 or older. None of these voter groups are among Obama's core nominating constituencies against Hillary, and the primary results show it. West Virginia Democrats aren't happy with Obama's lead in the nomination race, as more than half complain in the exit polls that they'd be dissatisfied if Obama won the nomination.

West Virginia's landslide gives Hillary a 20 to 8 delegate split. Earlier in the nominating race, this would have given her a big boost, but now it cannot change the trajectory of Obama's path toward the nomination. The *New York Times* headline after the voting is "Clinton Beats Obama Handily in West Virginia," but the reporting stresses "the continued long odds that she can secure her party's nomination." Still, Hillary declares at her West Virginia victory celebration that "I am more determined than ever to carry on this campaign, until everyone has had a chance to make their voices heard." And Pennsylvania Governor Ed Rendell, tells *CNN* that the "superdelegates have to have second thoughts" after her overwhelming win in West Virginia.

None of this posturing interests me as much as a *Wall Street Journal* report on Hillary's West Virginia news conference entitled "Clinton Focuses Anew on Florida, Michigan." The article says Clinton "offered a glimpse of what could be the next step in the controversy surrounding the Florida and Michigan delegations to the Democratic Party's nominating convention this summer," and that she pointed out that "under the rules of the Democratic Party, the Rules and Bylaws Committee makes the first determination [on seating delegates] and if people are not satisfied with that, they go to the Credentials Committee."

A credentials fight over the Florida and Michigan delegations in advance of the National Convention? That's the last thing

Obama or the Democratic Party needs, and is something I'll certainly be working to avoid in coming days.

Now, though, here are the delegate results for West Virginia:

Date	State	Election	Pledged Delegates	Delegate Results Obama	Clinton	Edwards	Obama Lead
	Prior Total		3036	1583.5	1426.5	26	157
13 May	West Virginia	Primary	28	8	20	0	-12
	New Total		3064	1591.5	1446.5	26	145

★   ★   ★

On May 20th, we have primaries in Kentucky and Oregon, two polar opposite states. Hillary can look to Kentucky for an easy win in another southern border state. It's a landslide for her, 65% to 30%, giving her a whopping 37 delegates to Obama's 14. Exit polls show her winning white voters 72% to 23% and Obama winning the smaller pool of African-Americans 90% to 7%.

In Oregon, we're looking at a much more favorable electorate. Here, the state's progressive politics fit Obama perfectly. A pre-election rally in Portland sets a state record for the highest attendance ever for a political event. The Oregon vote is unique in that it's the only state in the country that conducts its voting totally by mail. When the votes are tallied, Obama wins 59% to 41%, giving him a 31 to 21 delegate victory that takes some of the sting out of Hillary's big 23-delegate win in Kentucky. Unlike in some conservative states, exit polls show a solid majority of Clinton voters in Oregon—68%—say they will back Obama in the general election if he becomes the Democratic presidential nominee.

Here are the delegate results for Kentucky and Oregon:

Date	State	Election	Pledged Delegates	Delegate Results Obama	Clinton	Edwards	Obama Lead
	Prior Total		3064	1591.5	1446.5	26	145
20 May	Kentucky	Primary	51	14	37	0	-23
	Oregon	Primary	52	31	21	0	10
	New Total		3167	1636.5	1504.5	26	132

★   ★   ★

As we close in on the final leg of the nominating contest, I have to spend much of my time overseeing the selection of the actual individuals who will serve as our delegates. We've built a sizable team of young delegate trackers who are working with Obama loyalists in the states to select our delegates. Our trackers are doing their best to navigate sometimes choppy local political waters in picking our delegates. As Obama's chance for the presidential nomination has risen, the demand to serve as one of his delegates also has increased, with established politicos trying to fill positions alongside our grassroots supporters.

My main interest is in ensuring that every one of our delegates is loyal to Obama. While the Democratic rules enable a presidential campaign to ensure this type of loyalty, in some cases these rules can be difficult to implement.

In Pennsylvania, I'm informed by the state Democratic Party chair, T.J. Rooney—who is not related to the Pittsburgh Steelers-owning Rooneys—that Governor Ed Rendell, who chairs Hillary's state effort, will be selecting all of the state's delegates to the National Convention, no matter who the delegates support. I'm surprised. We never let anyone outside our campaign select our delegates, and certainly won't let a state chair for Hillary's campaign do so.

I need to clarify this situation right away. So, even though I'm on-site in Colorado embroiled in a battle with the Clinton campaign at the state's congressional district conventions, I walk outside to the parking lot to speak further with T.J.

"With all due respect to the Governor and you," I say, "the Governor cannot pick our delegates. We're still locked in a close national delegate race and there's no way a state chair of Hillary's campaign can choose Obama's delegates. I'm sorry, but I have to protect my candidate."

"I'm very surprised to hear you say that," T.J. replies. "I can assure you that the Governor will act in the best interest of all the presidential candidates in making the delegate selections. But if that's your answer, you'll have to tell him yourself."

With that, the conversation ends.

Obama won 73 pledged delegates in Pennsylvania's primary. Our national pledged delegate lead is hovering just under 150 delegates. Putting the loyalty of 73 Obama delegates at risk could mean—in the worst case—allowing half his national pledged lead to evaporate. And with an Obama pledged delegate lead under 100, we almost certainly would see Hillary contest Obama at the National Convention. Under Democratic Party rules, no delegate is legally bound to vote for his or her pledged candidate, and I can't take any chance that Hillary's campaign could unhinge the loyalty of our delegates by reminding them who picked them or who runs the show back home.

This danger could be all in my mind, but I'm sure flipping the loyalty of pledged Obama delegates already has been discussed within the Clinton camp. In a *CNN* story headlined "Pledged Delegates Up for Grabs," it's reported:

> For the second time in three days, Sen. Hillary Clinton told reporters that the pledged delegates awarded based on vote totals in their state are not bound to abide by election results. It's an idea that has been floated by her or a campaign surrogate nearly half a dozen times this month.

I'm not taking any chances. I arrange a conference call with a small group of Pennsylvania House members and election attorneys supporting Obama to figure out how to secure our delegates while still respecting the Governor.

"Governor Rendell wants to pick Obama's delegates from Pennsylvania, along with Hillary's," I tell my team. "That's not going to happen. I'm open, though, to any ideas on how we can best work with the Governor."

"Let us call the Governor and offer to talk," one of the group replies. "You can stand firm, and we'll work this out with him."

"Fine." I respond. "I'm in the middle of 20 other battles around the country and am more than happy to hand this off. But there can't be any question of loyalty for our delegates."

We end the call, and I slip back into the congressional district conventions in Colorado.

My Pennsylvania team calls the Governor's people to seek a way forward. After several discussions, my group calls me back.

"We've got a deal," my team says. "We'll work with you to pick Obama's Pennsylvania delegates. Then we'll take our list to the Governor and make sure it's okay with him. This way, he'll know we're not putting someone in the delegation who gives him heartburn, and you'll know only Obama loyalists will be delegates. But there's one condition to this deal."

"What's that?" I ask.

"You can't be in any discussion with the Governor. You're banned."

"Ha! If you guys can work this out, I don't need to be there. But no list goes to the Governor without my approval first—and I'm going to review every name on it."

With that, we've got a deal. Our Pennsylvania team and I hold a series of conference calls to put together our delegate list, with every position going to a deserving Obama supporter. When the team presents the list to the Governor, he sees they're all good Democrats, and accepts it. We all move on.

I don't think any more of our Pennsylvania delegates until I bump into David Axelrod in our Chicago office a little later.

"Hey, Jeff, how are we doing?" he quizzes me, as he typically does when we see each other. "Are our delegate numbers holding up?"

"Yeah," I reply. "We're hanging in there, but it isn't easy."

"Good. Sometimes you're the only guy I trust around here," he says with a chuckle. "By the way, I had a strange discussion with Governor Rendell. He complained about how you were handling our delegates in Pennsylvania."

"He wanted to pick ours and we don't let Clinton supporters do that anywhere," I explain. "I let our people in Pennsylvania run our list by him after we put it together. We worked it out."

"I thought there had to be more to the story," Axe replies.

Some weeks later, I cross paths with Governor Rendell when he addresses the Florida Democratic State Convention. We're face-to-face for the first time. He flashes a big smile at me and we embrace for a photograph. We're both Democrats and there are no hard feelings.

★ ★ ★

Questions about the loyalty of delegates can affect Hillary, too. One day, well into the spring of 2008, I receive an unexpected phone call.

"Jeff, we haven't met before, but I'm a supporter of Hillary Clinton. Some of us in my state can read the writing on the wall and want you to know that some Clinton delegates might be willing to support Obama, if your campaign would be interested."

"Hmmm," I'm thinking. "Why is he calling me with this kind of offer? What's going on here?"

I'm skeptical about even engaging in this conversation and respond nonchalantly, "Give me a call again tomorrow. I need to think about it."

After mulling this over for a few minutes, I decide to walk down to Plouffe's office to discuss the mysterious delegate switch offer with him. David and I readily agree that flipping any of Hillary's pledged delegates to Obama is too dangerous to consider at this point. Aggressive poaching of her delegates could open the door to a raid on our pledged delegates and de-stabilize the nominating race just when we're on the verge of winning it. Plus, we can't act counter to our view that the superdelegates need to respect the tally of the pledged delegates. This is a non-starter.

When the mystery caller dials me up the next day, we talk. When I try to get a handle on how real the offer is, I can't truly tell.

"Thanks, but no thanks," I say, when the moment is right. "We're not opening a Pandora's Box by taking in any of Hillary's pledged delegates. Not anywhere in the country."

I hang up the phone and turn my attention to the far more pressing issue of the still-simmering controversies over the early Florida and Michigan primaries.

17

One Last Showdown

AS SOON AS THE PLANS to re-do the early Michigan and Florida primaries collapse under their own weight, interest returns to whether any delegates from those two states will be seated at our National Convention. Of course, nothing has changed with respect to the rules violations that led the DNC's Rules Committee to strip both states of their delegates in the first place. But Democrats in the two states now are arguing that the pain caused by the loss of their delegates is too great to be allowed to continue.

Each state Democratic Party files a formal challenge with the DNC Rules Committee asking for full reinstatement of the lost delegates. Florida and Michigan Democrats, however, are not the only ones suffering from the elimination of delegates from these two states. Hillary Clinton must feel their pain. With the candidates approaching the end of the primaries, it's now increasingly clear that restoration of the Florida and Michigan delegates is the only real avenue left for the Clinton campaign to reduce Barack's pledged delegate lead and to stanch the hemorrhaging of super-delegates to him.

DNC leaders in Washington are not eager to revisit the unpleasant 2007 enforcement decisions against Florida and Michigan. These leaders have been waiting for weeks for voting results to end the duel between Obama and Clinton so there will be no need to discuss seating these two states while the tense fight between the candidates is still underway. But now that the re-do efforts have fallen flat, DNC leaders seem to believe they've run out of waiting time.

Plouffe is spitting mad that this issue will be brought up at all, much less in this eleventh hour in the nominating process. Neither he nor I believe the DNC has to take up the Florida and Michigan seating challenges before the nomination race is over. We're so close to clinching the nomination that it seems pointless to endure one more round of melodrama.

But the Clinton campaign wants an opportunity to argue for restoration of the delegates. And this opportunity will have value to Hillary only if it occurs before Obama wraps up the nomination. Holding a hearing in late May would give the Clinton team the chance to make their case before the end of the primaries, though it also would be very late in the game for them.

This is the DNC's idea of a compromise—and they set a meeting for May 31st to hear the two state challenges. We don't like it and I wouldn't be surprised if the Clinton team doesn't either.

I'm concerned that a decision in favor of Florida and Michigan could unleash a new dynamic in the nominating race as we head into the summer before the National Convention. Since our breakthrough in the mid-February primaries and caucuses, the public and press have come to believe that Obama's narrow, but steady, pledged delegates lead has placed him on an inexorable path to the nomination. The strength of this delegate lead is encouraging more and more superdelegates to view the race as effectively over and to throw in their lot with Barack.

The reality, though, is that as strong as Obama's delegate lead may appear, it could be undermined if the Rules Committee decides to reverse its earlier decisions against Florida and Michigan. As we approach the May 31st Rules Committee meeting, our lead over Hillary in the pledged delegate count has shrunk to 132 delegates. If the DNC were to fully restore the Florida and Michigan delegations, this pledged delegate lead would be sliced sharply.

Consider the math. Michigan at full delegate strength would have 128 pledged delegates. The January primary would allocate the state's pledged delegates at 73 for Clinton, 55 for Uncommitted and none for Obama, whose name wasn't on the ballot.

Florida at full delegate strength would have 185 pledged delegates. The January primary would allocate the pledged delegates at 105 for Clinton, 67 for Obama and 13 for Edwards.

If the two states had all their delegates restored and allocated by each of their primaries, the combined delegates from the two states would be 178 for Clinton, 67 for Obama, 55 for Uncommitted, and 13 Edwards. Clinton would gain a net pick-up of 111 delegates over Obama—not counting any edge either candidate might gain among Michigan's uncommitted delegates or the Edwards delegates—virtually wiping out Obama's 132 pledged delegates lead.

This scenario has a name. It's called the Nuclear Option, and I have no doubt that this is the option the Clinton camp will pursue at a DNC showdown over seating Florida and Michigan. The rationale for this option is that Florida and Michigan shouldn't have to suffer their loss of delegates any longer and that the DNC has no right to assign the Uncommitted delegates to Obama. In this way of thinking, some Uncommitted voters may have preferred Edwards or perhaps no candidate, and the Rules Committee has no business arbitrarily allocating them to Obama. This approach ignores the virtual certainty that nearly all the voters for Uncommitted were attempting to support Obama—besides the fact that the primaries in these two states were invalidated and uncontested—so their results shouldn't matter.

The Nuclear Option would reverse prior decision-making by the Rules Committee without justification and result in Hillary contesting the presidential nomination all the way to the National Convention. If this scenario were to materialize, Democrats would face a political donnybrook in Denver—probably worse than we saw in the 1980 Carter-Kennedy national convention—and could potentially lose the White House in November as a result.

★　★　★

In the weeks leading up to the May 31st Rules Committee meeting, the DNC undertakes talks with the Clinton and Obama campaigns, as well as Michigan and Florida Democratic Party officials, to try to broker a settlement of the two states' delegate seating challenges. The DNC staff floats proposals back and forth to the two presidential campaigns, but Plouffe and I believe the main dynamic in these proposals is that we concede delegates to Hillary in order to buy peace. We're trying to reach the Magic Number and these proposals would only push it farther away.

At one point, Plouffe and I get on the phone with Alexis Herman and Jim Roosevelt, the co-chairs of the Rules Committee, to explain how important it is for us to hold every delegate we have and add the last ones we need to get to end the nomination race. The call is tense.

"It's time to focus on the fall election, not the lingering challenge from Hillary Clinton," Plouffe insists. "The Rules Committee needs to wrap this process up, not start a new chapter thanks to Florida and Michigan."

The co-chairs, though, are determined to give Hillary her day in court. There is no immediate solution.

As we approach the week before the scheduled Rules Committee meeting, we're still spinning our wheels in the DNC's negotiations with the Clinton campaign. We're willing to yield more delegates to Hillary from Florida, where there was a normal-looking election, but only if the Michigan delegates are split evenly between the candidates, since Obama's name wasn't even on the ballot. This combined approach would protect our margin over Hillary while ending the lingering delegates dispute.

I expect that Florida state party leaders would accept this resolution, but Michigan Democrats may balk. They're under pressure from Clinton supporters in the state to obtain an advantage for her to reflect the state's primary results. State party leaders, though, seem to want to put this mess behind everyone for 2008, so the state's delegates can be seated at the National Convention.

Given where Hillary is in the nominating race, there's no obvious way for us to reach a deal with her campaign on Florida and Michigan. She needs to make up so much ground in the national delegate race that any settlement we'd accept wouldn't get her where she needs to go. This leaves the two campaigns at an impasse concerning the two state challenges.

By the time we reach the Wednesday before Saturday's Rules Committee meeting, I'm at my wit's end with the DNC's mediation efforts. We've been spinning our wheels in fruitless discussions, and now the May 31st Rules Committee meeting is almost upon us.

I tell Plouffe we need to change course. We have to transition from trying to negotiate a resolution to preparing for a showdown at the Saturday meeting.

David agrees, as he never thought much of any of the negotiating proposals on the table anyway. For him, we can't end that worthless process soon enough.

Now, I've got less than 72 hours to get things in order for the meeting. First, we need to deal with the rampant rumors that Hillary's supporters will be arriving from across the East Coast to lay siege to the Rules Committee meeting site at the Woodley Park Marriott Hotel in Washington, DC. All I can think of is the famous scene at the Miami-Dade Canvassing Board in Florida in 2000, when Bush campaign forces intimidated elections officials conducting a manual ballot recount into ending the recount.

I get on the phone with our Obama grassroots leaders in Washington, Virginia and Maryland to assess their resources to counter this potential Clinton threat. They're salivating over the chance to fight a Clinton siege of the hotel and offer to bring out so many supporters they could swamp the Clinton protesters.

I sit down with Plouffe to discuss how we're going to handle this outside game. We're concerned that the Clinton camp is risking the outbreak of violence at the meeting hotel just when we're trying to wind down the nomination race and reverse the acrimony it's created.

It's obvious that battling in the streets with Hillary's supporters would undermine our reconciliation efforts. On the other hand, I'm certain that Rules Committee members and reporters covering the meeting will have to run a gauntlet to enter the building and I want them to see support for Obama in addition to Clinton.

David and I agree that we should do what we can to prevent clashes inside or out of the meeting hotel, while bringing in enough supporters to avoid ceding control of the crowd to Hillary. I decide to bring in some of my most trusted lieutenants from northern Virginia to manage our supporters in the street and keep me posted on what's happening outside the building.

Inside the hotel, the DNC is careful to make sure both presidential campaigns have an equal opportunity to be represented in the meeting room. Each campaign receives a share of the seats in the spectator area. I want the right people in our seats in the room, as they'll need to be disciplined—in addition to vocal—as events unfold.

Our local grassroots units are disappointed we're capping the size of their presence at the Rules Committee meeting, but they're happy to receive an allocation of the seats in the meeting room. I empower their leaders to select those who'll be in the room, and they select their best people to serve in what is expected to be a tense, nationally televised showdown.

★   ★   ★

I turn my attention to the Florida and Michigan challenges that will be heard inside the meeting room. In light of the fact that the Rules committee voted unanimously against these states last year—and the reasons for doing this haven't changed—how can we lose these challenges? Could the Clinton supporters on the Rules Committee reverse their earlier votes—in order to knock Obama off his path to the nomination?

This might sound like a cynical thing to do, but the two states have argued that leniency for their delegates is now justified. Their arguments could provide the Clinton backers with the political cover they'd need to restore the two state delegations and implement the Nuclear Option.

The composition of the Rules Committee membership makes me uneasy. The Rules Committee has 30 members, including the two co-chairs Alexis Herman, former President Clinton's Secretary of Labor, and Jim Roosevelt, a Clinton appointee at the Social Security Administration. By tradition, the co-chairs will refrain from voting on any disputed matter. In addition, there is one member from Florida, Obama supporter Tallahassee City Commissioner Allan Katz, and one member from Michigan, state Democratic Party Chair Mark Brewer, both of whom will be prohibited from voting on their own state's dispute.

This means there will be 27 members, including Brewer, voting on Florida, and 27 members, including Katz, voting on Michigan. For both states, a majority of 14 votes is all Hillary will need to fully restore the Florida and Michigan delegations—and execute the Nuclear Option.

Unfortunately, I have good reason to fear this outcome. The 27 Rules Committee members who will be voting include a heavy representation of Clinton loyalists. I count 12 Clinton supporters among the 27 Rules Committee members, including consultants currently on the Clinton payroll and several who served in a governmental or political capacity during the eight-year Bill Clinton presidency.

They are not a monolithic group, however. I believe 5 are firm for any position that Hillary needs. Another 5 are open to compromise. And the last 2 are too inscrutable for me to categorize.

There are 9 supporters for Obama on the Committee, though one of them is Floridian Allan Katz, who cannot vote on seating the Florida delegation. We probably can hold all 9, although one or two might not be totally solid.

This leaves 7 uncommitted members of the Rules Committee. They are a political hodgepodge, each with his or her own identity and interests. While they likely will want to be consistent on Saturday with their earlier decisions to penalize Florida and Michigan, I can't be sure what they'll do when push comes to shove.

We need to win over nearly every uncommitted vote on the Committee to prevent a meltdown of the DNC's sanctions against Florida and Michigan. If we don't, Obama's pledged delegate lead could disappear in an instant.

Alice Germond, longtime Secretary of the DNC, is talking to the uncommitted members in search of a solution for the Rules Committee. Like other senior members of the Rules Committee, Alice believes the DNC must be consistent in its application of the rules, while finding a path that respects both candidates.

As for me, I'm grabbing a flight to Washington, DC on Thursday morning to ramp up preparations for the Saturday meeting. Plouffe and political director Matt Nugen also will come to Washington for the meeting. Plouffe wants to be on site if something big is going to come down, and Matt has years of experience as chief of staff to the DNC chair that can be valuable during the Rules Committee's deliberations.

Before I leave Chicago, I instruct our headquarters staff to set up a series of calls for me for that afternoon: "I want to personally speak with every Obama supporter and uncommitted member of the Rules Committee. I don't care how many hours I have to be on the phone."

When I arrive in Washington, I go straight home and make it in the door just before my call time begins. I've got only minutes to say hello to my family, do some hugs all around, and explain that they need to be quiet because I'm about to get on several hours of back-to-back phone calls. Then, I get started. One by one, I talk to each Obama supporter and uncommitted member of the Rules Committee.

I pace back and forth across the house as I talk on the phone. I listen to each person's views and stress the importance of maintaining the integrity of the DNC's rules and not using them at this late date to disrupt the nomination race.

Throughout the afternoon, different members of my family look in on me, hoping for a break in the calls so they can get a word in about school or other family matters. They don't know how many calls are scheduled, and over time must start to wonder if I've lost my marbles. All they hear and see is me relentlessly repeating the same words as I pace around the house.

I'm wound up, but as I speak with each of the Rules Committee members, including those who are uncommitted in the presidential race, I'm able to confirm their belief that this is no time for the Rules Committee to reverse its enforcement decisions from last year. There is little stomach for abandoning enforcement of the rules that they themselves wrote. By my math, as tenuous it might be, a one-vote margin now exists in the Rules Committee to stand firm against any effort to seat Florida and Michigan at the

National Convention, and if any Clinton supporter is willing to join our position, our margin will be even greater.

* * *

Having completed my hours of phone calls, I turn to the live testimony that has to be delivered on Saturday. The Rules Committee has bifurcated the Saturday meeting into two sessions, one on Florida and the other on Michigan.

The state Democratic Party and each presidential candidate will have the right to present testimony, with witnesses subject to questions from the Rules Committee members. Both campaigns are putting forward witnesses from the states that have filed the challenges. For us, this means Robert Wexler, our champion in Florida, and David Bonior of Michigan, the former Edwards campaign manager who is now backing Obama for president.

Both of these witnesses are highly respected Democrats in their respective states, but neither is expert on the issues at hand. I'm going to have to write their testimony, coach them on its content, and prepare them for cross-examination by the Clinton partisans on the Rules Committee. I've got a lot of reason for concern about how this will turn out, but I don't have time to worry about it.

I just need to start writing testimony.

After several hours of writing, I finish the draft testimony for each witness and send it off to Wexler and Bonior for their review. We meet up on Friday at our workroom at the Marriott to discuss their testimony and consider changes. Both witnesses are extremely gracious in spending several hours absorbing the material and practicing their response to expected questions.

DNC rules can be a dense topic, not unlike the Internal Revenue Code or federal pension rules. The willingness of our witnesses to throw themselves into the substance of the arguments says a lot about their personal depth and commitment to Obama. Of course, having served for years in Congress, both are accustomed to studying complex briefing materials for hearings at the last minute, so maybe I shouldn't be so impressed. But I am.

Our discussions produce a number of recommendations for

changes to the prepared testimony, which I'll make tonight. Matt Nugen says he'll do whatever is needed to get the final documents printed for the hearing in the morning, as long as I agree to get to bed at a reasonable hour. The last thing he wants is for me to be a sleep-deprived wreck for the hearing tomorrow. I feel the same way, and thank him for the help.

After catching some dinner, I'm back at the keyboard redrafting the testimony in our small, windowless workroom. As the hours go by while I work, a more interesting drama begins to unfold in another part of the hotel.

In a closed meeting room far from my location, the members of the Rules Committee are eating dinner together and discussing the issues that might arise in the public meeting tomorrow. The occasion has a social aspect to it and the wine has been flowing throughout dinner. After they finish eating, the DNC staff asks the Rules Committee members to take an informal poll of their views on whether to maintain or overturn the earlier decisions to penalize Florida and Michigan.

In a result that stuns the members themselves, the poll produces a near-tie vote, with several members abstaining. Obama supporter Allan Katz slips out of the room and calls me in my workroom. He's got a message I don't want to hear.

"Jeff, you're not going to believe this," Allan says. "The Rules Committee took an informal vote on the two state challenges, and there wasn't a majority of votes to defeat them. A few of the uncommitted members of the Committee are refusing to show their cards. They're abstaining. We're going to do more polling of the Committee members tonight, but people are getting drunk and some arguments are starting to get personal."

I nearly jump out of my chair.

"Allan, you're going to have to work to increase our vote total. Get our people together and get those abstainers on board. We can't let this vote get away from us. Stay away from the booze, and call me after the next poll."

I slump back into my chair and stare at the computer screen. It's getting late, and I've got to finish the testimony. But now my mind is starting to wander, wondering if the Rules Committee vote won't spin out of control. After a few minutes, I snap back and work at double speed to wrap up the drafting. Matt takes the documents to get them printed and I'm headed home.

My calls from Allan continue after each straw poll. The Rules Committee keeps informally voting through the night, struggling to reach a consensus for the meeting, when the country will be watching to learn what will happen next for Obama and Clinton.

According to the frontline reports from Allan, not one member has voted contrary to the intentions they expressed to me in my phone calls yesterday afternoon. It' hard for him to get a handle on the votes that are abstaining. I don't know why people are not voting, but until someone crosses over from our position, I still believe we can maintain our one-vote margin.

By two in the morning, I've had it. There's nothing more I can do tonight. So, I shut down to get some sleep.

In the morning, I scramble over to the hotel. I want to arrive early enough to scope out the situation outside the building and be available to visit with our supportive Rules Committee members and witnesses before the meeting begins.

True to their predictions, the Clinton campaign turns out masses of supporters who are determined to convince the Rules Committee to seat the Florida and Michigan delegates. Many of them are just mad as hell that Hillary has fallen behind Obama in the nomination race and letting everyone in earshot know it. Our grassroots supporters are arriving also and their leaders are working hard to keep things calm. Supporters of the opposing candidates taunt one another and put on a show for the TV cameras.

I finally get into our workroom and find a number of our allies on the Rules Committee lingering around and gossiping about the surreal events of last evening. I give Plouffe and Nugen a quick report on what happened and where I think things stand. Wexler and Bonior swing by the room and confirm they're okay with the final draft of their testimony.

Nugen leaves the room to take care of some arrangements at about 8:30 am. Then the phone rings. It's the DNC staff. They ask if we can come up to meet with them before the hearing begins.

"Of course," I reply. I grab Plouffe and we head for the hotel elevator. I figure this will be a standard last-minute pre-meeting check-in.

What's about to transpire, though, is far from standard.

As the doors to the elevator open, Plouffe and I are greeted by DNC staff who walk us down the hallway to a private suite. When we walk through the door, I see a lone figure sitting at a dining table. It's Howard Dean, the Chairman of the Democratic National Committee.

Dean motions to Plouffe and me to join him at the table. I sit at the end of the table opposite from Dean. Plouffe sits to my left between Dean and me, and Tom McMahon, the DNC's executive director, sits opposite Plouffe. The DNC's general counsel and its director of party affairs stand off to the side of the table.

Dean begins the meeting: "I don't know if you're aware, but the Rules Committee members had a private dinner last night and did a survey of opinion on how to resolve the seating of Florida and Michigan. I have to tell you the results concern me."

"We know, Governor," I respond. "I received reports from in the room and understand it was quite an evening."

Dean gets straight to the point: "Based on the straw polls they did last night, the Rules Committee lacks a majority for any solution. We can't go out there now and have a meeting that ends in chaos. We've got to cancel this meeting and re-set it for later this summer."

I'm stunned.

I came into the suite expecting to get what would amount to final pre-fight instructions from the referee. Instead, we're being asked to cancel the fight. If we don't hold this Rules Committee meeting now, we'll lose any chance of resolving the Florida and Michigan challenges until well into the summer, or even at the National Convention.

Cancelling the meeting would signal the Clinton campaign, the superdelegates, the national press and the rest of the country that we're unable to close off this threat to Obama's nomination. I know Dean is just trying to prevent what he thinks would be a disaster if the Rules Committee is unable to set a path forward for resolving the two state challenges. He wants to do what he thinks is right for the national Democratic Party. But I believe it would invite even more trouble in the form of Hillary contesting delegate credentials and the nomination itself at the National Convention.

I glance to my left at Plouffe, who has got to be as surprised as I am, and he nods, authorizing me to lead.

"With all due respect, Governor," I say. "There were a number of votes taken on different solutions last night and there were several abstentions. Today, when they get into that meeting room—and everyone votes—we're going to win this thing. You can't cancel this meeting."

Without hesitation, Dean objects: "You don't have the votes! You can't tell me you know what's going to happen out there."

"Governor, we're going to win by at least one vote." I reply. "It's not a big margin, but it's enough. We won't agree to cancel."

Seeing I won't back down, Dean changes tack: "I want to know your Plan B. What happens in that meeting room—on national TV—if you can't win this vote? I've got a right to know."

"Governor, we're going to win this vote, even if narrowly," I persist.

"You've already told me you think you can win," Dean responds sharply. "What's your Plan B if you're wrong?"

"Plan B will be to negotiate a different compromise with the Clinton campaign that gives them more delegates than we think they should get, but still doesn't block Obama's nomination."

Now knowing we're not hell-bent to drive the Rules Committee meeting straight off a cliff, Dean finally relents.

"Ok, the Rules Committee can't resolve these challenges," he says, "the Committee will recess to allow the two campaigns to work out that compromise. I hope you already have something in mind, because that's where we may be headed."

With that said and the Rules Committee convening downstairs, we all rise up from our chairs and head for the meeting.

★　★　★

When we enter the large multi-level ballroom where the meeting will be held, it's like entering a madhouse. The public is seated in tiers that take up a good half of the room, creating the appearance of a small arena. This area is packed to the rafters. Rowdy supporters of the two candidates are chanting, waving signs, and taunting each other, as well as targeting their shouts at the Rules Committee members.

At the front of the room is a horseshoe seating area for the Rules Committee members. The co-chairs and senior DNC staff sit in the center section, straight across from the witness table at the open end of the horseshoe. The Committee members, in no particular order, sit along the long sides of the horseshoe.

Rows of TV cameras positioned on risers are pointed at the Rules Committee members, looking like cannons set to fire a fusillade of cannonballs at the Committee members. It's as though the national press corps is ready to attack if the Committee fails to reach a resolution that will finalize the nominating race.

In fact, the cable news networks are planning to cover the Rules Committee meeting live from gavel to gavel. Top political journalists are in attendance from around the country. The *Washington Post* is here. The *Wall Street Journal* is here, as is *Politico*, and many others. Throughout the day, the *New York Times* is going to issue reports on its website from reporters inside the room.

As for me, the DNC staff has saved me a specific seat off to one side of the horseshoe. I want to sit within the clear view of my witnesses. As a failsafe, I've told both Wexler and Bonior to look at me if at any time they're confused or uncertain as to how to answer a question during their cross-examination. In most cases, I figure a nod of my head could be a lifeline to them.

DNC Chair Howard Dean opens the meeting with a short speech that acknowledges the accomplishments of both candidates in this historic chase for the presidential nomination. The Rules Committee then takes up the Florida challenge. Florida DNC member and sometimes rules gadfly Jon Ausman argues the Committee should restore half of the state's delegates to the National Convention, which is the automatic penalty under DNC rules for scheduling a primary earlier than allowed. The Rules Committee is permitted to expand this penalty, which it's done by stripping all of the Florida and Michigan delegates.

The Clinton Campaign's representative, Florida State Senator Arthenia Joyner, contends that all the delegates from Florida should be seated at full strength. She doesn't discuss the fact that her own candidate boycotted the primary because of its violation of national Party rules, and that the votes cast do not reflect a contested election.

Then our representative, Robert Wexler, sits in front of the microphone and proceeds to deliver a rousing oration not foreshadowed in our practice sessions. Wexler declares:

> The Obama presidential campaign supports a resolution today that will allow the DNC to preserve its nomination process and at the same time enable Democrats in Florida to participate in choosing our party's nominee and allow elected delegates from Florida to be represented at the Democratic National Convention.

Clinton partisans erupt in cheers upon hearing that we're going to support seating Florida delegates. Our position, though, is to grant leniency in line with Jon Ausman's request to use the primary results but with the standard penalty of a 50% loss of the state's delegate votes. We're not supporting the Clinton request that Florida be seated at full strength, an outcome that could make a significant cut into our national delegate lead.

When Wexler finishes, he receives a blistering cross-examination from Clinton backers on the Rules Committee. At one point, Harold Ickes, the most aggressive of Hillary's Committee supporters, hones in on Wexler. Harold wants to make a point founded on the "fair reflection" principle in our party rules, which requires that delegates be awarded directly in proportion to the presidential primary votes. Rather than explain the principle first, Harold goes straight to his question: "Congressman Wexler, are you familiar with the concept of fair reflection?"

For an instant, Wexler shifts in his seat, because he's not familiar with the jargon of DNC rules. My stomach locks up, as this is the moment I feared, where our rules novice is overwhelmed by the deep rules expertise of one of Hillary's top lieutenants. While

Wexler is unsure of what he's being asked about, he is certain he doesn't like being placed on the defensive by Harold's question.

Wexler musters the most contemptuous tone he can and replies: "Mr. Ickes, why don't you enlighten me?"

The room explodes in cheers from the Obama supporters, as Wexler has made clear he won't be intimidated. With his initiative lost, Harold decides not to challenge Wexler further: "That won't be necessary. I have no further questions."

The Rules Committee next moves on to the Michigan challenge. While I'm waiting for the testimony to begin, I feel someone poking me from behind. I turn to look, and see its Plouffe. He gestures to join him at the back of the room. The Ickes questioning of Wexler has him worried. Bonior has a tougher job. He'll be defending our insistence that Michigan's delegates be split evenly — with no recognition of the primary results.

"Can you walk Bonior through everything again?" he says.

"Sure," I reply.

There's no time to go back to our workroom, so I ask Bonior to follow me to the nearest exit door, unaware it opens to a barren emergency stairwell.

After the heavy metal stairwell door slams shut, I say, "David, the Florida questioning shouldn't concern you, but let's go through the key issues one more time to be safe."

And with that stilted introduction, I march him through the main elements of his testimony and the questions he's likely to receive. He's every bit as composed as I'd expect for a longtime leader in the U.S. House of Representatives. I'm convinced he's ready to step into the ring with Harold and the other Clinton backers on the Rules Committee.

When we get back into the meeting room, Michigan Democratic Chair Mark Brewer is in the midst of testifying that his state party favors full seating and voting rights for their delegates, with an allocation of 69 for Clinton and 59 for Obama. Brewer states that 594,000 Democrats voted in their January primary and that the state party proposal reflects all of these votes plus exit poll data that shows many voters who cast ballots for "Uncommitted" were expressing support for Obama.

Senator Levin speaks immediately after Brewer and endorses the state party proposal to give Hillary a ten-vote margin in the state. Levin says this is the best solution, if admittedly imperfect and non-scientific. He wants all of Michigan's delegates seated with full voting rights. He says he'll accept any division of the delegates between the candidates, if someone can come up with a better formulation than the ten-vote advantage to Hillary. While he has the microphone, Senator Levin reprises his criticism of the first-in-the-nation voting monopoly of Iowa and New Hampshire, but this isn't the issue today.

During the questions to Senator Levin, Harold Ickes takes another crack at using the "fair reflection" argument he started to employ with Wexler. Harold tells Senator Levin they're in agreement on seating the full Michigan delegation, but that allocating them to the candidates in a manner that is not based directly on the candidate vote totals in the January primary would fail to meet the "fair reflection" principle.

Senator Levin refuses the temptation to argue for allocating the delegates in accordance with Michigan's primary votes. He explains his reasoning simply: "You're calling for a fair reflection of a flawed primary." He doesn't say it, but the primary is flawed because the candidates didn't campaign in the state and Obama's name wasn't on the ballot—the steps we took many months ago to protect our campaign from the unauthorized early primary.

Bonior finally gets his turn at the witness table. The Obama campaign wants to split the delegates evenly between Clinton and Obama, he says. The January primary was "not anything close to a normal primary election," and its "serious flaws" mean it can't be used to allocate any extra delegates to Hillary. While not as dramatic as Wexler, Bonior testifies effectively and without error.

The Clinton camp attempts to rebut our argument by sending former Michigan Governor Jim Blanchard to the witness table. Governor Blanchard tells the Rules Committee that the primary was not "flawed" and that the Committee has "got to honor the 600,000 voters in Michigan." Blanchard says the delegates should be allocated to fairly reflect the preferences expressed by the voters in the January primary. He pleads that "it doesn't make sense to punish the voters of Michigan because you thought our party leaders were overly aggressive."

During Blanchard's questioning, he casually mentions that he's going to soon attend his mother's 98th birthday celebration. Committee member Donna Brazile sees this reference to his mother as an opportunity to make a basic moral point about the Michigan situation. "My momma always taught me to play by the rules," Donna says, and "when you decide to change the rules, especially in the middle of the game...that is referred to as cheating."

The room erupts in shouts, as the Obama supporters in the crowd realize that one of the most recognizable members of the Committee is taking their side. What they don't know is that Donna is one of the key Rules members who abstained from voting in the straw polls the night before. Now, she's on the record.

After Governor Blanchard finishes, the Rules Committee members take a late lunch break. Now is when they have to reach a solution behind closed doors. It isn't long before Allan Katz is calling me from their private lunch room. The Rules members are searching for a consensus and begin polling among themselves, as they did the night before. Those who abstained the night before now reveal their positions. The Clinton camp does not have the votes for the Nuclear Option or any vote that will undermine Obama's candidacy. Our support on the Rules Committee is as solid as I'd thought.

As the Committee debates possible solutions within their lunchroom, Allan relays the various proposals to me as I stand in the hallway outside the meeting room talking with Plouffe, Nugen and reporters. We're willing to negotiate, I tell Allan, but won't give up more delegates than necessary to reach a compromise. Every delegate we yield now we'll have to make up with a superdelegate later, if we're to reach the Magic Number.

When it comes to Florida, the two campaigns are not far apart. We're both looking at an allocation that provides Hillary with a 19-vote margin. Eventually, we agree to allocate all the delegate positions, but with half votes for each delegate. The resulting delegate votes are 52.5 for Obama, 33.5 for Hillary and

6.5 for Edwards. We're confident of picking up nearly all of Edwards's 13 delegates—each having half a vote—to mitigate the number of delegates we're yielding in the state.

On Michigan, we're at an impasse. The state Democratic Party wants a 69—59 split for Hillary, the Clinton campaign wants a 73—55 split for her, and we want to split Michigan's delegates evenly. We're now thankfully beyond arguing over how to treat the Uncommitted delegates. Obama is getting those delegates. If the Rules Committee can't agree on a solution, it could punt the whole controversy to the National Convention's credentials committee. Such a delay, though, could cause a lot of uncertainty for the National Convention, so we ask our Rules Committee supporters to work hard behind the closed doors to get us a deal. Allan Katz pleads with us to be flexible in what we'll accept.

My view is we can win a vote, so let's get it over. The Committee members should come out of their lunchroom and vote. Plouffe doesn't want to give an inch in negotiations, because we'll have to make up every extra delegate we give to Hillary. Allan keeps working with others on the Rules Committee to find a deal.

As time drags on, nerves are fraying. Finally, Mark Brewer, the chairman of the Michigan Democratic Party, agrees to support a plan to award Hillary 69 delegates and Obama 59, but each with only half a vote. This would produce a gain for Hillary of five delegate votes.

Plouffe won't buy it. He refuses to let Hillary take one extra vote out of Michigan, much less five. When I relay this to Katz, he's beside himself. Allan begs me to talk to David again and urge him to reconsider.

While we're grumbling in the hallway about what it's going to take to get the Rules Committee to come back to the meeting room and vote, I realize there might be one more move we can make to wrap this up. In addition to all the pledged delegates that Michigan is trying to get restored, Michigan has two unpledged add-on superdelegates that never were selected. If Michigan Democrats agree to select Obama supporters for each of these positions, Hillary's margin from Michigan would be reduced to a measly three delegate votes.

I pitch the idea to Plouffe, but he's not interested. She doesn't deserve any advantage from Michigan, and it just means we'll have to make up the three delegates.

At this point, like Allan, I've had it. With my nicest bedside manner, I tell David it's time to forget about getting an even split of the delegates. We're guaranteeing Obama the nomination today, so let her have the extra three damn delegates. It won't change a thing. Finally, David gives in.

There's a problem with this plan for the two unpledged add-ons, though. The state party expects to use one of them to get UAW President Ron Gettelfinger to the National Convention. Ron is uncommitted in the presidential contest and nobody in the state party is going to touch his delegate position.

"Oh, crap!" I say to myself, this meeting is never going to end.

To move things along, I call Dick Long, the UAW's longtime political director.

"Dick, I'm in a meeting in Washington and need your help," I say. "We want to assign the last two unpledged delegates from Michigan to Obama supporters. One of these spots has been saved for Ron and since he's uncommitted, I need you to fill that position and pledge it for Barack."

"Are you crazy?" he replies. "There's no way I'm taking my boss's delegate position—at least without asking him. I'll call him and we'll see what he says."

When Dick dials up Ron, who has just returned on an overnight flight from East Asia, Ron doesn't answer the phone. Dick calls me to say there's nothing he can do.

"Dick, I can appreciate your situation," I respond. "But resolving our situation in Washington depends on your taking this delegate position. I need you to make the executive decision to take Ron's delegate position for Obama. I'm begging you."

Finally, Dick relents. "Oh, the hell with it. I'll take Ron's seat, and he'll either have to understand or fire me."

And with that, I signal to the DNC staff that we have a deal. It's time to get the Rules Committee back in the meeting room.

The members file in. First up is the Florida challenge. The Clinton backers on the Committee want to show their support for full restoration of the delegates before conceding to the negotiated resolution. As soon as they make their motion to fully seat the Florida delegates, their supporters in the crowd, not knowing the motion is doomed to fail, cheer wildly.

When the vote on the motion is taken, only 12 supporting votes are mustered. The gleeful Clinton supporters in the gallery are stunned. Shouts of "Denver! Denver!" erupt. They want Hillary to take the fight to the floor of the National Convention.

The Committee next proceeds to a vote on the compromise to seat all of Florida's delegates, but with each having only half a vote. The motion passes unanimously.

With Florida done, the Rules Committee takes up the Michigan challenge. As with Florida, the motion is made to restore all the state's pledged delegates, but with each delegate to cast only half a vote. The motion fails. Next, the Committee votes on the compromise to give Hillary a ten-delegate advantage, but with half-votes only. This motion passes by a vote of 19 to 8, with several Clinton supporters on the Rules Committee crossing lines to approve the compromise—and Barack Obama as their party's presidential nominee.

As soon as the Michigan vote is taken, the Clinton supporters in the crowd erupt in a new round of protests. The Committee co-chair, concerned about the possibility of violence, asks security personnel to regain control of the room.

Harold Ickes takes to the microphone and charges that the grant of only half a vote for the Michigan delegates amounts to a "hijack" of the democratic process. As far as he's concerned, "This body of 30 individuals has decided that they're going to substitute their judgment for 600,000 voters."

Building up to a crescendo, Harold lays out the ultimate threat: "Mrs. Clinton has instructed me to reserve her rights to take this to the credentials committee."

I understand we're at the end of a long, hard-fought nomination fight and don't believe the Clinton campaign really would want a fight over delegate credentials. The fact is that the Rules Committee's decisions today eliminate any last chance Hillary can continue to contest the nomination. Harold's final words won't sit well with some in our campaign, but the nomination fight is over and we're going to need to put all this aside.

Finally, well into the evening, the Rules Committee wraps up. The ten-hour-long Rules Committee meeting is over. For Plouffe, Nugen and me, it's high-fives all around.

★   ★   ★

Our leaders and supporters serving on the Rules Committee have carried the day for Obama. I especially want to single out Floridian Allan Katz, who took on his own state party establishment to defend the national nomination system and the Obama candidacy. Our witnesses, Robert Wexler and David Bonior, for their marvelous representation of the Obama campaign, who had little opportunity to prepare for battle in the dangerous minefield of Democratic Party rules. I also want to give credit to our grassroots supporters who rose to the occasion once again to rally around the Obama candidacy. Their presence in the meeting hall has served to remind everyone involved of the passionate Obama following around the country and the need to act in a manner that would stand up as fair and justified under national party rules.

The Rules Committee, led by its co-chairs, Alexis Herman and Jim Roosevelt, and a number of its senior members, has stood up for its principles and defended the rules of our Party's nominating process. The Committee took a firm stand to apply and enforce its rules against Florida and Michigan in 2007 and today has reaffirmed the rules. This maintains the integrity of this year's nominating process and preserves the authority of the DNC and its Rules Committee for future presidential elections.

The decision to restore half-votes for the two states doesn't undermine the integrity of the primary timing rules, as the half-vote level is actually the standard penalty required under the rules. We can address the full restoration of Florida and Michigan's delegations at a time of our choosing closer to the National Convention, when it won't impact the nominating race.

The Clinton supporters on the Committee who voted for the

final compromise for Florida and Michigan also deserve recognition for standing by the nominating rules they helped to draft.

To me, though, the bottom line from today's events is that we've ended Hillary's last real chance to stop our momentum toward reaching the Magic Number.

★   ★   ★

After I finish thanking our grassroots supporters for coming out to show the flag for Obama, I hop into a taxi to head over to Nationals Stadium. I'm not going to see the Major League Baseball Washington Nationals. I'm going to see my son, Joe, take the field to compete in the DC high school championship baseball game. It's a rare chance for me to attend a family event, and only reminds me I've missed all the other games of his championship season. In August, he'll be heading off to begin college and I'll be left to wonder how I could've gone away for his entire last year at home.

I urge the driver to get to the stadium as fast as possible, I want to get there in time to see Joe be introduced and walk onto the baseball diamond with the rest of his team. When the taxi pulls up to the stadium, I bolt out the door and run through the stadium gate to get a glimpse of what's happening on the field. Thankfully, the players haven't been introduced yet. I've made it just in time.

When I find my family in the stands, it's an understatement to say they're relieved I made it to the game, much less being on time. We talk about how great it is to see Joe in his Wilson Tigers uniform on the Nationals' home field. Inevitably, the talk turns to today's Rules Committee meeting. It turns out my wife, Trish, and oldest daughter, Cassie, had come on their own to the meeting—proudly wearing their Obama campaign tee shirts—to witness the entire drama from the public gallery. They describe the boiling emotions of both the Hillary and Obama supporters. Trish and Cassie say that at times it seemed actual fistfights might break out between the two sides.

When Joe's game ends, we all head home together. I'm burned

out from the tension of the day and lack of sleep last night. Before I head to bed, there's one thing I need to do. I sit down at my laptop, open up my spreadsheet for the national delegate count, and add two new lines to reflect today's decision to restore half the delegate votes of Florida and Michigan:

Date	State	Election	Pledged Delegates	Obama	Clinton	Edwards	Obama Lead
	Prior Total		3167	1636.5	1504.5	26	132
31 May	Michigan	DNC Rules	64	29.5	34.5	0	-5
	Florida	DNC Rules	92.5	33.5	52.5	6.5	-19
	New Total		3323.5	1699.5	1591.5	32.5	108

How does this affect the Magic Number? With Florida and Michigan's delegates at half-delegate voting strength, the DNC adjusts the National Convention delegates roll to show Florida with 92.5 pledged delegate votes and 12.5 unpledged delegate votes and Michigan with 64 pledged delegate votes and 14.5 unpledged delegate votes. This change increases the national number of pledged delegates by 156.5 and unpledged delegates by 27. As a result, the National Convention now will have 3,409.5 pledged delegates and 825 superdelegates, for a total of 4,235.5 delegates to the National Convention.

The Magic Number rises from 2,026 to 2,118.

18

Reaching the Magic Number

BACK IN CHICAGO after the Rules Committee showdown, I re-join our staff for the final push for delegates to reach the Magic Number and claim the presidential nomination. With no scenario left for Hillary to resurge, the task now is to wrap up the delegate race as soon as possible. The sooner we get this done, the sooner we can focus all our attention on the coming campaign against Senator John McCain and the Republican Party.

We have a specific target date for reaching the Magic Number. It's the day of the last round of voting, Tuesday, June 3rd. When the primary voting ends, the remaining 200 or so uncommitted superdelegates will lose their last reason to continue sitting on the fence in the presidential race. They'll no longer be able to say, "there are still votes to be counted."

This rationale for superdelegates to remain uncommitted has been the cause of great frustration both within our campaign headquarters and among Democratic leaders in Washington, DC and elsewhere. In recent days, Democratic Party leaders, including Senate Majority Leader Harry Reid and House Speaker Nancy Pelosi, have been leaning hard on superdelegates to make up their minds and announce their decisions in the next few days.

Clinching the presidential nomination on the last day of the primary voting would have a certain historical importance. It was on the last day of primary voting in 1984 that Walter Mondale captured the presidential nomination, even though Gary Hart had won the California mega-primary earlier that day. Mondale's campaign had to scramble to overcome Hart's California win by recruiting enough superdelegates to reach the Magic Number.

This year, neither California nor any other major state will be voting on the last day of primaries. But we do have two more small rounds of primaries in which we can earn more delegates. First is Puerto Rico, which is the only contest to be held on Sunday, June 1st. The primary vote in Puerto Rico, a U.S. territory, is unlike the presidential primaries anywhere else in the U.S. Puerto Ricans do not organize their politics around the Democratic and Republican parties, but instead around their own political parties. The New Progressive Party supports statehood for Puerto Rico, while the Popular Democratic Party advocates continuing as a territory, or "commonwealth," as Puerto Rico also is known.

Since both statehooders and commonwealthers participate in Puerto Rico's Democratic Primary, I want to approach both groups of Puerto Rico's Democrats to ensure Obama has a basic level of support that will prevent the Clintons from locking up support with all the Island's Democratic leaders. There are a substantial 55 pledged delegates at stake, and I know we have to take Puerto Rico seriously.

★   ★   ★

With the primary not scheduled until June of 2008, how early do I have to start looking into our outreach to Puerto Rico? The answer: very early. With 55 pledged delegates to be allocated and the race between Obama and Clinton as tight as it's been from the start, a lopsided loss in Puerto Rico could change the dynamic of the national delegate race. The mere possibility this could happen concerns me.

Early in the spring of 2008, I begin making some inquiries around the campaign headquarters on whether anyone is reaching out to Puerto Rico's Democrats. I learn we're well into discussions with commonwealth leaders on the steps Obama would carry out if he wins the presidency. These talks—being mediated by Chicago Congressman Luis Gutierrez—are close to producing an Obama letter to commonwealth leader Governor Anibal Acevedo Vila. I obtain a copy of the letter recommend some changes and the letter is signed, paving the way for commonwealther support from the Governor and former State Senator Eduardo Bhatia, an Obama loyalist running for the state senate again.

Within hours after we issue Obama's letter, calls started pouring in from pro-statehood Obama supporters complaining that the commitments and language in the letter favor the commonwealthers. Andres Lopez, a member of Obama's National Finance Council, and others ask for a parallel Obama letter of commitments to the statehooders to show his neutrality on Puerto Rico's future. We agree to a second letter, but ask for a senior statehooder endorsement to match our top commonwealther support.

Lopez contacts Pedro Pierluisi, the statehood candidate for Congress, to see if he'll take the statehood lead for Obama. Within days, Pierluisi and his campaign manager, Andy Guillemard, are on their way with Lopez to Philadelphia, the site for Obama's major speech on race in America. There, at the conclusion of Obama's speech in Constitution Hall, Pierluisi and Obama—close in age and demeanor—meet and hit it off, sealing Pierluisi's endorsement for Obama on the spot.

Finally, we have the top-flight support from both commonwealthers and statehooders Obama needs to secure his position in Puerto Rico for the delegates that will be allocated months later at the beginning of June.

★   ★   ★

With June upon us, it's time for Puerto Rico's primary. Unfortunately, it's clear we can't match Hillary's support on the Island. Although our commonwealth and statehood supporters are working their hearts out for Obama, her aggressive personal campaigning and the popularity of her husband have given her a strong lead we can't overcome. With the delegate majority now virtually in hand, our campaign decides to concede Puerto Rico rather than fight hard to the finish. We'll take whatever share of the delegates Obama can win in the primary, and move on.

When the vote occurs, Puerto Ricans turn out in lower levels than many had projected. Some had estimated turnout could run as high as 1,000,000 voters, while others were looking for a still-substantial turnout of 600,000. In the end, only 388,000 voters come to the polls. Many on the Island had lost interest in the primary since Obama was set to claim the nomination. The low turnout denies Hillary the opportunity to build her national popular vote to buttress her contention that such a lead should determine the nomination.

Hillary wins a lopsided 68% to 31% victory that earns her 38 pledged delegates compared to 17 for Obama. While there is no glory in this result for Obama, he's avoided a shutout and taken enough delegates to push closer to wrapping up the presidential nomination.

Date	State	Election	Pledged Delegates	Delegate Results Obama	Clinton	Edwards	Obama Lead
	Prior Total		3323.5	1699.5	1591.5	32.5	108
1 Jun	Puerto Rico	Primary	55	17	38	0	-21
	New Total		3378.5	1716.5	1629.5	32.5	87

★   ★   ★

At last, we reach Tuesday, June 3rd, the final day of primary voting. Contests will be held in Montana and South Dakota. The voting on this first Tuesday in June is imbued with a tragic history from the Democratic primary in California decades ago. In 1968, Senator Robert Kennedy won the California Primary, which could have catapulted him to the presidential nomination—but for the bullet of assassin Sirhan B. Sirhan, who shot Kennedy as he departed from his primary night victory celebration.

The voting on this year's first Tuesday in June will be far less fateful. When the day begins, Obama is 41 delegates away from the Magic Number. Two lightly populated mountain states, Montana and South Dakota, will be closing out the national voting with primaries during the day. Pre-election polling indicates a split decision, with Montana going for Obama and South Dakota for Clinton. We can expect Obama to gain about 15 pledged delegates in these two states, but the votes in these states will not be counted until later tonight.

As the voters cast their ballots in Montana and South Dakota, our superdelegate trackers work to obtain more delegate commitments to get Obama to the Magic Number. For the still uncommitted superdelegates, there is no reason left to hold out. Very soon, there will be no more courting by top campaign officials, advisors and surrogates. Those superdelegates still holding out when the primaries end will be remembered for refusing to come off the fence for Obama all the way to the bitter end. A number of uncommitted superdelegates have assured us they won't fall into this category and will endorse Obama as soon as the last states vote.

As our trackers and others work the phones, new superdelegate commitments to Obama come trickling in. The first new commitment comes early in the morning and they continue throughout the day. We even pick up a superdelegate previously committed to Hillary. By the end of the day, Obama picks up 28 superdelegates casting 26.5 delegate votes (since Florida and Michigan superdelegates cast only one-half vote each).

The still-loyal Edwards pledged delegates are another source of new delegates for Obama today. With the Rules Committee decision to half-restore the Florida and Michigan pledged delegates, we have a group of new delegates to chase. In Florida, there are 13 pledged Edwards delegates, each with a half-vote. Allan Katz, our Florida warrior, takes the lead in reaching out to them, and a slew of others join the effort. With the full court press on to win over these orphan delegates, it doesn't take long before they start to realign to Obama. We claim 10 Edwards delegates for Obama, each casting one-half vote.

With a combined 38 delegate commitments casting 31.5 delegate votes, there is little drama whether we'll reach the Magic Number by the end of the day. We only need 9 more delegates from and Montana and South Dakota, and we project 15 from the two states. Obama will cross the finish line without question.

In Montana, a Rocky Mountain state with an increasingly liberal Democratic electorate, Obama wins with 57% of the vote to 41% for Hillary, giving Obama 9 more delegates for his push to the nomination.

In South Dakota, Hillary wins 55% to 45%, but with Obama still picking up 6 delegates thanks to the requirement of proportional representation.

Here are the Montana and South Dakota delegate results:

Date	State	Election	Pledged Delegates	Delegate Results Obama	Clinton	Edwards	Obama Lead
	Prior Total		3378.5	1716.5	1629.5	32.5	87
3 Jun	Montana	Primary	16	9	7	0	2
	South Dakota	Primary	15	6	9	0	-3
	New Total		3409.5	1731.5	1645.5	32.5	86

★   ★   ★

As a result of the 15 pledged delegates from Montana and South Dakota—in addition to the new commitments from superdelegates and Edwards switchers—Obama eases across the delegate race finish line.

In terms of pledged delegates, Obama beats Hillary by 1731.5 to 1645.5, for a total advantage of 86 pledged delegates, or just 50.7% of the pledged delegates—a whisker over the 50% mark.

Among superdelegates, the movement toward Obama since his success with voters in the January and February leaves him with a lead over Hillary of about 100 superdelegate commitments.

Almost 16 months after he announced his candidacy for President of the United States, Barack Obama has reached the Magic Number.

★   ★   ★

Today's push to secure the final delegate commitments to clinch the nomination has absorbed our campaign headquarters with an intense sense of mission. By nightfall, though, the feeling is different. Now, electric excitement is arcing through the headquarters, as all of us marvel at the magnitude of our accomplishment.

To celebrate, the staff heads over to a popular night spot, the Rockit Bar, just a few blocks north of the Chicago River. With an open bar tab, the drinking begins immediately and doesn't let up.

Knots of staffers gather around, hoisting beers, cocktails and shots to loud cheers. I make my way from one group to another, getting drafted to join in each round of drinks. There are red shots, blue shots and green ones. I have no idea what I'm drinking, and don't give a damn. Time after time, we lock arms, let out a yell, and send it down the hatch.

Plouffe makes his way to the raised DJ's spot at the front of bar to offer a few words to the campaign staff. At times, I can't hear what he's saying because of the shouting and laughing. David thanks everyone for the hard work put in over the many months we've fought together for the presidential nomination. Ever the realist, he takes a minute to warn everyone that after tonight there's a tough general election ahead and we need to close ranks with Hillary's supporters to succeed against McCain and the Republicans. But these sober thoughts can't intrude on the celebration for long. As soon as David leaves his perch, the crowd is back to partying for an achievement we'll never forget.

Finally, I've had all the drinking I can handle—and then some—and call it a night. I flop out the door and into a cab, then I'm out for the night.

The next morning, I feel almost as drunk as the night before. By 11 am, I finally get onto a bus, anchoring myself in for the ride to the office. I have a chuckle when I see another staffer slither onto the bus a few minutes later, looking even more worn out from last night than me. In the office, almost everyone is moving slowly. I'm not surprised.

It was quite a party last night.

19

Getting Ready
for the Big Show

IT'S JUNE, the start of summer, and the end of the primaries. Back home in Washington, this month brings the arrival of lightning bugs in our backyard. But here in Chicago, I don't see much of the world outdoors or focus much on things back home.

One other aspect of June, though, doesn't escape my notice, and that's the start of my kids' summer vacation from school. All four of my kids know exactly what they want to do, which is come to Chicago for a few weeks. My wife will have to stay in Washington to attend to her job, but the kids are old enough to travel and camp out with me. Joe will work for a second summer in the Information Technology department, while the girls shop, go to the Lake Michigan beach, and eat their favorite foods.

When they arrive at my apartment, each child finds their own niche for their summer bivouac at Camp Dad. It isn't but a few hours before we make plans to get dinner that evening.

What do you guys want to eat tonight?" I ask.

"Pizza!" they shout in unison. "Deep dish!"

Deep dish pizza is a religion in Chicago. The temples of this cuisine, Giordano's, Gino's and Uno's are peppered throughout the area just north of our campaign office and the Chicago River. We meet at my office and walk to the restaurants. The neighborhood streets rise up to feed traffic onto an old bridge that crosses the river. Underneath these streets is a labyrinth of dimly lit roads so creepy that they were used this past winter for the filming of Batman: The Dark Knight. The kids are justifiably edgy as we make our way over the river and onto the roads below.

Eventually, we arrive at the first of the pizza palaces, and see a line out the door. I look directly across the street at another pizza place, and their line is just as bad. I'm not sure I'll have the patience for this.

"Ok, guys," I say. "If you want deep dish, we'll be waiting an hour just to get seated. Can we eat something else?"

"No! We want pizza!" they answer. And so we wait.

We finally get seated. They're full of questions about what's happening at the campaign headquarters, and I fill them in as best I can until the food arrives. Then the conversation goes silent. The big, thick pizzas glisten with oil from the melted cheese. We all dig in with the zeal of the converted. Chicago deep dish pizza is renowned for a reason. It's amazingly delicious.

As everyone advances to their second piece of pizza, the conversation restarts and I ask the kids to tell me what's been going on at home. They recount their successes in the classroom, on the athletic field and in the staging of school plays. As I listen to their stories, I want to smile, but it's not easy, as I'm reminded an entire school year has gone by for them and I've missed every day of it.

There isn't much I can do about that now, except to try to find the time to sneak out for lunch and join them for dinner as much as I can. In a couple months, summer vacation will be over and we'll be separated again, so I want to make the most of my time.

★   ★   ★

During the summer, our staff will be putting the finishing touches on preparations for the National Convention. The National Convention team still has to raise an enormous amount of money to help the host committee complete the financing of the four-day gathering. Additional work still is required on a host of logistics, including the staging for the Pepsi Center and Mile High Stadium, the preparation of credentials and the arrangements for housing and transportation. Media and messaging experts will work on the all-important speeches and programming that will be televised to the American public. The list of tasks to be completed seems endless.

For me, as the campaign's delegate director, the focus will be on working with the delegates to complete their business at the National Convention. I'll guide the Credentials Committee in finalizing the roster of delegates, the Rules Committee in writing the rules for convention voting and for possible changes to the Party's presidential nominating process, and the Platform Committee in preparing the Party Platform. My goal in all these cases is to get the delegates' work done with the least amount of controversy.

The mission of the Convention is to present a clear picture of Barack's candidacy to the American people, and we don't want internal disputes muddying this image. National political conventions have changed over the years. There was a time when these quadrennial gatherings of state and local leaders debated national policies and chose their candidates for president and vice president. Now, national conventions are a coda to a nominating process whose outcome already has been determined, with the delegates doing their business quietly during the day and providing a useful backdrop for the primetime television programming at night.

For 2008, the first item on my plate for the delegates is to revisit the dispute over seating the delegations from Florida and Michigan. The last time we addressed this nagging challenge was at the May 31st DNC Rules Committee meeting in Washington, where the delegates were restored but with only half-votes for each delegate. Now, Democrats in the two states want their delegates restored to full voting strength, with no penalty for their early primaries.

Of course, at this point, the nomination fight is over. Whether they cast half-votes or full votes, or even double votes or no votes, doesn't matter to anyone but them. I tell anyone within earshot that there's no point in continuing the penalties, and within our campaign, there's no disagreement on this issue.

It's a simple matter to resolve. We'll have Barack formally ask the Credentials Committee to restore Florida and Michigan to their full delegate voting strength and then the Credentials Committee can approve the change when it meets on August 24th, the day before the National Convention begins. The DNC staff and general counsel agree with me on this approach and it's going to be a slam dunk to get it done. The Florida and Michigan controversies finally will be over—at least until the next presidential election.

The Credentials Committee promptly concurs with Obama's request and votes to fully restore the delegate votes for Florida and Michigan. With this action, below is the revised—and final—tally for the pledged delegates:

Date	State	Election	Pledged Delegates	Obama	Clinton	Edwards	Obama Lead
	Prior Total		3409.5	1731.5	1645.5	32.5	86
24 Aug	Florida	Credentials	92.5	33.5	52.5	6.5	-19
	Michigan	Credentials	64	29.5	34.5	0	-5
	New Total		3566	1794.5	1732.5	39	62

I step back from my day-to-day preparation for the National Convention and look at the delegate landscape after we fully restore the delegates from Florida and Michigan. Nobody else notices—and it doesn't matter now that Obama owns the nomination—but privately I marvel at the closeness of the final pledged delegate count.

With the Florida and Michigan delegations back to full strength, Obama's national pledged delegate lead has shrunk to a total of 62 delegates. He has just 50.3% of the total number of pledged delegates, barely over the 50% threshold. After counting the pledged delegates of every state and territory, this is where we're left.

I imagine Hillary and her campaign leaders can only wonder what might have been had Florida and Michigan simply followed the rules and voted during early February, or if the two states had managed to get their delegates counted on a timely basis. We'll never know, but fully counted wins in two of the biggest states might have affected Obama's momentum coming out of Super Tuesday or perceptions of the national delegate race at a time when there was great uncertainty about the outcome.

These states could have mattered.

★   ★   ★

A little more interesting is the preparation of the Democratic Party Platform. Several weeks before the National Convention, we solicit help from an old hand at drafting Party Platforms, Michael Yaki, a politically astute and maximally energetic attorney in San Francisco, and Dan Carol, a longtime Democratic policy advisor. We also pull in Karen Kornbluh, who served on Obama's Senate staff, to do most of the actual writing of the Platform. Karen knows Obama's issue positions and phrasing as well as anyone.

Yaki arranges two days of presentations at the DNC office in Washington for every interested constituency group within the Party. No recognized group will be precluded from offering input. But they only get a few minutes each to make their case. This is assembly-line policy development, but it works.

Following tradition, we also appoint a special drafting committee of 15 prominent Democrats from around the country to advise on the policy positions in the Platform. Leading the committee will be Arizona Governor Janet Napolitano and Massachusetts Governor Deval Patrick. The committee meets several times before the National Convention to review Karen's Platform draft and the issues raised by the constituency groups. While we're at a meeting in Cleveland, Governor Napolitano and I, both born in 1957, decide to take a break from our work and visit the musical exhibits of our youth at the Rock and Roll Hall of Fame. It's a short break from the Platform drafting tedium, but we both get a kick from Elvis Pressley's classic car and music, Jim Morrison's handwritten lyrics for the Doors, and everything in between.

One idea that comes up during our campaign's discussions of the Platform process is to add a new wrinkle by obtaining policy recommendations directly from our grassroots supporters. Why not empower grassroots Democrats throughout the country to hold their own hearings and send in reports to the Platform Committee for inclusion in the Platform?

Plouffe loves the idea. It reinforces the campaign's approach to encourage rank-and-file Democrats to participate and organize for victory in the 2008 elections. Others in Chicago are more wary. What if the most fringe elements of the Party capture the microphone at these events and steal the media spotlight?

David and I are convinced that the danger of this happening is minimal. Our communications specialists can manage the risk. Any risk is more than outweighed by the benefits of grassroots empowerment and the positive image that will be conveyed from this new type of direct participation in the policy process.

Devoted grassroots manager from New York City, Deborah Slott, oversees the development of the Platform hearings, and by the time the last one is completed, our supporters have held hundreds of hearings located in every part of the country. Ordinary people tell their stories, how they've been affected by national policies and how these policies can be improved for everyone. A number of their policy recommendations are included in the Platform.

* * *

The last area of delegate activity I have to work on is the report of the National Convention's Rules Committee. This committee recommends procedural rules for the National Convention and changes to the Democratic Party's nominating process for future elections. I consult with Plouffe on the changes I'd like to see in the national nominating rules to address some of the issues that arose during 2008. The primaries and caucuses, beginning right after the Christmas and New Year's Day holidays on January 3rd started too early. They opening of voting needs to be pushed back a month. Democrats should review the operation of caucuses and conventions to improve their functioning. Finally, we should lessen the role of the superdelegates, who clouded the outcome of the nominating process for months. David talks to Barack about it and we get the go-ahead to recommend changes.

Given the need to unify the Democratic Party for the fall campaign, we decide not to make changes during the National Convention that could roil components of the Party. Instead, I draft a resolution with DNC staff and counsel to create a special commission to review these issue areas and recommend changes to the DNC's Rules Committee and the full DNC. We might not get all the changes we'd like to see, but hopefully we'll get some that will improve the nominating process for the future.

As for the procedural rules for the 2008 National Convention, there's not much to do in the Rules Committee report other than make a few minor updates to the rules that were used in 2004.

Why else would we change the convention nominating procedures for 2008?

20

Unity in Denver

IT'S LATE AUGUST and a euphoric time in the Obama world. Democratic delegates are gathering in Denver for the National Convention that will nominate Barack Obama for president. The Convention will include four days of televised speeches and presentations designed to rally Democrats, Independents and maybe even a few Republicans for the Obama-Biden ticket.

I want my family to come to Denver to see the National Convention and know why I've had to be gone all these many months leading up to it. I've been to almost every Democratic National Convention since I began my presidential campaign career in 1984 with John Glenn. But this is the first time I've gone to a National Convention for the winning presidential candidate. No doubt, this Convention experience will be different from all my others.

The many months of competition between Barack and Hillary leading up to the National Convention has been intense and sometimes bitter. Both candidates have led their supporters in a historic chase to be either the first African-American or the first female presidential nominee of a major American political party.

Obama's supporters are full of satisfaction over his impending nomination, but many Clinton supporters remain disappointed. The most extreme of these disappointed Clinton backers form a group called "Party Unity My Ass" and call themselves PUMAs. While the PUMAs are just a tiny portion of the millions of Hillary supporters, their reluctance to support Barack is a warning sign that more work needs to be done to unify Democrats behind him in November.

Questions remain over how enthusiastically the Clinton delegates will embrace Obama at the National Convention. There are a huge number of delegates supporting Hillary and, in fact, many of them are among the most stalwart of her supporters. Plouffe is convinced, though, that these delegates can help draw Hillary's voters in behind Obama for the fall election. He wants them to send a signal to Hillary's voters everywhere that they should back Obama for the fall election.

A message comes over my blackberry from Plouffe.

"Can you come to the staff room in the Arena?" he asks.

When I arrive, David says: "we need to pull the delegates together in the convention hall for Barack. There's nobody better to lead the effort than Hillary. Can you work with her people to have her release her delegates and call for a unanimous nomination vote for Barack? And can you pull this off so it happens during the evening network news shows so we can reach the maximum home TV audience?"

At first, I can't believe what he's asking. A unanimous convention vote, known as nomination by acclamation, hasn't been done for a Democratic presidential nominee since Lyndon Baines Johnson was nominated for president in 1964. Moreover, arranging for this procedure to occur during the thirty-minute evening news would be like parachuting out of a plane at 10,000 feet and hoping to land in a bull's eye the size of a beach blanket.

"Hmmm. This isn't going to be easy to pull off," I respond. "I don't have to tell you there's a lot of Hillary delegates in the hall who still haven't come to terms with losing the nomination. Plus, this will require the state delegations giving up their chance to speak and cast their votes during the traditional roll call vote."

"I know, but it would mean a lot to Barack to unify Hillary's voters behind him. Can you do it?" he asks.

"I hope so," I reply, wondering if it really will be possible.

And that's the end of our discussion.

The first thing I need to do is get Craig Smith on the phone. He's the longtime political hand of the Clinton family from Little

Rock, Arkansas. He served as Political Director for the Clinton White House during President Clinton's first term in office. Hillary has tasked Craig to work with the Obama team at the National Convention to prevent problems in the hall and smooth them out when they occur. I dial up Craig.

"Craig, it's Jeff," I say. "I've got a new proposal to run by you. Let's meet in the convention hall and take a walk together to discuss it."

Within minutes, Craig and I are meandering down the concrete hallway that circumnavigates the arena floor behind the public seating areas. When I make my pitch to Craig for the acclamation vote, he's flabbergasted.

"Are you kidding?" he asks. "We'll have a damn riot in here if we try to prevent Hillary's delegates from voting for her. They fought for her through months of a losing campaign, traveled across the country to Denver to be here for her, and now you want Hillary to tell them not to vote for her? I'll run it up the chain, but I'm not sure we can do this."

Hillary, though, apparently has no doubts about the wisdom of helping Obama with her voters and quickly agrees to do the acclamation motion. She's concerned though about the sensibilities of her delegates and still wants her name entered into nomination and speeches made on her behalf before the acclamation vote so that her delegates will have at least this opportunity to celebrate her candidacy.

With her assent in hand, maybe this procedure will be easier to accomplish than I thought.

Next, I need to coordinate with DNC officials, who have years of experience in managing the traditional nomination roll call vote. They know best how much the state delegations treasure the opportunity to showcase their political stars, deliver their remarks and vote for the presidential candidates. They warn me that state leaders will not be happy if the nomination roll call vote is not held and they lose this opportunity.

The Convention programmers, who plan the Convention to maximize the impact of all the speeches and other programs to boost Obama's image for the fall campaign, want to spend as little time as possible on the nomination voting process. It can take hours to get through the traditional nomination roll call vote, and having state leaders wax on about their great cities or natural wonders doesn't do much for advancing Obama's candidacy. The bottom line is that they want the nomination vote to take no more than two hours from start to finish.

This amount of time won't stretch very far. It's customary for each presidential candidate to have multiple nominating speeches. And DNC leaders are insisting that at least some states get to cast their delegate votes, so that the tradition of this process is not completely abandoned. After some delicate discussions, we collectively agree that at least some states will cast their votes before Hillary cuts off the roll call. From a staging perspective, this would allow for an element of surprise when Hillary calls to interrupt the roll call for a unanimous vote to nominate Obama.

But how many states should we have vote before Hillary asks to end the roll call? DNC leaders want as many states as they can wring out of the programmers. The more states that get to vote, the fewer that will feel cheated of that opportunity.

Based on an estimate from the DNC that each of the states will talk for a few minutes at the microphone before announcing their votes, we determine we'll let around ten states vote before Hillary makes her acclamation motion. With the several nominating speeches beforehand, that should consume about the two hours allotted for the nomination vote.

After considering the best place in the alphabet to end the roll call, it occurs to me that there might be a little magic in letting the vote run through 13 states to Illinois and then have Barack's home state yield to New York, Hillary's home state, for her to bring the acclamation motion. I run this by Plouffe, the programmers, Hillary's team, DNC officials and other interested Democratic leaders. Everyone agrees this plan could be a home run for our television audience and Barack. The plan is set.

It's Wednesday, the day of the nomination vote, and all systems are go for the vote to start at 4pm Mountain Time. Hillary has decided to convene a meeting early in the afternoon with all her delegates to let them know she is releasing them to vote for

Barack if they'd like to do so. It's their choice, she tells them, but that's what she recommends.

At the request of our parliamentary experts, I plan a quick motion at the beginning of the roll call to lay the procedural basis for Hillary's acclamation motion. The maker of the motion and the person seconding it are to locate themselves just in front of the main podium so they can be heard in the noisy hall by the Convention Chair. I also place another delegate near the podium to second the motion that Hillary will make to nominate Obama by acclamation. I expect it will be nearly impossible to hear the second to Hillary's motion over the roar of the delegates, but I want it made any way.

As we get closer to the start of the procedure, I go onto the podium to make sure everyone directing the proceedings is comfortable with the nomination plan. The podium is nothing like a normal podium you might see at a business conference or neighborhood meeting. Instead, it's a huge elevated area big enough on which to play a basketball game. For the nomination vote, there will be a small lectern with a microphone in the front for the Convention Chair and a small desk to the side for the Secretary. To the rear is a long line of desks where the Convention programmers and other officials sit, directing the podium activity that is seen by the television audience. Behind the desks is a stairway that runs down to a back-office area, where a cluster of staffers do the support work for what goes on up above.

While talking to the podium personnel, the Convention Parliamentarian, Helen McFadden, tells me she's worried about one thing. She knows there's opposition among some state delegation leaders and Clinton delegates who've heard rumors the nomination roll call will be cut off. She warns me that once Hillary makes her motion, it will take only one delegate to shout for a point of order to pull the whole Convention into an extended debate on how and whether to approve the motion. This would be precisely when we're supposed to have our nomination climax for the national television audience. I've known Helen for years from other DNC meetings where she's assisted and take her warning seriously.

Presiding over the nomination vote will be the Convention Chair, Speaker Nancy Pelosi. The Speaker is a seasoned parliamentary leader and the best person to hold the gavel during what could be a tricky procedure.

After hearing Helen's concern about the possibility of a parliamentary dispute when Hillary cuts off the roll call, I decide to consult with the Speaker one more time on what is about to unfold. I briefed her yesterday on the details of what we're planning to do, so she's generally up to speed. Now, the Speaker is not at all fazed by my warning to her to avoid any parliamentary objections to Hillary's acclamation motion.

"Please make sure you move fast after Hillary's motion," I tell the Speaker. "It could be a disaster if anyone interrupts the process and blows our timing for the TV audience."

Pelosi responds without losing a beat: "Don't worry. I know how to handle the gavel and I know how to handle it fast."

We each flash a smile, and we're ready to begin the roll call vote. I take a podium seat next to the Parliamentarian and the DNC's General Counsel. They want me at their elbow in case anything unexpected happens.

Below the arena stands, Paul Tewes, the caucus leader who led us to victory in Iowa, is in charge of the boiler room, the nerve center for coordinating our campaign operatives on the convention floor. Paul has been nervous since the start of the Convention because his expertise is turning out voters for elections more than managing convention operations. He's asked me to be available to help if issues arise in the boiler room and I've assured him I will. Until now, I've attended a few meetings with him and we've had some informal conversations, but nothing more than that.

Speaker Pelosi gavels the delegates' attention and introduces the first of the nominating speeches. I'm comfortably settled into my seat on the podium stage and listen to the opening speech, when Craig Smith comes over and tells me there's a complication.

"What are you talking about?" I ask him.

"You're not going to be happy," he replies, "but Hillary doesn't want to make the acclamation motion. She's decided it would be a disservice to her delegates to cut off the roll call and their right to vote. The disenfranchisement of the delegates from Florida and Michigan was such a big issue, that she's decided she just can't do it."

I'm stunned, but immediately reply: "It's too late to turn back, the nominating procedure's begun. We've got to find a solution so she'll be comfortable going forward. And we've got to do it within the next few minutes, because the states are about to start voting."

Craig and I hustle down the podium stairs and huddle together to come up with a formula to keep things on track. Even though the acclamation motion will have the effect of terminating the voting through a single unanimous vote of all the delegates for Obama, I tell him we still can physically count the paper ballots that will be formally submitted by the state delegations. We can release the tally after the televised roll call is over.

"Craig, tell your folks we can do this. I'll have the Speaker announce to the Convention that all the ballots submitted by the state delegations will be counted and the totals released to the public. This will protect Hillary from any complaints that she disenfranchised delegates by cutting off the roll call."

Craig consults with others and then returns to say: "Hillary will make the motion, but only if we approve the exact language you'll give to the Speaker. We won't take any chances on this."

As I hear the nomination speeches droning in the background, I quickly write out the Speaker's statement. Craig relays it for approval, as my eyes stay riveted to the clock. We're almost out of time to wrap this up.

Craig gets the ok and I hand the statement to the DNC staffer operating the teleprompter that will display the text on the podium above. Disaster averted, I return to my podium seat, now more on edge than before. When it's time for the Speaker's statement, I listen intently.

That moment comes. And then it goes. But the Speaker says nothing about counting all the ballots.

"Holy crap!" I say to nobody in particular, as I jump out of my seat and go flying down the podium stairs.

"What happened to the statement I saw you typing?" I ask the teleprompter staffer.

"It must have been too late for the teleprompter to display it at the podium," the staffer replies.

"Why the hell didn't you tell me it might be too late," I grumble as I scramble back up the podium stairs. I've got a printed copy of the short statement in hand.

As the final nominating speech nears conclusion, I motion a young aide to take the paper to Speaker Pelosi and tell her I need her to read it immediately—before the roll call starts.

The Speaker looks down at the paper, as the aide whispers in her ear. She nods and addresses the Convention.

"Ladies and gentlemen, that concludes the nominations for our presidential candidates. We will now proceed to the roll call of the states to nominate the Democratic Party's candidate for the 44th President of the United States. Following the roll call, all tally sheets will be collected and all delegate votes will be counted...."

With these few magic words uttered—"the votes will be counted"—our nomination deal with Hillary is back on track and the roll call vote begins.

That was more excitement than I wanted. But now I'm back in my seat, looking out at the excited delegates happily embarking on the longtime tradition of voting for their nominee for president. Alabama, Alaska, American Samoa, Arizona, one by one, the states and territories cast their votes for the presidential nomination. Arkansas, after announcing its devotion to its home-state Clinton heroes, in a classy touch, casts all 47 of its delegate votes for Obama.

When California's turn to cast its 441 delegate votes arrives, State Democratic Party Chair Art Torres announces: "California passes!"

What is California doing? Why did they just pass?

Rather than dwell on this surprise, my attention turns to the speed with which the states are moving through their voting. After the first few states have made their remarks and announced their delegate tally for the candidates, it's becoming clear the states are moving faster than was anticipated.

Ordinarily, a quick pace of voting on the convention floor would be of no concern. However, this year's convention isn't an ordinary one. We're trying to achieve a nomination by acclamation during a narrow time window for the evening news. At the speed they're going now, we're going to reach the handoff from Illinois to New York before the evening news broadcast even begins.

As it soon becomes clear, this fact is not lost upon those coordinating the activity on the convention floor.

While I'm looking out at the delegates and thinking about ways to slow down the voting, Paul Tewes, who's managing the convention floor from the boiler room, appears on the podium.

When he spots my location, he comes straight over and says: "Jeff, the voting is going too fast! We need you in the boiler room! Now!"

I wheel out of my seat in an instant, telling others on the podium I'm headed to the boiler room.

Paul and I go barreling down the podium stairs and into the back hallway that circumnavigates the arena. Together, in our business suits and wingtip shoes, we run as fast as we can to the boiler room on the other side of the convention hall. It feels like a foot chase scene from a Hollywood movie, as we avoid crashing into convention personnel, carts and boxes.

When we reach the boiler room, true to its name, it is a cauldron of heated activity. There are a dozen or so round tables in the room, each outfitted with telephones and staffers seated shoulder-to-shoulder around its periphery. I quickly move through the room to what looks like the front and shout out, "Who can tell me where we are in the roll call?"

One of the staffers at the tables shouts back that we haven't reached Illinois yet, but we're getting damn close. It's still too early to do the handoff to New York.

Seated at a table to my right is Jenny Backus, a veteran Democratic Party press expert. She's on a dedicated phone line with the major television networks. She wants to give me a report.

"The networks know about our plan for Illinois to handoff to New York during the evening news, but think we're going to miss the time frame," she says. "They're nervous and want to know if we're going to ditch the plan."

"Tell them to hang in there," I respond. "We're going to get this done."

"Listen up everyone!" I shout to the staff on the phones. "Tell your state delegations to slow down. When it's their turn to speak, they have to extend their remarks. I don't care what they say, but they have to keep talking. Spread the word on the convention floor."

Out on the convention floor, our operatives immediately scramble. The phones can't always get the word out. The floor can be chaotic. The delegation chair may have left the state podium or the noise can make it impossible to hear the phone ring. Our floor operatives—wearing brightly colored vests—are deployed to designated zones to make sure we can direct the state delegations even when the phones don't work.

As the states continue through the roll call vote, our floor operatives now are doing everything in their power to instruct the states in their zone to keep talking. One operative, Michael Yaki, the San Francisco lawyer who helped write the Party Platform, is determined to get the word to his delegations.

The podium area for one of his states is on the other side of a seating section. Yaki looks at the aisles that go around the section and sees they're jammed with delegates. The aisles are impassable. Seeing no alternative, he dives into the seating area and claws his way across the delegates, stepping on feet and climbing over laps. The delegates are shocked and try to beat him off with their bags and signposts.

Yaki keeps going, screaming, "Help me get through! I have orders from the convention manager!"

Finally, battered but determined, he reaches the other side, where he shouts to his delegation chair, "When you get the microphone, keep talking! Damn it, don't stop talking!"

Back in the boiler room, the staff on the phone with the California delegation yells to me, "California is now ready to vote! Senator Boxer is on the phone demanding we return to California."

"No way!" I respond. "We've got enough trouble getting the roll call timing back on track. We're not jumping in reverse and making this more complicated. Tell her whatever you want, but we're not going backwards to California."

"They weren't ready to vote when it was their turn," the staffer shouts back. "The Senator insists we come back to them so they can cast their votes."

"No!" I reply in an instant.

We're getting perilously close now to Illinois, and we're still going too fast to hit our landing zone for the network evening news.

Having no choice to save the handoff to New York, I shout, "Tell Illinois, they have to pass! We'll return to them to handoff to New York when the time is right."

And with that, the roll call jumps beyond Illinois to Indiana and the "Great Unknown." As Iowa, Kansas and Kentucky get their turn on national television, my attention turns to Hillary, the key to the acclamation vote.

"Where's Hillary?" I ask Craig Smith, who has taken up residence next to my shoulder.

"You're not going to like this," he tells me. "They brought her downstairs from her suite earlier, when the roll call was moving towards Illinois. When the boiler room wasn't ready for her, we had nowhere to put her, so they took her outside to the parking lot. She's in a parked car without air conditioning, getting emails from governors in the back of the state alphabet begging her not to cut off the roll call."

"She has to stay strong," I tell Craig. "We'll have her out of the car as soon as we can."

As we move through Minnesota, Mississippi and Missouri, a staffer shouts to me from across the boiler room: "I'm getting a rumor that some of the states in the back of the alphabet are going to walk off the convention floor if we cut off the roll call vote."

For an instant, my stomach sinks. A walkout would destroy our nomination vote on national TV. But it's got to be a bluff. No state delegation will have the nerve to do it.

"Ignore the threats. They won't do it," I shout back. "Let's keep our eyes on the ball. We're almost ready to handoff to New York."

Montana, Nebraska and Nevada cast their votes, as we get closer and closer to New York in the alphabet. We'll have to return to Illinois before New York, so Illinois can do the handoff from Barack's home state to Hillary's home state. We're now approaching the drop zone for the network news and we need Hillary near the entrance to the convention floor.

"Craig, move Hillary out of the car and get her in position to go on the floor," I tell him.

"She's already left the car and is on her way," he responds.

That's some good news.

As New Jersey finishes voting, we get ready to move to New Mexico, the state before New York.

"Craig," I ask, "is Hillary in position to enter the floor?"

"I can't get her on the phone," he replies. "I don't know where she is."

They've lost Hillary. And we're only minutes away from the handoff to New York. My stomach sinks, again.

On the Convention floor, New Mexico, the state before New York, is in the process of yielding backwards to Illinois.

New Mexico Chairman Brian Colón, after having waxed eloquently about their "wonderful land of enchantment," announces "All of us together yield to the beautiful state of Illinois, the home of the next President of the United States, Barack Obama."

DNC Secretary Germond calls for Illinois to cast its 185 delegate votes. Mayor Richard Daley from Chicago takes the microphone and begins his prepared remarks, proudly lauding the choice of Senator Barack Obama to be our next President. It's a great moment for the Mayor and Obama's home state.

Back in the boiler room, I instruct our Illinois desk: "Tell the Illinois podium that the Mayor must keep talking while we find Hillary. Under no circumstances can he stop!"

I look to my left and my right, surveying the packed boiler room as I decide our next move. The tension is overwhelming, as I try to hold the roll call vote together the best I can.

"The television networks are beside themselves," Jenny Backus tells me. "They say we're not going to pull this off!"

"Just tell them we're going to do it," I respond.

For an instant, I think of our convention programmers on the podium and how they're handling the uncertainty. I know they've been in regular touch with the boiler room—though I don't know who they're talking with—and must be helping any way they can.

Our staffer in touch with New York shouts: "New York doesn't have Hillary! They want to know what to do!"

Hillary is missing, and we can't do the acclamation motion without her. With no alternative, I shout to our New York desk, "Tell New York to prepare to pass!"

We'll have to skip them and return when we find her. If she reappears too late, the handoff to New York will come after the national news hour and the national TV audience that Plouffe wants for Obama's nomination.

For the moment, though, Mayor Daley should be able to speak for some time about his state's favorite son until Hillary surfaces.

Or so I think.

Facing me from the back wall of the boiler room and above everyone's heads are a bank of television screens that give me a view of what's being broadcast by all the national TV networks.

I make it a point to keep one eye on Mayor Daley as he speaks.

I also hear an audio feed from the arena floor. This allows me to stay abreast of the Convention proceedings when I have to pull my full attention away from the screens.

Without warning, I hear Mayor Daley say, "...we yield to the great state of New York, home of Hillary Clinton."

I can't believe my ears. It seems he's hardly spoken ten words before passing off to New York. I told the Illinois podium to have him keep talking.

There's not a second to waste, though, dwelling on what just happened.

DNC Secretary Germond dutifully calls out from the main podium: "Thank you, Illinois. Thank you, Mayor Daley. Thank you, Illinois. Thank you, Mayor Daley. New York, New York, you have 282 votes. How do you cast them?"

I instantly decide that New York is going to have to pass. If not, our whole plan to nominate Barack by acclamation will collapse.

Before I can give the order to pass, a cacophony rises up on the audio feed from the convention floor. I look up to the television screens and see a flash of commotion on the Convention floor.

As the cameras zoom in on the center of the tumult, I make out a phalanx of security officials emerging from one of the tunnels under the seating stands. Then I see a woman dressed in powder blue behind them. She is waving broadly to the cheering crowd in the Convention hall.

"It's Hillary!" the boiler room erupts. After disappearing into the bowels of the arena, she's now sweeping across the Convention floor toward the now-jubilant New York delegation.

We're back on track! The convention programmers on the main podium have helped locate Hillary, and now she's right where she needs to be with a few minutes still left in the national news hour. The Speaker of the New York State Assembly, Shelly Silver, proudly calls Hillary to the New York podium to speak to the delegates and the national television audience.

Hillary is beaming. Keeping faith with her commitment to Barack Obama and our presidential campaign, she says:

Madame Secretary, on behalf of the great State of New York, with appreciation for the spirit and dedication of all who are gathered here, with eyes firmly fixed on the future, in the spirit of unity, with the goal of victory, with faith in our Party and our country, let's declare together in one voice, right here, right now, that Barack Obama is our candidate and that he will be our President. Madame Secretary. Madame Secretary. I move that the Convention suspend the procedural rules and suspend the further conduct of the roll call vote. All votes cast by the delegates will be counted. And that I move Senator Barack Obama of Illinois be selected by this Convention by acclamation as the nominee of the Democratic Party for President of the United States.

Bedlam explodes on the Convention floor. Jubilant delegates applaud wildly and chant "Hillary! Hillary! Hillary!"

I look up at the televisions displayed across the back of the boiler room. Still in the heart of the national news hour, the words "BREAKING NEWS" flash on the screens.

Then, as if on cue, the words "Hillary Clinton calls for Nomination of Obama by Acclamation."

Back on the Convention floor, Speaker Pelosi addresses the delegates from the main podium:

Thank you, Senator Clinton. Senator Clinton has moved in the spirit of unity to suspend the rules of the Convention and to nominate Barack Obama by acclamation as the presidential candidate of the Democratic Party. Is there a second?

My planted second screams "Yes!" at the top of his lungs just in front of the podium. He is drowned out by the thousands of delegates and guests in the hall who spontaneously shout, "Yes!"

Speaker Pelosi says: "All in favor of the motion to suspend the rules and nominate by acclamation Barack Obama as the Democratic Party's Presidential candidate, please say "Aye."

"Aye!" the throng of thousands in the Convention hall shout back.

Speaker Pelosi asks, "All those opposed, say no."

Then, without letting a second go by that could allow a challenge to the acclamation motion, she announces "Two-thirds of the delegates having voted in the affirmative, the motion is adopted." And pounds her gavel on the lectern.

"It is with great pride," she declares, "that I announce that Barack Obama is the Democratic nominee for President of the United States by acclamation."

Clouds of balloons drop from the ceiling and celebratory music rises up. The delegates and guests chant euphorically: "Yes we can! Yes we can! Yes we can!"

With Obama's historic nomination vote completed, I grab my son, Joe, and bolt out of the boiler room. I'm determined to climb to the top balcony of the arena, where the rest of my family has been watching in a guest seating area.

When I reach them, far from the delegates below, they're pumped with excitement at Hillary's leading the way to Barack's nomination.

"Hillary was fantastic," my wife, Trish, says.

"Yes," I agree. "She was truly gracious."

Reunited, my family and I make our way out of the convention hall. It's time to celebrate together.

Epilogue

THE NEXT EVENING, Barack Obama accepts his nomination for president at Mile High Stadium in Denver. His acceptance speech brings the house down. I can't see him very well from my position on the field far to the right of the stage. I'd rather move to a better view closer to the center, but I've been asked to stay here so I can exit the field quickly.

As Barack finishes his speech, the secret service signal me that it's time to begin moving off the field. My path through the bowels of the stadium has been pre-cleared and I'm rushed to the Denver Broncos locker room. The room is empty when I arrive. There's a bare table and a few chairs, which I re-arrange to create a small working area.

I unload a satchel of papers on the table. These are the official filings the presidential and vice presidential candidates must sign after they've accepted their nominations. With Obama now having completed his acceptance of the presidential nomination, and Vice Presidential nominee Senator Joe Biden having done so the day before, it's time for the two Democratic nominees to complete their paperwork.

I've just finished laying the paperwork out on the table when I hear a commotion coming down the hallway. At first, I don't see the nominees. Instead a phalanx of photographers and videographers bust into the room with the families of the candidates. I keep everyone at a distance from the papers to avoid having to play a game of 52-card pickup with the many pages of documents.

Then, the noise rises yet again, this time even louder. Finally, Obama and Biden make their way into the room. Each of them comes over to the table, smiling and hugging everyone within reach. It's a wonderful moment being captured by snapping and whirring cameras.

When the candidates are ready to focus, I ask Obama to step to my left and Biden to come to my right, each facing the papers aligned for their signature. Michelle wraps her arms around Sasha and Malia, as they watch the scene from the side. As soon as the signings are finished, like the storm that just rolled in, the nominees and their families and friends blast back out to celebrate their big night.

Alone, I gather up the now-completed documents and make my way out of Mile High Stadium.

★   ★   ★

In the subsequent weeks, the Republicans hold their own nominating convention. John McCain is nominated and chooses Sarah Palin for the vice presidential slot on his ticket. Then Lehman Brothers files for bankruptcy and the financial system swoons due to years of poor lending practices and loose regulation. As the public focuses on the financial crisis and concern over the strength of the economy, McCain pulls out of a debate with Obama and suspends his campaign to participate in bank bailout legislation. The legislation fails to pass amid questions of whether McCain contributed sufficiently to its negotiation and passage.

Obama and Biden, in contrast, manage their response to the financial crisis and economic downturn without missteps and put in solid debate performances.

On November 4, 2008, Obama and Biden achieve a landslide victory, taking a whopping 375 electoral votes to 173 for McCain and Palin.

The 2008 election is over, with Obama and Biden headed to the White House.

Acknowledgments

I HAVE MANY PEOPLE TO THANK. First, I want to thank my family for sharing me with the Obama campaign. From the start, I feared I'd be unable to return home from Chicago very often, especially once the pace of the campaign quickened. And that's exactly what happened. I'm sorry for being away for such a long period of time and for missing so much that went on in my absence. Thank you for your willingness to let me go and your support while I was away.

Every presidential campaign reflects the personality and leadership of its candidate. This was particularly true for the Obama campaign. President Obama was an inspiring candidate who campaigned with focus and discipline to return Democrats to the White House. We on his campaign staff followed his example the best we could and worked hard, with minimal drama, to get our jobs done. It was an honor to be part of the President's team.

None of our success in 2008 would have been possible without the President's highly committed grassroots supporters. There is a long roll call of rank-and-file heroes who helped win the presidential nomination. The delegate operation relied on the guidance and hard work of Obama supporters in almost every state. I was able to recount only a small fraction of these contributions in *The Magic Number*. To everyone who signed or circulated a petition, organized support efforts, counseled us on strategy or served as a delegate, whether at the precinct, county, congressional district, state or national level, thank you for making Barack Obama's success in 2008 possible.

Among our staff, I want to first thank David Plouffe, our campaign manager. David's no-nonsense approach kept us working productively and in unison. His sharp judgment navigated us through every difficult decision the campaign faced. I wouldn't have been able to do my work without David's guidance and support.

I want to thank the rest of our campaign organization and external consultants for the opportunity to work together with you on our mission to elect Barack Obama to the White House. Your collaboration and esprit de corps made our success possible and, when we weren't stressed out, entirely enjoyable. Special thanks to Matt Nugen and our Political Department for the nearly limitless assistance you provided to the delegate operation.

Of course, I want to thank all the staff of our delegate operation. We started out as just three people, myself with deputy director Myesha Ward and Mike Robertson—and we stayed as three people throughout 2007. Our small group grew over time to include delegate trackers Ian Adams, Steven Brokaw, Danielle Cendejas, Liz Emanuel, Andrei Greenawalt, Emily Jacobson, Jen Koch, Toni Morales, John Paul Rollert, Bobby Schmuck, Deborah Slott, Daryl Sprague, Jennifer Parrish Taylor, Khalil Thompson, Jenn Watts, Matt Winters and Dave Zikusoka. Christine Turner joined to direct traffic for us and keep us productive. Thanks to all of you. I hope the experience was one you'll never forget.

We would not have held our delegate gains so effectively in the many caucus states without the expert work of our small caucus and convention team. Brandon Hurlbut managed this effort with Mike French and Mitch Wallace to protect our campaign's success, as we made our way through the often byzantine caucus and convention process. Thank you, Brandon, Mike and Mitch.

Another group who was critical to the success of the Obama delegate operation was our data team, an eclectic group of statisticians, computer and Internet experts, and politically savvy thinkers. Thank you to Peter Appel for your leadership of the team, and to Ken Strasma, Michael Simon, Luke Peterson, and others who provided such important support to the delegate effort.

⋆   ⋆   ⋆

Several people assisted in the creation of *The Magic Number*. Thank you to fellow Obama 2008 staffers David Plouffe and Matt Rodriguez for reading the manuscript and supporting the book. Thanks to friends Phil Brenner, Bill Carrick, Marsha Cranberg, Peter Kirby, Waldo McMillan, Dave Russell, Jim Stewart, and Sam Wolff for reading the manuscript. Thanks also to family members Alan Berman, Joe Berman, Rubin Berman and Trish Berman for reading the manuscript. Thank you, Oliver Munday, for designing the exterior cover of *The Magic Number*, and Joe Berman and Walton Mendelson for formatting the book's interior.

I had a unique vantage point for the Democratic presidential delegate race in 2008. Much of the material for *The Magic Number* comes from my recollection of the actual events, plus notes and materials produced during or about the events of 2008. Scenes and conversations described in the book are accurate to the best of my recollection and capture the essence of what I saw or heard.

There is no index included in *The Magic Number* in recognition of all the Obama campaign staff and supporters around the country whose names might not turn up, but who made invaluable contributions to our joint effort.

Finally, I want to thank my family once again for their support—this time not for the campaign—but for my decision to write *The Magic Number*. It was a dicey proposition for me to ask for the personal time needed to write this book after all the time I'd been away in Chicago, but my family was there for me again. Thank you, Trish, Joe, Cassie, Annie and Molly for supporting me in this project.

About The Author

JEFF BERMAN SERVED as the National Director of Delegate Operations for the 2008 Obama presidential campaign. After the 2008 elections, Jeff was elected to the Democratic National Committee and its Rules and Bylaws Committee. He was appointed by then-DNC Chair Tim Kaine to the Democratic Change Commission to recommend changes to the Democratic Party's presidential nominating process. Jeff previously served as an advisor to presidential candidates Dick Gephardt in 2004 and 1988 and John Glenn in 1984.

Jeff is married to Trish Berman, a registrar for the District of Columbia Public Schools system. They have four children, all of whom campaigned and cheered for Obama during 2007-08. Joe, the oldest, interned in the campaign's Information Technology department for two summers and attends Carnegie Mellon University in Pittsburgh. Cassie, the next in line, attends the College of William and Mary in Virginia. Younger daughters, Annie and Molly, like their siblings before them, attend District of Columbia public schools.

Jeff currently is an attorney in Washington, DC and a graduate of Brown University and Harvard Law School.

Made in the USA
Lexington, KY
30 June 2015